AF228445

MAKING THE RENAISSANCE MAN

MAKING THE RENAISSANCE MAN

Masculinity in the Courts of Renaissance Italy

TIMOTHY McCALL

REAKTION BOOKS

Published by
REAKTION BOOKS LTD
Unit 32, Waterside
44–48 Wharf Road
London N1 7UX, UK

www.reaktionbooks.co.uk

First published 2023
Copyright © Timothy McCall 2023

Printed and bound in India by Replika Press Pvt. Ltd

A catalogue record for this book is available from the British Library

ISBN 978 1 78914 785 8

CONTENTS

1 Francesco del Cossa, 'Ferrarese courtier, seen from behind',
c. 1470, pen and brown ink.

Introduction:
Making Renaissance Men

In Renaissance Italy, as today, power seduces. Ugo Caleffini, a chronicler and notary from Ferrara, characterized the town's lord Niccolò III d'Este as 'more courtly than a beautiful lady'. Women who 'saw this noble lord', he asserted, 'fell in love with him more than with their husbands'. Caleffini was writing decades after the fact; he was barely old enough to walk at the time of Niccolò's death in 1441. His value as a source lies less in the truth it tells us about how anyone felt about Niccolò, than in what these claims reveal about the ways that aristocratic status and authority were eroticized, and that elegance and courtliness were celebrated. Caleffini also professed – about Borso d'Este, Niccolò's son and second successor, whom the notary knew well – that he was 'so very in love with' or 'enchanted by' Borso.[1] In fifteenth-century Italy, love and admiration directed towards noble men sustained power and its supporting fictions. Social status and sexual desirability were not strictly differentiated but echoed and amplified each other. Aristophiliac subjects – men and women seduced by manifestations of aristocratic status – fell in love with their rulers on sight, because of their nobility and courtliness.[2] Or, at least, this is what lords and their propagandists hoped for.

This book explores the constructions and performances of elite masculinity that embodied power and captivated subjects in fifteenth-century Italy. It asks how noble Renaissance men were made and how they set themselves apart from those they ruled. This study investigates the experiences, images, objects and even animals that contributed to the fashioning of seigneurial, or lordly, masculinity in the Quattrocento, and it inventories, analyses and critically interprets the material culture and activities through which boys became men

7

and princes became lords. These men fought each other in violent battle and in spectacular jousts; they seduced mistresses; they flaunted splendour in lavish rituals of knighting; and they demonstrated masculine prowess through the ferocity of the hunt. These were not frivolous diversions or carefree leisure activities. They were politically charged displays of privilege, virility and the right to rule. Lords exercised and visualized their dominance over other men, often quite ostentatiously, and they likewise enacted control over members of both sexes through the seduction of women – sometimes girls or very young women. This book closely observes the prince and his representatives, whether courtiers or falcons, and explores the pivotal role of gifts, such as branded dogs and burnished armours, in forging the violence that underlay the cultural veneer of Italian Renaissance courts. Not only people, but animals and objects also exercised and manifested the agency of lords.[3]

As familiar as the idea of the 'Renaissance man' is, it is not one that many fifteenth- or sixteenth-century Italians would have understood. The archetypal Renaissance man, Leonardo da Vinci, appears throughout these pages, and Chapter Four provides a crucial new perspective on one of his most famous paintings, yet *Making the Renaissance Man* investigates representations and ideals of manhood beyond that of, and sometimes contradictory to, the well-rounded and extraordinarily gifted polymath. Dominant manhood emerges here not as embodied in a singular intellectual individual, but as shared by a class of men whose authority was fundamentally based upon exhibiting models of elite masculinity. Elsewhere, I argued that beauty, adornment and radiance embodied in fair skin, sparkling gems and lustrous brocades served patriarchy.[4] So too did experiences and performances of manhood. Noble male bodies, and their demonstrations of masculine elegance, prowess and virility, were charismatic and seductive, drawing gazes and desires towards them. Male display and spectacle engendered power.

For scholars and in popular culture, masculinities are increasingly visible analytically, rather than merely existing as unspoken norms. The study of Renaissance and early modern masculinities is flourishing and provides the foundations for this book.[5] It is best to speak of plural masculinities, for no culture has only one paradigmatic or normative ideal of what it means to be a man. Multiple constructions of masculinity always compete for cultural prominence, and any single ideal of manhood is far from monolithic or fixed, but rather has conflicting, overlapping, ever-shifting and often ambiguous meanings. Theorists of gender and sexuality such as R. W. Connell, Jack Halberstam and Judith Butler, among others, allow us to appreciate the socially and historically contingent rather than essential or static nature of masculinities.[6] Societies recognize and identify maleness through culturally determined – rather than innate or natural – markers of manhood reproduced through the embodied practices and repetition of everyday life. Masculinities are made and are always being made; they are continuously in process, socially performed and coming to be through bodies, experiences and even representations. In fifteenth-century Italy, the *signore* presented a dominant and domineering model of manhood, one that still looms large in our imagining of the Renaissance (though I am uncertain if we can label this normative masculinity, since it was available to so few). Some, but not all, attributes of noble masculinity resonate with contemporary ideals. Aggression, sexual prowess and virility will seem familiar to readers, though an emphasis on beauty and elegance might be less so. Yet these values sat together comfortably for lords and their subjects.

The charisma of Renaissance rulership was erotically charged and visualized. Art provided a 'staged eroticism of power'.[7] Fifteenth-century Italian courts were, by and large, homosocial spaces where groups of men, the lord and his adherents, maintained significant authority – and where, of course, some dynamic and privileged women did as well. Courtliness was broadcast and embodied in the prince and his male attendants, as we see, for instance, in scenes from Palazzo Schifanoia's Salone dei Mesi (Room of the Months) in Ferrara (illus. 2). For fifteenth-century oligarchies, as in many homosocial spaces, it is often not possible to differentiate between the sexual, erotic, affective and intimate.[8] This book centres Renaissance homosociality and explores its configurations in a number of ways: by investigating men and boys looking at and being watched by other men in jousts and hunts; by examining lords bonding over exchanged dogs, horses and armour (what we might call 'mail bonding'); by interpreting mistresses situated and manoeuvring between men; and by revisiting one prince's infamous bachelorhood at a court organized around the promotion of beautiful youths in spaces that were almost exclusively inhabited by men. Sharpening our gaze on the fundamental importance of male homosociality for Renaissance sovereignty allows for new perspectives on the history of sexuality. We can better appreciate why Ugo Caleffini would describe himself as 'in love' with his lord Borso d'Este, and why, decades later, Matteo Bandello would define Borso's father Niccolò, sire of dozens of illegitimate children, as the 'most womanly man' of his time, because 'as many women as he saw, that many he desired'.[9]

Today, we are ever more wary of gender binaries. Sex and gender, as they are understood and embodied, are increasingly fluid and unstable, and were so in the fifteenth and preceding centuries to a greater extent than we have generally recognized.[10] Yet, of course, the dichotomies of male/female and masculine/feminine structured power and culture in Renaissance Europe, as they continue to do. Though this book primarily scrutinizes the experiences of men and boys, it also considers women – and centres them in Chapters Three and Four. In doing so, I aim to shift attention to the interdependent, inter-relational nature of gender. Studying men in isolation from women – or vice versa – can only produce a fragmentary impression of the cultural operations and power dynamics of sexual difference.[11] That said, it is important to recognize that masculine authority and identity were multi-relational; they were fashioned not only through opposition to femininity, but simultaneously through competition with and domination of other men (who enjoyed the benefits of the 'patriarchal dividend' even when disempowered or subordinated in relation to some men).[12]

This book's title explicitly prioritizes gender and masculinity as categories of analysis, but equally crucial in its pages will be class and status. The experiences investigated in this study and celebrated in Renaissance culture – including hunting, jousting and the seduction of noble women – were all intended to be the preserve of the aristocracy. They were performed and displayed to separate rulers from the ruled, to maintain class divisions and to bolster supremacy. Though lords often advertised concern for their subjects, and now and then may have been sincere, sources and voices frequently reveal utter disdain for the commonfolk. For instance, an apologist of the Este dynasty, Antonio Cornazzano, ridiculed the supporters of Niccolò di Leonello d'Este – who waged a futile attempt to usurp control of Ferrara from his uncle Ercole – as 'savage men born in forests and rocks' who literally nauseated him.[13]

Qualities that separated lords from their subjects were identified as *courtliness* (some version of the word *cortese*), *nobility* (*gentilezza*) or *polish* (*politezza*, a concept that encompassed class resonances suggested by *politeness*). These ideals were fundamentally structured by distinctions of status and class, and they were often located in models that we would label chivalric. In fifteenth-century Italy, chivalric discourses and modes of courtliness were at once political, martial, amorous and resolutely gendered. They were fundamental components of power's representation in visual and literary form and provided organizing principles around which patriarchal authority was broadcast and amplified. Chivalric imagery and traditions – be they Greek, Roman, Arthurian or Carolingian – remain somewhat obscured in scholarly and popular understandings of Renaissance Italy, eclipsed as they often are by the focus on the rebirth of classical or ancient culture, art and literature. Returning to Ferrara and briefly examining two medals, relatively early examples of a new art form that developed in the Italian courts, will clarify my point. Leonello and Borso d'Este, who successively governed Ferrara between 1441 and 1471, are familiar to art historians as representatives of opposite sides of the conventional division between, on the one hand, humanism and Latin literature, and, on the other, chivalric vernacular traditions. This binary is a false dichotomy, because chivalric texts were steeped in ancient Roman and Greek traditions, yet it still frames our understanding of the Este princes' artistic patronage. Indeed, since the publication of Werner Gundersheimer's *Ferrara: The Style of a Renaissance Despotism* in 1973, scholars have not uncommonly characterized these brothers, and their successor, Ercole, according to the individual personalities that Gundersheimer assigned them: the learned Leonello, the vain Borso and the pious Ercole.[14]

This was a laudable attempt to rehabilitate the reputation of lords previously marginalized and disparaged in modern historiography as tyrannical despots, but the 'despotic styles' of these three Este rulers have in some scholarship crystalized, at times narrowing our interpretative framework for Ferrarese court culture. Due in large part to Angelo Decembrio having set the anti-vernacular *De politia litteraria* at his court, Leonello d'Este has emerged as the epitome of the fifteenth-century humanist prince. Yet Leonello was firmly entrenched within chivalric culture (and, of course, humanist texts and traditions could be as erotic as chivalric ones).[15] Like Borso, he deployed amorous

2 Borso d'Este's court, from Francesco del Cossa, *March*, late 1460s, fresco, east wall, Salone dei Mesi, Palazzo Schifanoia, Ferrara.

imagery from all of these cultural fonts to support his authority. Indeed, both classicism and chivalry enlivened courtly masculinities, which, as we will increasingly appreciate, were fluid and dynamic, adaptive and resilient.

The complicated and challenging reverses of Pisanello's medals of Leonello d'Este are often taken as proof of the lord's learned personality. Crucially, the medals likewise reveal the value of the sensual display of courtly bodies for even this most humanist of princes, and their obscurity and multivalence invite further speculation and contradictory readings. One reverse exhibits a naked, lithe male body for the viewer's perusal (illus. 3). When casting the medal, Pisanello consulted his earlier sketch of a burly marble Saturn (a figure that is in fact a monumental second-century CE Tigris River god, now outside the Palazzo Senatorio (illus. 4)), but the medal's reclining figure is much more slender and slight.[16] Tellingly, Pisanello removed the drapery covering Saturn's lower body to reveal the youth's lissome, poised legs, conspicuous markers of courtliness that embodied contemporary ideals of male beauty. Male legs were erotically charged in fifteenth-century Italy, while women's were hidden under long, voluminous dresses.[17] The beholder strains to guess the meaning of the flowering vase with one broken and one unbroken anchor. Not only the naked male body with its gracefully crossed legs, but also the surface and finish of these hand-held objects encourage prolonged, possibly sensuous looking and touching.

On the reverse of a slightly later medal, Pisanello represents Leonello in the guise of a lion (illus. 5), the eponymous animal with

3 Pisanello, *Leonello d'Este* (obverse) and *Nude Youth* (reverse), 1440s, bronze.

4 Unknown artist, *River Tigris* (often identified as *River Tiber*), 2nd century CE, marble, Palazzo Senatorio, Rome.

which the prince was compared in painted portraits through his mane-like coiffure. The courageous and noble lion receives instruction from Cupid, who displays to the beast a scroll marked with musical notations. This medal was produced for Leonello's second marriage, to Maria of Aragon, the daughter of the Neapolitan king Alfonso of Aragon, yet discussions of the imagery in terms of the lord's musical pursuits often neglect amorous valences and dismiss politics or dynastic concerns. Love and marriage have been written off as 'polite fiction[s]' and as jokes for knowing insiders, demonstrably inauthentic and even laughable in relation to Leonello's genuine interest in music.[18] This reverse, however, may have been related by viewers to Ovid's *Ars Amatoria*, a text adapted in medieval works such as the *Romance of the Rose* and well known at Ferrara, where a court poet described Ovid as 'our guiding light'. The Este library held the *Ars Amatoria* in multiple manuscripts.[19] From the very start of the work, Ovid underscores his identity and duty as the teacher of love: 'ego sum praeceptor Amoris'. In Pisanello's medal, Cupid serves as Leonello's 'praeceptor' or teacher in all things amorous, instructing the lion in love and taming the ferocious beast.[20] The allusion must be evaluated within the context of Leonello's amatory enterprise and the construction of the lord's persona as poet and lover. His two surviving sonnet fragments, in fact,

5 Pisanello, *Leonello d'Este* (obverse) and *Lion Instructed by Cupid* (reverse), 1444, bronze.

lament Cupid's cruel domination of the lover, and numerous authors composed love elegies and other amorous poetry for Leonello.[21] We will see throughout this book that princes broadcast their authority through erotic and amorous imagery. Seigneurial masculinity was sensual and seductive.

Niccolò Machiavelli is often thought to have said that it is better to be feared than loved. In fact, Machiavelli asserted that the prince should be both, and only if 'one of the two had to be relinquished', he added, then it would be 'much safer to be feared'.[22] Indeed, subjects had much to fear from their own and other lords. I want not only to underscore the importance of seduction, charisma and enchantment to aristocratic masculinity, but equally to highlight the brutality, violence and cruelty inflicted by ruling oligarchies and by individual princes. It is tempting to romanticize Renaissance men as either enlightened patrons of art and culture, or chivalrous and chaste knights protecting the powerless. Yet we must not be 'blinded by the light reflected off shining armour'.[23] In many ways, violence served as the foundation of lordship and elite masculinity. Violence was meted out not only to bring about specific, material ends, but as a means to articulate and enact status and privilege through domination, intimidation and coercion. This book, then, is not a celebration of the Renaissance man. It makes plain the callous attitudes and ruthless manoeuvres that engendered and maintained authority.

Rule was never invulnerable or absolute for Renaissance Italy's noble regimes, nor was it ever entirely based on pure domination by force. In fifteenth-century Italy, lordship was typically legitimated by a measure of consent from the people (*popolo*) and from civic institutions, who had to be persuaded that those in power deserved to be. A council of 'wise men' (the *Savi*), for instance, ostensibly granted the approval of Ferrara's *popolo* when they elected the town's lord. The relationship between subjects and sovereigns was forged through a balance between 'conflict, compromise and consensus'. Lords had to convince subjects of their aristocratic privilege, and they needed to provide protection, economic opportunity and the impression, at least, of justice.[24] Otherwise, the ruled could and would revolt. Renaissance Italians, the historian John Najemy reminds us, 'did not find it quite so easy to forgive their nobles everything in appreciation of [their] cultural achievements'.[25]

Subjects could indeed strike back, by rioting or by shifting loyalties. Princes were butchered, most famously Milan's duke Galeazzo Maria Sforza on the feast of St Stephen, the day after Christmas 1476. In 1431, the fourteen-year-old Sigismondo Malatesta was attacked in Fano by rebels in the thrall of a charismatic priest. Sigismondo had been sent to Fano to calm the townsfolk, but his presence did just the opposite. This violent assault may explain why Sigismondo's right radius bone (the shorter of the two in the forearm) was discovered to have a break, likely a defensive wound, when his body was exhumed centuries later.[26] It was good to be the lord, but a bull's-eye was forever on his back.

In 1482, Ferrara's duchess Eleonora of Aragon wrote to her husband Ercole d'Este warning of a potential rebellion triggered by violent abuses suffered at the hands of Este mercenaries quartered in the ducal hunting park. If Ercole did not keep his troops in check and punish those guilty of murder, robbery and the general mistreatment of their subjects, Eleonora foresaw a 'most manifest danger' from the *popolo* who were so terrorized by the soldiers 'with very little in their heads' – including some who killed a man after first stealing his pig – that they were left with 'no alternative but a popular uprising'. Este subjects did sporadically revolt. In Reggio in 1469, for example, a fire that burned down the ducal stables coincided with the presence of visiting Este officials in town and was at the time interpreted as a 'premeditated act' against the regime.[27] As we will see, for horse-crazy princes, the ducal stables were no random target but a significant and resonant site. These flames were intended to sear Este hearts.

Baldassare Castiglione's *Book of the Courtier* (*Il Cortegiano*), first published in 1528, looms large in studies of both Renaissance courts and masculinities – and with good reason, given its proliferation and influence across Europe in the sixteenth and subsequent centuries. Here I must provide that most tiresome of features of an introduction – caution about what this book is not. As I indicated, it is not an exploration of individuals who best fit our category of the 'Renaissance man'. Nor is it an account of Castiglione's ideal male courtier, nonchalant, unaffected and dissembling. The models of courtly masculinity that emerge here were separated by decades from *Il Cortegiano*, but additionally, and perhaps more significantly, by many years of foreign invasion and occupation – the disastrous Wars of Italy – that heralded a sea change in ideals of normative manliness among elite Italians.[28]

Our narrative ranges primarily over the north, but sometimes the south, of the peninsula; it delves into many rather than a single dynasty or city. The Este of Ferrara, Sforza of Milan and Gonzaga of Mantua predominate throughout the book, but other houses contribute to our story as well, including the Aragonese kings of Naples, Rossi of Parma, Montefeltro of Urbino, Bentivoglio of Bologna and Malatesta of Rimini, and various courtiers and cadet branches of these clans. Frescoed rooms adorning their castles and palaces – notably Andrea Mantegna's Camera Picta for Ludovico Gonzaga and the Salone dei Mesi at Palazzo Schifanoia, commissioned by Borso d'Este – are familiar to both scholars and tourists and will be seen in new light in these pages.[29]

Fifteenth-century Italy's most spectacular monumental cycle of chivalric imagery may be Torrechiara's Camera d'Oro, one of the period's best-preserved multimedia spaces. Between the mid-1450s and 1463, artisans led by the Bembo family of Cremona painted this marvellous 'Golden Chamber' for Count Pier Maria Rossi, on the *piano nobile* or 'noble floor' of Torrechiara, a castle dramatically perched on a hill 16 kilometres (10 mi.) south of Parma (illus. 6). In the hall's frescoed vaults, Rossi's mistress Bianca Pellegrini wanders her lord's territory in the guise of a pilgrim (*pellegrina*), a pun on her aristocratic family name. Just below, in the four lunettes, the mistress ennobles Pier Maria through rituals of courtly love (illus. 7).[30] Originally polychromed and gilded terracotta tiles bearing Rossi emblems cover the lower walls, which are interrupted only in the room's southeast corner by intarsia panelling and *terra verde* frescoes of illustrious men, remnants of a study or *studiolo*. The walls and azurite frescoes above,

6 Torrechiara Castle, built *c.* 1448–60.

7 Camera d'Oro, Torrechiara Castle, decorated *c.* 1460 by Bonifacio Bembo and workshop.

sumptuously adorned with metallic leaf and gilded pastiglia, manifest splendid, noble materiality from floor to ceiling.

In the north lunette, Pier Maria Rossi and Bianca Pellegrini stand triumphantly within an elaborate pavilion, extravagantly attired and backed by the Rossi castles of San Secondo and Roccabianca (illus. 8). A crown suspended above the *pellegrina*'s head and a golden orb near her face signal her nobility, as does the adjacent, newly built castle Roccabianca, whose name echoed her own. Traces of gold and silver can be seen on Bianca's white gown and headdress, once seemingly further enriched with a golden brooch and a string of pearls, now vanished. Bianca is, at once, a pilgrim (*pellegrina*); noblewoman; mistress; and fair or white (*bianca*) damsel. Pier Maria, for his part, is garbed as a courtly, youthful knight. Enclosed in shining armour with two swords at his side, the blond prince delicately grasps the baton of command with his index finger and thumb, with a graceful gesture we will see repeated by other lords. This image of Rossi may have visually evoked a large marble portrait once decorating Torrechiara's exterior, in a niche above the castle's entrance. He is juxtaposed with his castle of San Secondo, and thus viewers may have recognized not

8 Bonifacio Bembo and workshop, *Pier Maria Rossi and Bianca Pellegrini Triumphant*, *c.* 1460, fresco, north lunette, Camera d'Oro, Torrechiara Castle.

only a courtly lover and warrior, but a pious knight recalling the early Christian St Secundus, who enjoyed active devotions in and around Parma.

The frescoes of the Camera d'Oro are not straightforward declarations of love from a lord to his mistress. Much more is at stake in this dynamic visualization of aristocratic charisma and authority. This book brings to light chivalric models and images familiar to contemporary audiences from spectacles and art. These representations were mediated through ideals of courtliness and through literary and verbal description in various media. In Italian Renaissance courts, art bolstered social hierarchies by proclaiming and promising that lords embodied model paradigms of elite manhood. When interpreting Renaissance art, we should ask not only what it means but how it works, and to what ends. The images and experiences that made Renaissance men also worked to secure their dominance.

1

Chivalry and Courtly Masculinity

From their earliest years, Renaissance lords hunted and fought together. They competed against one another in jousts and dances. They penned amorous poetry, slew deer (or even bears) and commanded horses, inspired by Cupid, Roman heroes and chivalric knights. Princes took lessons from art in an array of media and wielded material culture (and materiel) in spectacles, thrilling audiences with their prowess. They read and studied vernacular romances, Latin grammars, fighting manuals and ancient histories – in books often illuminated with scenes of war alongside images of love and seduction. Through these and other courtly experiences, noble boys became noblemen.

In palaces, piazzas and hunting parks, and likewise in visual imagery, models for young princes ranged from lithe, adolescent Cupids inspiring love, to robust, mature ancestors and elders presented as exemplary hunters and jousters. Amorous verses, rituals of dubbing and depictions of combat provided organizing principles around which Renaissance masculinities were formed and performed. These chivalric images and experiences were martial and erotic, violent and alluring. Lords seduced both subjects and peers with displays of virility and elegant courtliness. By embodying ideals of aristocratic masculinity that were assertive and bellicose yet endowed with enchanting charisma, at every turn princes distinguished themselves from those they ruled. Peers and subjects expected and even demanded that they do so.

Amorous Bodies, Chivalric Forms

Chivalric texts and frescoes supplied Italian aristocrats the visual language and symbolism on which they built their authority. These narratives and paradigms were not the static, irrelevant fantasies of a decaying class; nor were chivalric, vernacular texts mere entertainment waiting to be surpassed by humanist, Neo-Latin literature on the Renaissance's inevitable march to modernity. Within fifteenth-century Italian courts, Latin and vernaculars were read side by side, serving as vital sources for displays of distinction, privilege and cultural refinement.[1] Indeed, this book emphasizes the political importance and expediency of chivalric cultural productions. These traditions were vibrant and dynamic; there was no singular 'vernacular' in fifteenth-century Italy, moreover, but instead multiple vernaculars.[2]

Court libraries teemed with chivalric narratives of all sorts, including myriad versions and translations of Arthurian legends, Carolingian tales and Trojan histories, in numerous European vernaculars (variants of French, Spanish, Italian, Franco-Veneto and diverse tongues in between).[3] Lords commissioned or were presented with countless chivalric romances, and with dynastic histories and genealogies, many of which were lavishly illuminated. These books were not considered poor reflections of authentic Northern European prototypes, but were valued by readers in their own right. Leonello d'Este's illegitimate son Francesco, who had been resident at the Burgundian court for fifteen years, borrowed chivalric codices from the Este library when he visited Italy in 1459–60 as part of Philip the Good's embassy to the Council of Mantua. Francesco valued these manuscripts because of their connection with his family, though this case also suggests that even lords north of the Alps savoured French books from Italy. When Francesco briefly returned to Ferrara in 1467, he made sure to take back to Burgundy an additional tome, a *Lancelotto*, from the Este library.[4]

Many of the chivalric frescoes that adorned Renaissance courtly spaces are known to us primarily from inventories. They are slowly emerging, however, from behind layers of plaster and in recent responses to decades of scholarly indifference. In both the literal and Foucauldian senses, the archaeological excavation of courtly art is flourishing. Noteworthy rooms include Torrechiara's Camera d'Oro

9 Pisanello, *Knights and Chivalric Mêlée*, 1430s, fresco, Sala di Pisanello,
Palazzo Ducale, Mantua.

(illus. 7); Pisanello's frescoed *sala* in Mantua (illus. 9); an Arthurian cycle from Frugarolo (in Piedmont); Margherita Gonzaga's 'chamber of Lancelot' in Ferrara; and an interior decorated with the tale of Tristan and Isolde at nearby Fossadalbero, among many others.[5] Luminous tapestries woven with metallic threads were much more expensive than frescoes, and they too depicted subjects from chivalry and romance. The Este of Ferrara displayed costly tapestries with scenes from the *Romance of the Rose*, in addition to magnificent hangings portraying courtly tournaments and the siege of the castle of love.

Fifteenth-century lords, moreover, were commonly named after chivalric heroes. Borso, a protagonist of Pisanello's frescoes, and Leonello were brothers both in Arthurian legend and in Ferrara's ruling dynasty. Borso d'Este, in fact, possessed a large codex of the deeds of *Re Borso*.[6] Throughout their lives, Italian princes were compared to chivalric heroes of old. A chronicler, for instance, asserted that Sigismondo Malatesta's son Roberto seemed to be another 'Count Roland'.[7]

Noble boys and men read or at least possessed chivalric romances and histories in Italian and French. These manuscripts were often richly illuminated with exemplars and models to ponder. Borso d'Este commissioned images for vernacular books of the deeds of Lancelot and Merlin, and he sent for a French *Lancelot* to compare with an Italian-language version. A mid-Quattrocento *Tavola Ritonda* profusely illustrated with 289 pen drawings by Bonifacio Bembo, or perhaps one of his brothers, reminds us of the sort of codex that Borso said brought him more pleasure than the acquisition of a city.[8] The manuscript has been associated with various Lombard and Emilian courtly centres and patrons, including Pier Maria Rossi of Parma. Depictions of battles and hunts, prophetic dreams and demonic visions, courtly seduction and pious prayer all entertain the reader. The action is brutal. Swords pierce armour and slice through helmets. Heads roll. Here we see the knight Palamedes dramatically flattened on his mount by a lance blow delivered as his opponent's horse lunges into the fray (illus. 10). Palamedes struggles to hold on, and one foot desperately grips the stirrup as his horse slams on the brakes with its straight left legs. Lively, if not living, creatures adorn helmet crests and horse bards, and two knights witness the assault, including one at far right turning into our scene for a better view.[9]

Though the patron of this fabulous *Tavola Ritonda* is unknown, the book's ideal audiences would have included princes young and old – boys and men who typically studied Latin alongside various vernaculars. Indeed, as a precocious child, the count of Pavia and later duke of Milan Galeazzo Maria Sforza greatly impressed Emperor Frederick III, Pope Pius II and audiences throughout Italy with his accomplished Latin orations. Galeazzo's recitation for the emperor of an oration composed by Francesco Filelfo – delivered in Ferrara in 1452, at the tender age of eight – was described as 'stupendous and miraculous'.[10] His sister Ippolita was equally astonishing. Their mother reported that Ippolita's performance as a fourteen-year-old at the 1459 Council of Mantua elicited stupor and admiration. Galeazzo commented that it was 'something supernatural, considering [Ippolita's] age and sex'.[11] Nevertheless, Galeazzo's parents worried tremendously about his commitment to his studies, as tutors struggled to keep him on track (or at least to convince his parents that he was).

During a boat trip along the River Po to the Council of Mantua, Galeazzo listened to a lecture on Dante described as a 'beautiful thing'. Two years prior, in 1457, thirteen-year-old Galeazzo was preparing to travel to Ferrara. He wrote to his father to ask if he could

10 Circle of Bonifacio Bembo (attr.), perhaps Ambrogio or Lazzaro Bembo, 'Palamedes flattened by a lance blow', illustration from *Tavola Ritonda*, c. 1446.

take two French manuscripts from the Sforza library in Pavia to help pass the time during the impending days-long riverboat journey. Galeazzo assured his father that he preferred Latin over French texts, though he added that 'from French books I will take delight together with the entire group'.[12] The homosocial male world of mid-fifteenth-century courts preferred chivalric narratives, and these tales were best suited – in one young prince's mind at least – to entertain his 'compagnia' during a tedious voyage along the Po.

Tales and poems involving Cupid were equally resonant for Renaissance lords who understood that power was exercised through love, seduction and domination. As we saw in the Introduction, Cupid was a familiar accomplice, foe and intermediary for Quattrocento poets and lords. Leonello d'Este, made blind by the cruel god of love, slandered Cupid as enemy, following Ovid. Basinio di Parma, in the *Liber Isottaeus* celebrating the love between Sigismondo Malatesta of Rimini and his mistress Isotta degli Atti (see illus. 62), composed an epistle sent from Sigismondo to 'Amorem'.[13] A hovering, blind cupid with rainbow-coloured wings takes aim at Alessandro Sforza in an illuminated manuscript of Sforza's *Canzoniere* – a poetic text much indebted to Petrarch (illus. 11). Radiant and lordly, Alessandro is encased in gleaming armour. He busily pens sonnets, about to be struck for a second time by *amore*'s arrow. Alessandro Sforza was one of numerous lords who constructed a seigneurial identity as both military hero and author of courtly verses. After being made ruler of Pesaro with the support of his brother Francesco in 1445, Alessandro remained closely connected to the culture of luxury book production at the Milanese court for decades, as both patron and reader. In 1471, he requested the loan of Petrarch's famous Virgil illuminated by Simone Martini (then in the Sforza library in Pavia and now in Milan's Biblioteca Ambrosiana). Three surviving fifteenth-century manuscripts of Sforza's *Canzoniere* seem to have been decorated in Milan.[14]

Rogier van der Weyden, or his workshop, also portrayed Alessandro Sforza, in a small triptych painted when Sforza was in Flanders in 1458. Rogier's naturalism is visible in the luminous armour (with gilt buckles and virtuoso reflections of the pious lord's folded hands and golden sword hilt) and in Alessandro's balding, slicked back hair (illus. 12).[15] Indeed, his face is painted on parchment (or paper?), glued directly onto the ground. Alessandro's improbably narrow waist aligns

11 Illuminator close to Bonifacio Bembo (the Pesaro Sforza Master?), also attributed to the Master of Ippolita Sforza, 'Alessandro Sforza in armour composing poetry', illumination from Alessandro Sforza, *Canzoniere*, c. 1460s.

with Italian expectations about the depiction of lords' lithe bodies. So too do the waists of his son Costanzo and modestly dressed daughter Battista, shown with a green velvet belt worn high and very tight. Battista is represented here at the age of twelve or thirteen, not long before her marriage to Federico da Montefeltro of Urbino (25 years her senior) and thus twelve years and nearly as many children before her more famous portrait in Piero della Francesca's Uffizi diptych, painted just after her death at age 25 (illus. 13). Costanzo wears a snugly buttoned doublet underneath his opulently frilled tunic, and the graceful curves of his slender right leg are suggested by the multicoloured hose's delicate lines of blue.

At the festivities of Costanzo's wedding to Camilla Marzano of Aragon a decade and a half later, a boy outfitted as Cupid fired arrows

12 Workshop of Rogier van der Weyden, *Alessandro Sforza and His Children Costanzo and Battista Kneeling before the Crucifixion*, central panel of the *Sforza Triptych*, c. 1460, oil on oak panel.

13 Piero della Francesca, *Battista Sforza and Federico da Montefeltro*, c. 1472, diptych, tempera on panel.

from atop a float, perhaps feigning to take aim at the bride and groom.[16] Indeed, Quattrocento viewers beheld Cupid in representations of the Triumph of Love and in other scenes of love's instigation in various media: frescoes, *cassoni* (see illus. 82), manuscripts, ivories and tapestries.[17] In *August*, from the Palazzo Schifanoia's Room of the Months (Salone dei Mesi), two *amorini* – archers with bows drawn, perched atop the cornice in the fresco's central pavilion – point their arrows at members of Borso's gallant court, perhaps even at the lord himself (illus. 14). Within an illuminated Milanese wedding oration (*epithalamium*), commissioned by the Sforza courtier Gaspare Vimercati, the splendidly dressed beloved are brought together by a fair god of love, naked save his blindfold, bow and quiver. Above, Venus spills roses and violets on her son and on the blond couple he joins together, while beautiful and elegantly attired young men with golden locks look on (illus. 15).[18] Just below, Cupid takes aim at the pair across the page. In the initial 'O', the bride, Elisabetta Vimercati (the patron's niece), and the groom, Pietro Conte, both gesture to the arrows now fixed in their hearts.

14 Cupids taking aim, detail from unknown artist (sometimes attributed to Gherardo di Andrea da Vicenza), *August*, late 1460s, fresco, north wall, Salone dei Mesi, Palazzo Schifanoia, Ferrara.

Cupid also instigates amorous rituals within Torrechiara's magnificent Camera d'Oro. In the chamber's east lunette, idealized figures of Pier Maria Rossi and his mistress Bianca Pellegrini face one another, in profile from the viewer's perspective (illus. 16). Stepping into the Camera d'Oro, no doubt drawn by the golden chamber's visual splendour, the viewer first sees the lord and his damsel flanking a blindfolded Cupid. This golden-haired god of love stands atop the gilded capital of a column illusionistically painted to suggest rich, polychrome marble. He seems to smile as he incites love by smiting the pair with arrows. Cupid – fair skinned and naked save his blindfold and the red belt holding his quiver – radiates light from his entire body. His wings may originally have been gilded. Significantly, Torrechiara's god of love is not the familiar chubby, infant Cupid, but rather a lithe and dazzling youth. He parallels, for instance, a similarly gorgeous and radiant *Amore* described in verses dedicated to Isabella d'Este a few decades later. Niccolò da Correggio's brilliant Cupid from his Apuleian *Favola di Psiche* likewise possessed resplendent eyes and golden locks. He

15 Pesaro Sforza Master or the Master of Ippolita Sforza (attr.), 'Cupid weds two lovers', illuminated page from Bonino Mombrizio, *Epithalamium de nuptiis Petri Comitis et Helisabeth Vicomercatae, c.* 1460.

16 Bonifacio Bembo and workshop, *Cupid Instigates the Love between Pier Maria Rossi and Bianca Pellegrini*, *c.* 1460, fresco, east lunette, Camera d'Oro, Torrechiara Castle.

shone brighter than the sun at midday, and his 'lascivious beauty' surpassed even that of Narcissus.[19]

Spectacle, Prowess and Violence: Fashioning Courtly Masculinity

Torrechiara's Cupid may be about the very age at which beautiful males most attracted men's gazes and desires, from what we know of sodomitical practices and cultures in Renaissance Italy.[20] Only Cupid's mythological status allowed for the visual display of his naked body

– actual humans would have been clothed, if so prominently represented. Similar bodies dressed in *calze*, doublets and tunics magnetically drew looks to beautiful young men. These paragons of courtliness seduced audiences at events celebrating marriages, feast days, births, baptisms, peace accords, conferrals of knighthood, military victories and arrivals of illustrious guests. At these politically significant spectacles, men and boys were meant to be looked at. Like magnets, they pulled gazes towards themselves, seeking distinction and admiration, and they looked back, sizing up and emulating one another. They exercised and manifested courtliness and authority through exhibitions of noble masculinity and chivalric prowess, captivating audiences across the peninsula. The display of men was fundamental to the operations and erotics of aristocratic power in Renaissance Italy.[21]

In Bologna, competing jousts staged by the rival Bentivoglio and Malvezzi dynasties advertised and promoted each family's seigneurial aspirations. The tournaments were commemorated and mythologized in frescoes within the Bentivoglio palace shortly after they took place.[22] Chivalric spectacles were thus indispensable tools for the negotiation of dynastic power with that of civic institutions, local adversaries and regional lords. Though they served to bolster esteem and admiration for *signori*, spectacles could equally be utilized as political invective intended to defame. A farcical performance of the *condottiere* and lord Bartolomeo Colleoni riding a 'most fat pig' was purportedly performed in Paris in 1474, after he had insulted the French king Louis XI in the presence of royal falconers passing through Brescian territory. Duke Galeazzo Maria Sforza – Colleoni's nemesis – and Milan's ambassador in France widely publicized the event on both sides of the Alps.[23]

Chroniclers and diplomatic correspondents provide abundant details about the jousts and other spectacles that dotted the Renaissance calendar. Not surprisingly, given the contemporary value of opulent fabrics, the prize for public, chivalric competitions was typically a *palio* (in English pall, or *pallium*, from Latin), a length of brocaded, luxury cloth, which famously gives its name to the civic horse races at which the brocades were also awarded (to be explored in Chapter Two).[24] In 1469, for Milan's St George's Day joust, the triumphant man of arms was awarded a stretch of cloth of gold, while his squire received silver brocade. Two years later, to the winner on the feast of St George went two 'pieces' of silver brocade.[25] In May 1475, Costanzo Sforza won a *palio* of cloth of silver on account of his prowess with the lance during his wedding festivities at Pesaro, but also for his shimmering noble 'polish' or 'politeness'. The groom comported himself admirably during this multiday gala. Numerous 'splendid, great-hearted knights' participated, yet 'in the general opinion of everyone who discussed it, he [Costanzo] was thought one of the most beautiful and polished soldiers and knights seen for a long time'.[26]

Among the scores of jousts that the Este staged in Ferrara were those held to celebrate Leonello d'Este's birth in 1407 and his second wedding, to Maria of Aragon, in 1444. Indeed, jousts often marked the rites of passage of a lord's life. No expense was spared to put on these showstoppers. Wooden 'giants' and castles were constructed for jousts held in the mid-1460s (and both painters and carpenters had to be paid). In 1480, horses meant to look like lions were outfitted with 'big tail[s]' and with 'manes on their head'. The popularity of these events is suggested by a three-day tourney organized by Borso d'Este in May 1464, in an attempt to draw back to Ferrara citizens who fled during an outbreak of the plague.[27]

Jousts and tourneys were frequently represented on palace walls. Contests featuring mounted knights wearing brilliant armour and elaborate crests – and taking place in the centre of Ferrara, as the town's cathedral and castle seem to be visible – are depicted in the damaged frescoes on the south wall of Schifanoia's Salone dei Mesi, between the months of *January* and *February*, but more importantly between windows from which privileged viewers watched similar spectacles. The frescoes of this wall were painted *a secco*, directly on dry plaster, and were illegible even before the room was whitewashed in the eighteenth century (and eventually served as a tobacco ware-house). The detail illustrated here seems to show a well-armoured jouster and his horse 'going full tilt' – that is, running along a wooden barrier known in English as the tilt (illus. 17). We can make out, from behind, the sprinting horse's front hooves lifted in the air, plus the rider's mantle fluttering in the wind, both suggesting the dynamic energy of the charge. In 1485, the duchess Eleonora of Aragon took in a joust from just this vantage point inside Schifanoia, while her husband Ercole d'Este observed on horseback below. In frescoes from the villa of Belfiore, a Neapolitan knight and a Frenchman were portrayed jousting in front of a large audience, and a 'most beautiful tournament of arms' was painted among the cycle glorifying Eleonora's

17 Knight going full tilt in Ferrara, detail from unknown artist, *Urban Scene*, late 1460s, fresco, south wall, Salone dei Mesi, Palazzo Schifanoia, Ferrara.

wedding to Ercole in July 1473. The nuptial celebrations had been marked by days of jousts, including one won by the groom's brother Sigismondo, who was awarded 20 *bracce* (12 metres/40 feet) of 'beautiful gold brocade' after seven hours of jousting involving sixty rivals. Eleonora watched from above, and she participated in dances and in a fabulous meal with sugar sculptures depicting 'buildings, castles, damsels [and] animals'.[28]

It seems likely that Ferrarese frescoes would have represented the Este heroes and half-brothers Sigismondo and Alberto performing feats of chivalric valour. Alberto, an illegitimate son of Niccolò III and Filippa della Tavola, was one of the dynasty's most skilful combatants and a veritable knight in shining armour (a symbol that looms large in our imagination of the Middle Ages but actually a Renaissance man who only existed from the mid-fifteenth century, when plate

armour eclipsed protective mails). Numerous payments in the late 1450s and throughout the 1460s document Alberto's armours and brocades, including a tunic embroidered with silver threads representing the Este diamond impresa and a crimson satin garment embellished with gilded silver hooks. Cosmè Tura painted and applied gold and silver to some of this jousting attire. Alberto's tunics matched his horses' bards.[29]

A green silk garment produced for Alberto d'Este in 1458 was adorned by the painter Gherardo di Andrea da Vicenza with images of Apollo driving the sun on his chariot. The golden rays of the sun suffused the knight's clothing and the horse's barding, and they were echoed by the gilded flames that Gherardo applied to two lances. Given Alberto's courtly splendour, perhaps it is no surprise that it was he, rather than the more soberly dressed Ercole d'Este, whom Galeazzo Maria Sforza hoped would be made duke of Ferrara following the death of their brother Borso in 1471. Ercole sought to forestall Alberto's claims by rewarding him – or, rather, buying him off – with territories and palaces, including Rovigo, Lendinara, Sassuolo and the Palazzo Schifanoia (where he is doubtlessly portrayed, even if we no longer recognize his visage). In May 1474, however, Ercole had consolidated his position in Ferrara and ordered Alberto to Naples, ostensibly because of disobedience.[30]

A *cassone* in the Yale University Art Gallery (illus. 18) depicts a clamorous joust in Florence's Piazza Santa Croce. The scene has

18 Apollonio di Giovanni, *Tournament in Piazza Santa Croce*, *c.* 1440–60,
cassone panel, tempera on panel.

been recently interpreted as an evocation of the *mêlée* of 29 April
1459 organized by Cosimo de' Medici to celebrate the visit to Florence
of the fifteen-year-old Galeazzo Maria Sforza, though it may represent a more generic tournament.[31] Dozens of radiantly armoured
and outfitted men and horses battle, pose, charge and strut about.
Opulently dressed women and respectable men observe from above,
and, indeed, a contemporary poet described the construction of special viewing balconies. Near the very centre of the panel, six men
augustly arrayed in crimson assess the proceedings below, accompanied by a notary dressed in black, ready to register and tally the scores.
As the poet tells it, 'in the middle were the honest judges [*buon
giudicatori*] . . . [with] the notary . . . [who] with paper, pen and ink-
well . . . noted the jousters' blows'. Boys and young men separated
from the boisterous tourney by a wooden enclosure determinedly
view the action by standing on benches and stools, or by peeking
through holes in the fence. Though decent seats for the three-hour
spectacle were much in demand, they could be had: one Florentine
reported that he paid twelve *soldi* for his sons' tickets. The poet's
claim that 100,000 souls viewed the joust is no doubt an exaggera-
tion, yet the specificity of his description of, for instance, the horses'
barding made of crimson velvet embroidered with silver and pearls
reveals an attentive and discerning eye.[32]

Lorenzo and Giuliano de' Medici were the shining stars of the Florentine jousts of the 1460s and '70s. Artists such as Botticelli and Verrocchio manufactured visual ephemera for these courtly spectacles, which poets including Politian and Luigi Pulci celebrated in verse.[33] The rich, chivalric 'materiel' culture of republican Florence is affirmed by Medici inventories. Dozens of gleaming components of armour – breastplates and helmets, in addition to arm, thigh, shoulder, elbow and neck defences – are identified specifically in relation to jousting ('da giostra'). Gilded branches and figures of Cupid, Pallas and a golden damsel decorated helmet crests, some of which were prizes won during these jousts. Splendid headgear was awarded at the joust held in Piazza Santa Croce in 1459: for first place, a 'rich and beautiful' helmet covered or lined in crimson, surmounted by an eagle crest made of pearls, and valued at over 200 ducats; for second, a sallet bedecked with worked silver and a stunning pennache, estimated to cost about 100.[34]

Seigneurial armouries were stocked with instruments of ritual combat. In 1490, just months before he was murdered by a rival painter, Giovanni Bianchini gilded and burnished a shield for the teenaged Alfonso d'Este to carry in a joust celebrating the marriage of his sister Isabella. Lances were often painted or decorated with gold in Milan and Ferrara, as were Alberto d'Este's flamboyant lances mentioned above or those for which Costantino da Vaprio received payment for gilding in 1475.[35] Lances were commonly adorned to match or complement the rider's and even horse's clothing. At a few days of jousting accompanying a combined double wedding uniting the Sforza and Este dynasties in January 1492, Annibale II Bentivoglio of Bologna wore a green satin doublet and wielded lances painted green, while his horse's barding was gold-brocaded green silk.[36]

Subjects and peers recognized armour in portraits of *signori* as specifically jousting armour, outfitted with lance rests. The marble rest is broken in Sperandio's portrait of Ercole d'Este to be discussed in Chapter Two (illus. 52), while in Andrea Mantegna's painted *Madonna della Vittoria*, now in the Louvre, the lord Francesco Gonzaga's rest parallels his piously folded hands.[37] In a remarkable, full-page depiction of Ludovico Sforza illuminated by Ambrogio de Predis (illus. 19), the dark, gleaming plate armour seems to have been blued, and it echoes or reiterates il Moro's equally lustrous and black (or almost dark blue) flowing locks. Ludovico's lance rest audaciously passes through the portrait's frame, calling further attention to the painter's artifice and to Sforza's chivalric paraphernalia and prowess. These conspicuously jutting metal rests – whether painted, sculpted or forged – further attest to the cultural prominence of the joust. They work to convince viewers of lords' triumphs and derring-do.

19 Ambrogio de Predis, 'Ludovico Sforza', portrait in Aelius Donatus, *Grammatica* (or *Ianua*), *c.* 1498.

In 1489, in Pavia, Galeazzo Sanseverino broke nineteen lances and took home the gold-brocaded *palio* for unseating his adversary. Second place at this joust, and a stretch of silver brocade, went to another of Ludovico's courtiers, who splintered eleven lances. The day's real winner was Ludovico il Moro himself, however, whom the Ferrarese ambassador called the tourney's 'big fish [*gran pesce*]'. Galeazzo Sanseverino was a close confidant of Ludovico Sforza – both the lord's (first) cousin (once removed) and the husband of his niece. Ludovico and Galeazzo often dressed in matching garments. Similarly coordinated attire was commonly worn by allied jousters in these years.[38] In 1490, Francesco Gonzaga, lord of Mantua, and Giulio Cesare Tassoni, an Este courtier, were described to be 'both wearing the same fashion' at a joust celebrating Francesco's marriage to Isabella d'Este.[39]

More than two decades prior, in April 1464, Francesco Sforza had presided over a spectacular mock siege during which his sons defended a wooden castle, with ravelins on all four sides, against their oldest brother Galeazzo, age twenty. The boys are not specifically named but may have included Filippo, Sforza Maria, Ludovico, Ascanio and Ottaviano (ages fourteen to five, respectively). They were all 'entirely armed', as was Galeazzo. Their father, mounted atop a horse barded in cloth of gold, served as referee and judge. After two hours Galeazzo damaged sufficient wooden planks to enter and conquer the castle and safely put an end to the 'delightful spectacle'. Our source, the Mantuan ambassador in Milan, clarified that the fracas was executed with dulled weapons and lances without iron tips. It was a 'pleasing sight, and with little danger', a comment offered, no doubt, because these spectacles were often violent, even if swords were blunted and lances were inspected and regulated.[40] Indeed, jousting lances were subject to approval and certification before their use, and though they were often outfitted with the iron tips or lance heads that we still see in armoury collections, lances were commonly made of a soft wood that would break and shatter easily, and dramatically, upon impact. Many helmets and lances described in seigneurial inventories were damaged, in fact, suggesting the force of collisions.[41] As Patricia Simons has argued, in the performance and artistic representation of jousts, audiences enjoyed sexual metaphors of orgasm and ejaculation enacted by bursting and breaking lances.[42] These bodily metaphors would have been all the more resonant and enthralling when jousts and other chivalric spectacles accompanied nuptial festivities and, of course, because aristocratic participants customarily dedicated their exhibitions of courtly masculinity to noble women to whom they were devoted, sometimes chastely, sometimes not.

Princes and knights striving for glory in Quattrocento jousts were at times maimed, or worse. Most famously, in a series of profile portraits, Federico da Montefeltro (illus. 13) shields one side of his face from the viewer, hiding from us a nasty injury suffered during a joust held in honour of Francesco Sforza. A man at arms of the Mirandola court suffered a violent injury upon hitting the ground, flattened by a lance blow delivered by Galeazzo Sanseverino at a Ferrarese joust in 1493.[43] In January 1475, the Milanese ambassador in Florence described to his lord Galeazzo Maria Sforza a perilous lance blow breaking through Luigi della Stufa's helmet during the *giostra* won by Giuliano de' Medici. This son of Angelo della Stufa, a Florentine who had a few years earlier been made a knight of the golden spur by Galeazzo, emerged from the incident unscathed, though the ambassador characterized the blow as somehow improper or disgraceful.[44]

Two decades prior to Angelo's near miss, Sigismondo d'Este had been wounded in the thigh during a joust held in Naples. His elder brother Ercole reassured their mother, Ricciarda da Saluzzo, that Sigismondo was 'out of danger', yet the injury was severe enough that she pleaded with their half-brother and lord Borso to use his authority to make his siblings give up these 'perilous jousts'. They could not be convinced to do so, however, and we saw above that Sigismondo would take first prize at a joust marking Ercole's wedding festivities in 1473. Many of the dozens of rules issued by Francesco Sforza in 1465 for jousts celebrating his daughter Ippolita's nuptials with Alfonso II, duke of Calabria, aimed to protect both horse and rider by regulating lances, shields, saddles and armour. Saddles, for example, were inspected to ensure that no hidden straps or harnesses could keep combatants from being unseated. Indeed, for all their safety precautions, these contests, and their elaborate scoring systems, rewarded violently dismounting and disabling one's rival.[45]

In 1518, at Amboise, the teenaged Federico Gonzaga suited up for a series of jousts organized by King François I of France. Federico's father Francesco was distressed to learn that the lad would joust in the hazardous French style, which he considered to be 'very dangerous

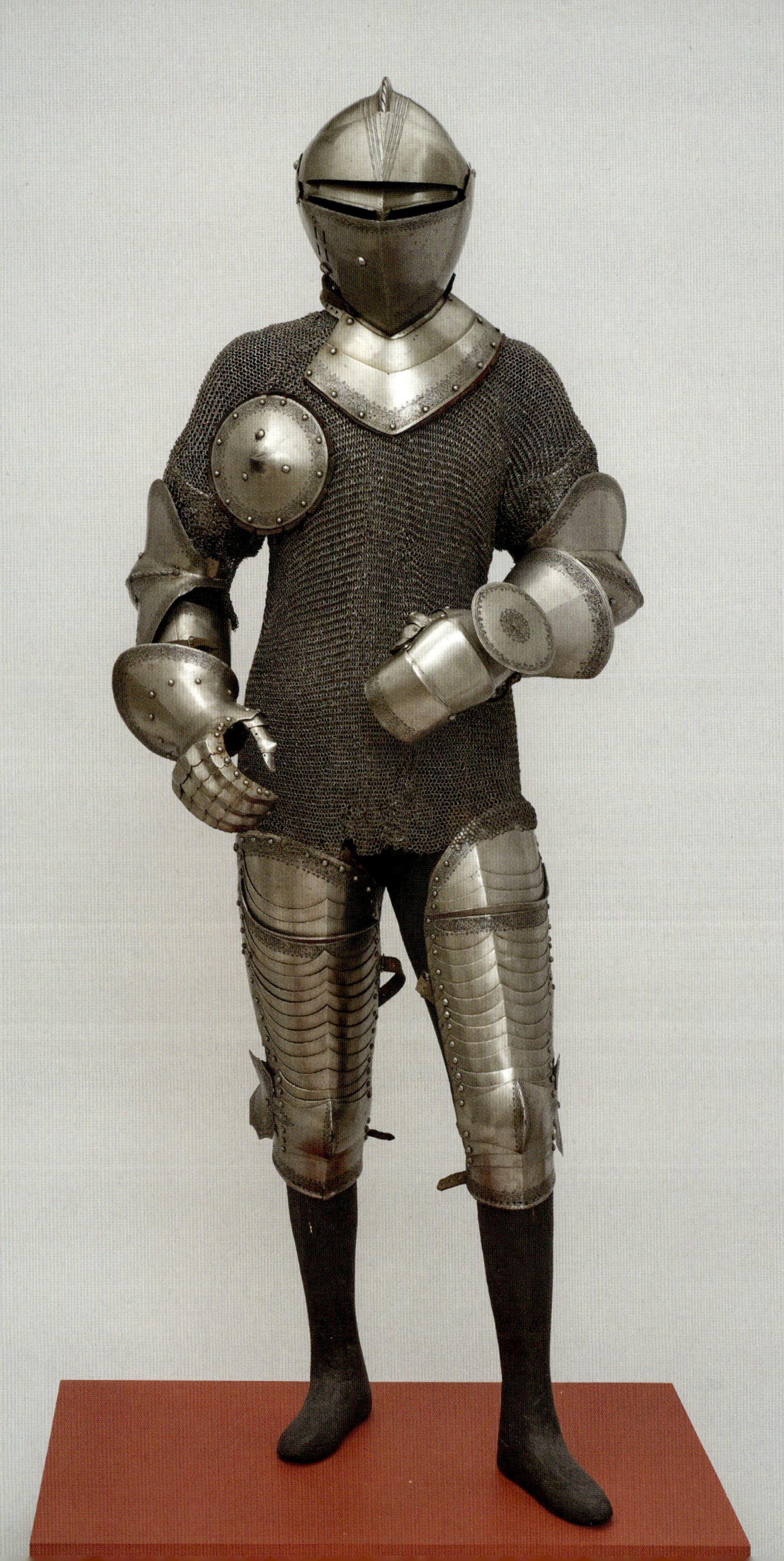

. . . we warn you not to enter, so that some disgrace not befall you, because that would cause us too much pain'. Not just Federico's honour, but that of the entire Gonzaga dynasty was at stake. To emphasize this point, Francesco instructed the boy's handler at the joust, each and every time that he gives Federico the lance before a run, to tell the young prince, 'Remember, you are the son of Lord Francesco Gonzaga, *marchese* of Mantua.'[46]

François I – who by then had shared a friendship with Federico Gonzaga for a few years, and on both sides of the Alps – requested that Federico joust arrayed in French royal livery. Though these garments have not survived the ravages of time, various components of armour and a mail shirt – allowing for relatively fluid movement – have been associated with Federico and dated to about a decade after this French tournament (illus. 20). At Amboise, Federico showed his mettle and on the first day broke two of his five lances and additionally scored three touching blows. On the second day of jousting, he improved, shattering four of his five lances, and scoring a blow with the other. As Federico informed his father: 'I did not fail to make my mark and among the other things that inspired me to do honour to myself was reminding myself that I am the son of Your Excellency from whom I have many honourable things to imitate.' The model and image of the father loomed large in the son's mind. Federico, however, had sliced his leg during one of the early runs. He insisted in a letter to his mother, Isabella d'Este, that it was 'nothing', yet he came down with a high-grade fever from the wound's infection. His father was relieved when informed that Federico would thus sit out the upcoming mock castle assault and sword duels: 'we console ourselves because the illness was nothing and maybe it was by divine disposition to avoid some greater evil in those dangerous games.'[47] It is impossible to say if Francesco Gonzaga worried more about his son's health or his dynasty's honour.

From an early age, men at court learned to hunt, ride horses and wield weapons with vigour and skill, but simultaneously with restraint, decorum and caution. The young prince must practise martial arts but, as Francesco Sforza admonished his son Galeazzo, should not 'joke around' with weapons: 'non schirzare con ferri, saxi o bastoni'.[48] In 1459, the fifteen-year-old Galeazzo punctured the palm of his right

20 Presumed armour of Federico Gonzaga, Northern Italian, *c.* 1531, iron, leather and silk velvet.

hand precisely while joking around – grabbing a piece of melon that a ducal sword bearer had set on the point of a blade. The Mantuan ambassador in Milan – our source – notified his lord, whose daughter Dorotea was at the time promised to Galeazzo, that the prince was intact and well cared for. In a letter sent the following day, the envoy reiterated that Galeazzo's hand was fine. Five years later, Francesco Sforza was no doubt reassured when another son – Ludovico, at age twelve – recounted a dramatic deer hunt in Pavia's ducal park or *barco* and insisted that he had closely minded his weapons so as to not harm himself, when he hurriedly mounted his horse to chase two large deer.[49]

As James Schultz recently reminded us, speaking of late medieval Europe, 'fighting is the activity by which noble men define themselves, as a gender and as a class.'[50] Knowledge of hand-to-hand combat was expected for young Renaissance princes, and they appreciated and enjoyed wrestling and other violent contests throughout their lives. Borso d'Este and Ludovico Gonzaga were entertained in 1458 by two brawling men who pummelled each other until so much blood flowed that Borso had to stop the *mêlée*. The fighters were rewarded with expensive tunics for their performance.[51] Borso's father, Niccolò III d'Este, possessed at least three copies of Fiore dei Liberi's fighting manual *Il Fior di Battaglia* (The Flower of Battle), some of them gifts from Gian Galeazzo Visconti. *The Flower of Battle* provided instruction on armed and unarmed combat and demonstrated wrestling techniques such as the 'boar's tooth' and the 'iron gate'. In one profusely illustrated codex belonging to Niccolò – and no doubt used by his sons – nimble youths dressed in armour and tight-fitting clothing battle each other with swords, daggers and knives of all sorts. On one page, we see a *bastoncello* or small baton deftly wielded in various offensive and defensive manoeuvres (illus. 21).[52]

Depictions of battle and war supplied foundational lessons in the education of Renaissance princes. Young lords simultaneously attained literacy and learned to fight assisted by grammar manuals filled with violent imagery. Ancient Persian, Greek and Roman warriors appear as splendidly armoured fifteenth-century knights in an illuminated manuscript with text copied by the precisely fifteen-year-and-four-month-old Ludovico il Moro Sforza. The reckoning of the book's inscription – 'Ludovicusmaria Sfortia Vicecomes annorum xv ᵐ/ et mensuum iiijʳ manu propria die xxvij Novembris / 1467 /

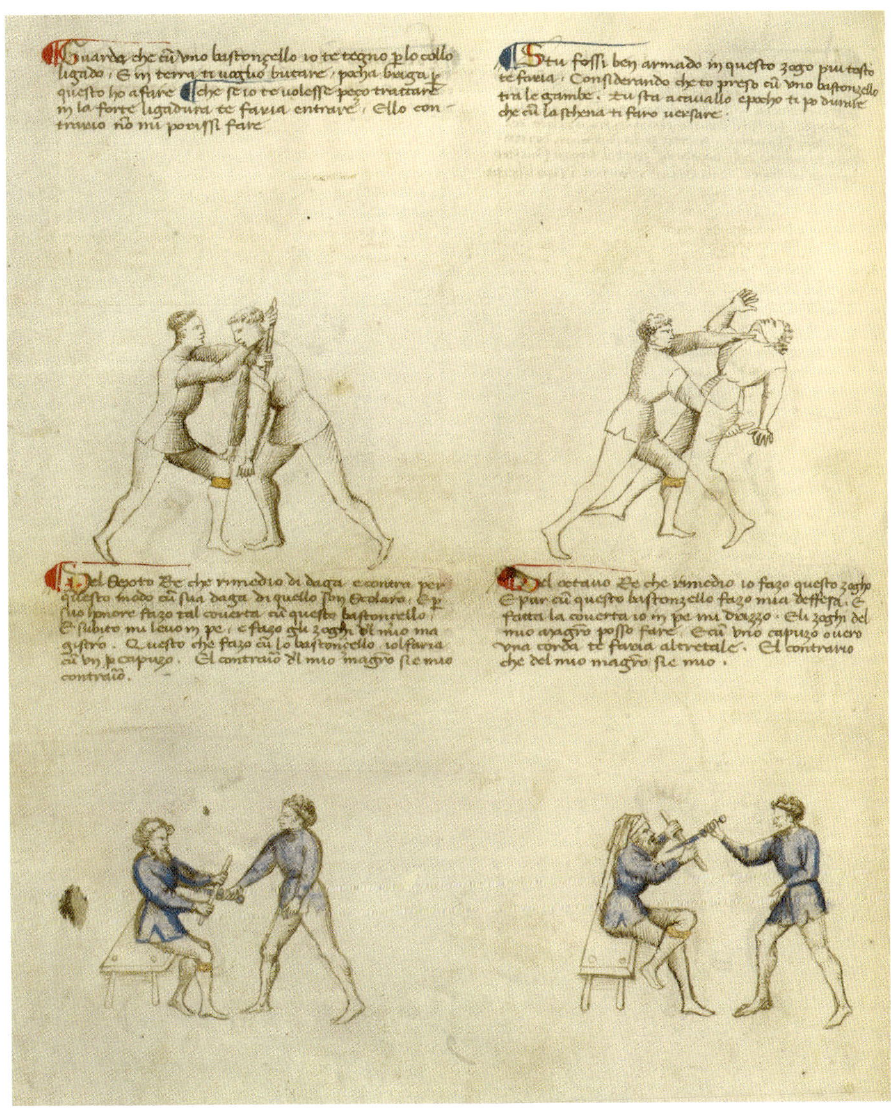

21 Unknown artist, 'Fighting manoeuvres with a *bastoncello*', drawings from Fiore dei Liberi, *Il Fior di Battaglia* (*c.* 1410).

Cremone' – is exact as Ludovico was born on 27 July 1452. Ludovico's tutor Francesco Filelfo directed this writing exercise perhaps commissioned by the boy's mother, Bianca Maria Visconti Sforza.[53] The young aristocratic scribe wrote out Filelfo's commentary on the *Rhetorica ad Herennium*, a popular treatise on rhetoric believed to have been authored by Cicero, and one that encompasses courtly and Latin traditions.[54] The book's final page displays Ludovico hunched

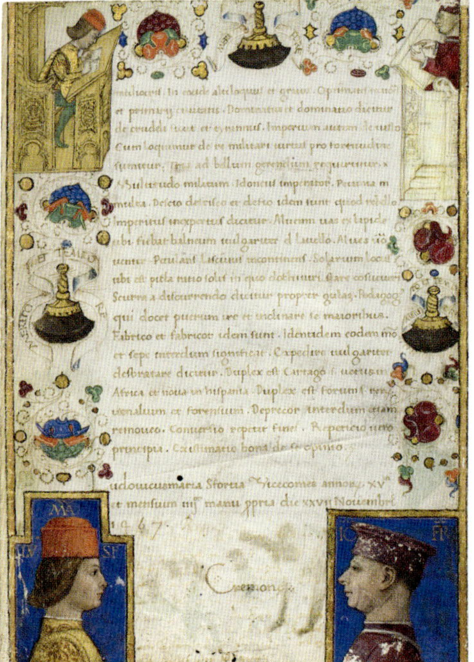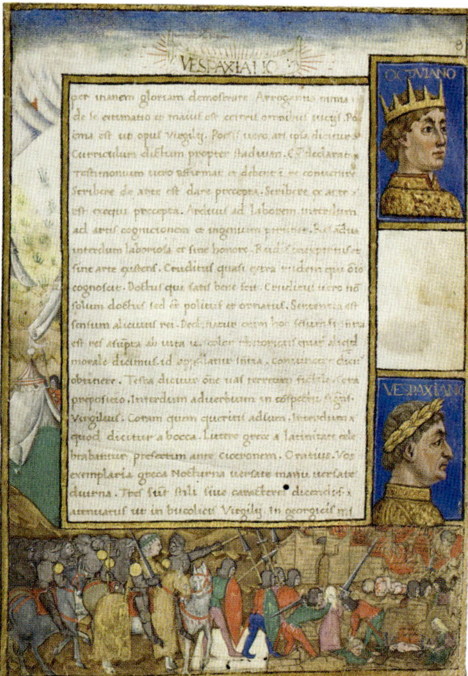

Clockwise: Cristoforo de Predis and Ambrogio da Marliano (attr.), illuminated pages from *Commentario de Rhetorica ad Herennium*, 1467: 22 'Ludovico Sforza as student and scribe, with tutor Francesco Filelfo'; 23 '"Vespaxiano" with the Sack of Jerusalem'; 24 '"Camiles" with Camillus defeating the Gauls'; 25 '"Romulus" with the Rape of the Sabine Women'.

over a desk wearing green *calze*, a red *berretta* and a gold-brocaded doublet and tunic (illus. 22). The teenager diligently copies the text opposite Filelfo, who, seated at a small *cathedra*, gestures with his fingers while rehearsing the grammar's rhetorical exercises. Below, two representations of Ludovico's brush device (*la scopetta*) and an additional pair of portraits of the pupil and teacher in decorous profile ornament the page.

Accompanying the text copied by the prince, portraits of ancient warriors and emperors co-mingle with those of Ludovico's illustrious Visconti and Sforza ancestors. These men served as exemplars for the boy. One folio depicts Titus's sack of Jerusalem in 70 CE. On the lower right, flames rise from the city (or perhaps Solomon's Temple), dead and bloodied bodies are strewn about, and soldiers assault and violate their victims (illus. 23). In the representation of Marcus Furius Camillus's defeat of the Gauls in 387 BCE (described in Book Five of Livy's *Ab urbe condita*) (illus. 24), Ludovico saw episodes of hand-to-hand combat like those found in Niccolò III d'Este's fighting manual (illus. 21). Trampled corpses and a dismembered body gruesomely suggest actual warfare in the grammar primer, however. The codex's scene of the Rape of the Sabine Women (illus. 25) presents numerous fashionably dressed fifteenth-century couples – fair damsels in long, cascading dresses and blond lads with tight *calze*, fashionable tunics and narrow waists. The serenity of the dance below works to efface the violence of the rape itself, which is suggested in the left margin by one man forcibly holding and lifting a woman from behind just outside the dance hall, adjacent to the depiction of a marriage ritual.

Alison Nogueira connected the manuscript's wedding celebrations to those of Ludovico's parents, Bianca Maria Visconti Sforza and the recently deceased Francesco Sforza, and interpreted the figure of the mounted Titus commanding the brutal sack of Jerusalem (illus. 23) as a portrait of Francesco.[55] The identifications provide further evidence that these and similar images and books were intended as models of belligerent masculinity for their young readers. So too were the scenes of ancient combat and armoured heroes that the Augustinian friar Nebridio illuminated in Cremona in a manuscript of Sallust's works also produced for Ludovico. Indeed, lordly 'materiel' culture very much preoccupied the boy. Ludovico requested that his armour be sent to him in Cremona, where he had been living almost as prince of the town following the death of his father Francesco in March

26 Ambrogio de Predis, 'Massimiliano Sforza', portrait in Aelius Donatus, *Grammatica* (or *Ianua*), *c.* 1498.

1466, and through 1467, with significant diplomatic and political responsibilities. Il Moro wanted 'to keep it [his armour] close to me, as is the custom of each good and valorous man of arms'.[56] Armour was of course *de rigueur* for any lord in the making. Ludovico's nephews

Gian Galeazzo and Ermes, at the ages of four and five, had satin-lined armour produced by Antonio Missaglia. In 1489, Ludovico presented to the twelve-year-old Ferrante d'Este gilded armour manufactured in the Missaglia *bottega* known in Milan as the Casa dell'Inferno (House of Hell), so-called because of its infernal din and fire. For Ferrante's elder brother Alfonso, a goldsmith embellished a breastplate with gilded silver when the lad was eight.[57]

Ludovico passed down to his sons the lessons that he had learned as a boy. About three decades after his portrayal hard at work as a scribe, the adult Ludovico (illus. 19) was depicted by Ambrogio de Predis in shining armour at the end of Aelius Donatus' *Grammatica* (or *Ianua*) produced for his son Massimiliano (illus. 26). This was a popular Renaissance grammar manual for adolescent lords. In 1417, for instance, the text was illuminated in a manuscript intended for the five-year-old Ludovico Gonzaga.[58] The Sforza codex opens to a tightly cropped profile portrait of young Massimiliano, who is like his father portrayed by Ambrogio de Predis with glossy, luminous hair and wearing lustrous armour. Massimiliano literally looks towards his paternal exemplar at the book's end – the pair of images recently was called 'the most monumental illuminated portraits of the Renaissance'.[59] Between these two striking portraits are pages of verb conjugations and other grammatical exercises. In full-page illuminations, Massimiliano saw himself travelling on horseback through Milan, so that the town's women could view and fall in love with him (*amo*, I love); listening to his tutor, Gian Antonio Secco da Borella, and studying (*doceo*, I teach); dining and delighting among friends (and a chained monkey) (*edo*, I eat); riding a triumphal chariot accompanied by a spirited troupe of musicians (*gaudeo*, I rejoice); and, finally, pledging himself to virtue. Grammars were tools for practising Latin, of course, but they simultaneously – and just as importantly – steeped the boys who would become lords in the essential ideologies of courtliness, violence and seduction upon which their authority and rule were based.

Making Knights

In the south lunette of Torrechiara's Camera d'Oro (illus. 27), the damsel Bianca Pellegrini pledges love and loyalty to Pier Maria Rossi by presenting him with a sword, a traditional symbol of fealty and knighthood. Bianca inspires her lord's martial deeds, confers military honour and thus confirms his authority.[60] The blond knight's plate armour covers what seems to be either rich fabric or perhaps mail. Because his upper body is here depicted in profile, Rossi's unfolded lance rest is conspicuously visible, suggesting to viewers glory in the joust, perhaps one at which he dedicated himself to Bianca. Pier Maria's silver spurs likewise stand out prominently against the green background. His love and devotion to the damsel, moreover, are visualized by a heart suspended between his chest and the sword presented to him.

Though we might consider them the stuff of Romance or earlier centuries, rituals of knighting and the sword's bestowal were often performed by Rossi's peers. The Camera d'Oro's depiction of a woman dubbing her lord was an imaginary scene, however, an inversion or reversal of that linking a prince and his (male) subject.[61] These homosocial, male experiences formalized bonds between lords and vassals, but additionally, when family members of noble mistresses were involved, those between lords and lovers. Borso d'Este presented a kneeling feudatory with a ducal sword and invested him with various castles after receiving an oath of fealty in 1453. Twelve years later, Francesco Sforza ennobled a number of men during celebrations for his daughter Ippolita's nuptials.[62] Francesco's son Galeazzo, in turn, knighted a dozen young men, all scions of aristocratic families from Lombardy or throughout the peninusula (plus his illegitimate son Alessandro), to mark the betrothal of his first-born, legitimate daughter Bianca Maria.[63] Not yet two, Bianca was at this time promised to her cousin Philibert of Savoy, who died when she was ten. Her uncle Ludovico considered marrying Bianca first to John Corvinus, son of King Matthias Corvinus of Hungary, and then to King James IV of Scotland, before arranging an ultimately miserable union with Maximilian, king of the Romans and later Holy Roman emperor.

In 1445, Pope Eugenius IV knighted Sigismondo Malatesta in Rome and presented him with sword and chaplet. This lord took golden – actually, mercury gilt – spurs to his grave. Well before he ended up there, however, Sigismondo dubbed Antonio degli Atti, his mistress Isotta's brother, with a sword. Sigismondo granted Antonio golden spurs, silver vessels, brocaded clothing and, through Isotta, 200 golden ducats.[64] Antonio's pledge to serve his lord loyally reassured Sigismondo that he had secured the support of the family of his favoured mistress. To this end, similar honours and gifts were bestowed

27 Bonifacio Bembo and workshop, *Bianca Pellegrini Awards Her Knight Pier Maria Rossi a Sword*, c. 1460, fresco, south lunette, Camera d'Oro, Torrechiara Castle.

upon family members of other aristocratic mistresses, as I discuss in Chapters Three and Four. Indeed, chroniclers described rituals of knighting because they powerfully publicized and reinforced hierarchies of political alliance and dependence, as did, for instance, the ceremony in which Federico da Montefeltro was made duke of Urbino by Pope Sixtus iv. In Old St Peter's Basilica, Sixtus presented Federico a scintillating, gold-brocaded robe and awarded him golden spurs. The newly promoted duke dramatically waved a gleaming sword through the air after the pope laid it on his shoulders.[65]

On the end panel of a *cassone* dating circa 1460–70 (but destroyed at Bath in 1942), Emperor Frederick iii dubs a kneeling knight, perhaps one who paid for the honour during one of the emperor's visits to Italy, in either 1452 or 1469. The reverse of Bertoldo di Giovanni's medal of the emperor, moreover, represents Frederick's conferral of knighthoods on Rome's Ponte Sant'Angelo in January 1469. In Ferrara, Borso's courtiers made knights by the emperor in 1452 included Niccolò Ariosto, the poet Ludovico's father who we encounter again in Chapter Five; and the one-year-old Niccolò da Correggio, who would become a well-known poet and a much lionized combatant, called the 'invincible jouster' following his heroic defence of Cupid in a Ferrarese spectacle of 1478 (and, indeed, his lance rest is conspicuously extended in Sperandio's portrait medal struck at about that time).[66]

These rituals marked significant political and military alliances and, when celebrated in chivalric spectacle, poetic unions of fealty and love. In 1413 Pietro Rossi, Pier Maria Rossi's father, was knighted by Niccolò iii d'Este in the church of the Holy Sepulchre in Jerusalem. Accompanying Pietro and Niccolò was Feltrino Boiardo, grandfather of the poet Matteo who would commemorate the pilgrimage decades later in his epic *Orlando Innamorato*. Boiardo imagined frescoes celebrating Niccolò's journey with 'counts and barons setting sail/ upon a sacred course to see/ the Holy Land and other realms'.[67] Niccolò d'Este had been given golden spurs at age nine, at his father's deathbed. In Jerusalem, he girded Pietro Rossi and others with swords and placed spurs on their feet. While in Cyprus on this journey, the lords made vows over a feast of peacocks, mirroring late medieval crusading bird oaths such as that narrated in Jacques de Longuyon's *Les Voeux du paon* (The Vows of the Peacock). Much like knights of lore, these men swore to perform feats of valour and acts of devotion. Pietro

Rossi vowed never to lie, except on behalf of his lord's state or to save his own life or that of a close friend. Rossi further pledged to recite an 'Ave Maria' whenever he saw a painted image of Mary, which provides revealing evidence of one of the many ways that Renaissance art activated responses from beholders.[68]

Stakes were high when promises of allegiance were made visible. In 1509, Troilo Rossi (Pietro's great-grandson) exiled one hundred men and confiscated their goods for having pledged loyalty to his cousin Filippo Maria Rossi by ritually touching his hand.[69] Spectacles attending rituals of dubbing and investiture, moreover, afforded men the opportunity to both create and display courtly bodies glittering in gold. On Christmas Day 1464, Borso dubbed his courtier Teofilo Calcagnini knight of the golden spur. Teofilo organized an extravagant joust to commemorate the honour the following day, for which he ordered eleven painted lances and a stretch of taffeta (adorned with his arms in gold and silver) to be placed above the crimson, silver-brocaded *palio* awarded as first prize. On Easter of 1471 in Old St Peter's Basilica in Rome, Teofilo accompanied his lord as Borso was formally invested with the duchy of Ferrara by Pope Paul II. Paul girded Borso with a sword and presented him a golden necklace, a gilt *bacchetta* (baton or sceptre) and a fur-lined mantle of gold brocade that Borso referred to in a letter as 'ducal attire'. The gleaming sword in particular caught the attention of those present: one source called it 'resplendent' and 'that relucent and so lordly sword'.[70]

Borso's brocades worn at the Easter ceremony seem to have been fabricated by Antonio di Boccaccio da Cremona, father of the painter Boccaccio Boccaccino. Following Borso's death a few months later, Ercole d'Este tried to get out of paying Antonio for this work and for the large quantity of silver that had been furnished by a goldsmith.[71] Ercole, who as a child had been knighted by Emperor Sigismund, may have been reluctant to pay his brother's debts, but he, like Borso, utilized dubbing rituals to instil loyalty in his knights. Not long after the tournament celebrating the first anniversary of his succession, Ercole ennobled a number of men and outfitted them with swords, golden spurs, gold chains and gold-brocaded tunics. At least two of these courtiers were invested with lands that had been confiscated from disgraced officials convicted of lese-majesty, including one accused of stealing from Borso and falsifying account books.[72] Ercole also solidified alliances with aristocratic dynasties beyond

28 Lorenzo Costa, *Bentivoglio Altarpiece* (*Madonna and Child with Giovanni II Bentivoglio and His Family*), 1488, tempera on canvas.

Ferrara through rituals of knighthood. On New Year's Day 1492, he raised the teenaged Ermes Bentivoglio to knight and presented him with a golden necklace enhanced by a magnificent gem. The ceremony took place in the Bentivoglio chapel in San Giacomo Maggiore in Bologna, and thus in front of Lorenzo Costa's votive image in which Ermes could see his slightly younger self (illus. 28).[73] Privileged audiences for these rituals witnessed noble Renaissance men in the making.

2

Aristocratic Animals
and Men at Court

Lords and ladies, courtiers and kin, and men-at-arms and mistresses all composed the Renaissance court. So too did non-human companions who were accorded aristocratic status: horses, dogs, birds of prey and, sometimes, cats. Indeed, princes formed intense bonds with domesticated animals and were, even as boys, expected to exhibit mastery over them. Doing so confirmed their rank and manhood. This chapter investigates the hounds, stallions, cheetahs and falcons whose presence and prowess made Italian Renaissance men, and the affective relationships shared between beasts and their lords, to better understand ideologies of rule and dominance exercised over animals and human subjects alike. Renaissance relationships to animals sometimes seem bracingly familiar and conform to our own sentimental attachments to pets. At other times, they demonstrate a stomach-churning brutality (which, of course, is equally a fundamental condition of our treatment of and lives entangled with animals).[1]

This chapter traces the expansive global networks that these creatures inhabited and traversed, and explores the ways that they bound elite men together through collective experiences and shared knowledge and expertise. The hunt, for example, was not merely an essential noble pastime substituting and training for war, though it certainly was that. It was likewise an indispensable mechanism for spectacle, surveillance and rule. Crucially, animals were cherished gifts that mediated alliance and exchange. Aristocratic animals contributed much to and at times shaped Renaissance politics, diplomacy and ideals of masculinity.

Before looking closely at hounds, hawks and horses, an examination of one carefully managed conferral of gifts intended to prompt a counter gift of stallions will illuminate the ways that lords calculated as they orchestrated acts of gift-giving, scheming to acquire the most desirable animals. Ferrara's lord Borso d'Este provided fastidious instructions to two ambassadors sent to the court of Abu 'Amr 'Uthman, the Hafsid caliph of Ifriqiya (Tunisia), in the spring of 1464.[2] Francesco Gattamellata and Giovanni Giacomo della Torre were tasked with presenting prized Sicilian mules and other gifts to Uthman and prominent Tunisian courtiers, and with obtaining for Borso coveted Barbary horses. Borso advised not only what should be given to whom, but additionally about the manner and order in which the precious objects – ivory boxes, scissors, brocaded chairs, opulent dog collars and leashes, even wheels of cheese – would be carried, displayed and bestowed. Borso urged his envoys to prepare their letters of presentation meticulously and to apprise their interpreter of the ceremony's details in advance. Francesco and Giovanni were directed to introduce Borso as a 'lord in Italy, and not a minor or middling one'. They should prepare Borso's gifts 'in a pleasing and beautiful way, displaying them suitably, and making sure to have enough people to carry everything'.

These gifts and their materials manifested distinctions of rank. Caliph Uthman would be given two hunting horns 'made for a king'; a silk and gold hunting bag 'as for a king'; and a 'king's sword'. Uthman would receive eight Sicilian mules with mantles of brocaded silk; his son two mules draped in silk (without brocade); and a key customs official (the *caydameth*) wool mule mantles. The timing of the presentation was complicated by the fact that the envoys reached Tunis before the mules, which were being transported from Sicily by an Este farrier. Borso d'Este assessed both opportunities and risks in this lag, just as we might recognize promise and peril in all diplomatic acts of gift-giving. On the one hand, Borso understood that, the 'appetites of men being as they are', Uthman or his son might become impatient and press to know about or peek at the gifts. If the ambassadors suspect this, Borso advised, then they should solicit Clemente Ciceri, a Genoese representative resident in Tunis, to describe the gifts secretly to the caliph, 'as if by his own initiative'. This would satisfy Uthman's curiosity yet allow him to maintain the pretence of surprise during the formal unveiling.

The cunning Borso also perceived advantages afforded by the delay. He instructed his men to be alert to, and ready to size up, Uthman's and his courtiers' horses while they awaited the mules' arrival: 'Do not hesitate . . . to look around and examine what horses there are in the court and in the lands of nobles, if you ever see something that would seem good for us.' Borso only wanted the finest animals: 'if they are not beautiful and well-bred as specified above, we would rather go without.' 'You should do this,' Borso advised, 'since in the time you have with the king, he might ask you and say, "look around and see if there is something your lord might like" and then you will be able to say, "in fact, yes, there is this horse and that horse that our lord would like".' If Uthman did not make this offer, Borso encouraged his agents to pre-emptively indicate to Ciceri 'tactfully, that such and such a horse with such and such a name would be good for us', anticipating that the Genoese envoy could finagle a horse or two. Borso d'Este left nothing to chance. He methodically manoeuvred to maximize the reception, presentation and value of the gifts he gave, and of those he reckoned would be given in return. The duke's gambit paid off. By year's end a Tunisian ambassador arrived in Ferrara accompanied by a dozen or so attendants bearing Barbary horses, greyhounds and 'delicate textiles'.[3] Renaissance princes were clever gift-givers and recipients, indeed.

Borso's peers thoroughly understood the inclusions and exclusions activated and advertised by acts of giving. They deftly navigated the networks and relations forged by the presentation, reception or even refusal of gifts. Florence's *signoria*, for instance, measured the worth of brocade and armour given in 1432 to the hero of the battle of San Romano beyond their monetary value. According to a chronicler, these sumptuous objects were presented to Niccolò Mauruzzi da Tolentino – leading the charge at the centre of Paolo Uccello's spellbinding panel in London – to 'make him more submissive in our service'.[4] Gift-giving's attendant rituals produced and reflected domination and submission, dependence and obligation, distinction and division. Gifts materialized alliance, yet they likewise negotiated rivalries and inflamed tensions.

Even very young lords were expected to demonstrate magnanimity and liberality. In June 1467, the fifteen-year-old Ludovico Sforza pledged to give his tutor Franchino Caimi one of his own horses, as a 'sign of gratitude' for Franchino's instruction. Ludovico had already, a few years prior, requested a painted portrait of a horse, to impress his father and demonstrate filial respect.[5] This image of the horse that he described as 'beautiful enough for a king' may have been the first artistic commission of the boy who would become Leonardo da Vinci's patron for the *Last Supper*. In 1498, more than three decades after Ludovico's early plans for a horse portrait, the duke's five-year-old son Massimiliano recounted to him a play date with his illegitimate half-brothers Cesare (son of Cecilia Gallerani, Leonardo's *Girl with an Ermine*) and Gian Paolo (son of Lucrezia Crivelli, perhaps Leonardo's *Belle Ferronnière*).[6] Sforza boys and girls were taught to compose letters to their often-absent parents from a young age, assisted by their tutors, and thus to practise both literacy and diplomacy. Massimiliano proudly reported that he had offered Gian Paolo a wooden horse, but that the toddler was already too big for the saddle. Massimiliano took 'singular pleasure' in his act of generosity, as did the entire 'company' of boys, he asserted. Massimiliano clearly wanted to please his father with this precocious display of largesse.

Canine Courtiers

Noble Renaissance men loved horses, yet their affections for hounds did not lag far behind. In December 1470, the 21-year-old Lorenzo de' Medici thanked Ludovico Gonzaga for 'very beautiful' dogs from the Gonzaga kennels, and the following month Lorenzo sent Galeazzo Maria Sforza three black bloodhounds and apologized that he had no other well-bred dogs to offer. Angelo della Stufa, the Florentine ambassador in Milan, had recently informed Lorenzo that Galeazzo was obsessed with a particular breed of greyhound: 'a wild passion for greyhounds has come over the duke and he thinks of nothing else.' Angelo advised Lorenzo to send Galeazzo a pair. The Medici envoy additionally reported that Galeazzo's son Gian Galeazzo – then a toddler – had been depicted throughout the Sforza castle in Pavia surrounded by greyhounds.[7] Scenthounds of various breeds (the *bracco* and *segugio*) and also sighthounds (the *levriero*, greyhound) are the dogs that recur most frequently in princely correspondence. When lords hunted, these dogs often worked in tandem. Scenthounds, with muzzles to the ground, located prey by smell and then drove it to the speedier greyhounds, who chased quarry by sight. We will see the two breeds in court frescoes, and as Francesca Borgo elucidated, this sort of hunt served as a crucial metaphor in Leonardo da Vinci's understanding of vision.[8] Leonardo's optical science was fundamentally informed by Sforza cultures of hunting.

Renaissance frescoes often depicted dogs who sometimes viewed these very images. Francesco Gonzaga's hound Superbo darted towards and tried to bite a representation of Plaxi, perhaps his nemesis, with painting underway in the Camera dai Cani (Room of the Dogs) of the dynasty's palace at Marmirolo in 1486. This incident recounted in a report on the artists' progress to their patron echoes Pliny's tales of birds pecking at fictive grapes or horses neighing at painted stallions – and Giorgio Vasari tells a similar story in which a lifelike image of Turco, so-named because the dog was a gift from the Turkish sultan, was assailed by a Gonzaga hound who was 'most inimical' to Turco. The overseer of the work at Marmirolo, our source, did introduce doubt about the authenticity or extemporaneity of Superbo's aggression.[9] He asserted that the (unnamed) painters must have incited the dog and clarified that he did not witness the event himself but relied on what they had told him. Maybe Superbo did bark and bite at Plaxi's image. Alternatively, the cagey painters may have concocted a story that they thought would amuse or impress their lord by demonstrating their life-like skills and knowledge of ancient tropes celebrating artistic artifice.

Dogs had long been central to Italian politics and propaganda. As Pavia starved during a blockade by the Visconti dynasty in 1359, the Augustinian preacher Giacomo Bussolari expelled women, children and the infirm and elderly. The poet Petrarch, a Visconti partisan, condemned Bussolari, yet reserved his most histrionic pleas not for Pavia's miserable townsfolk, but for its dogs. Petrarch implored the Augustinian tyrant not to slaughter the animals as he had vowed, but instead to hand them over to the Visconti, whom they would loyally serve. The dogs would ask as much themselves, the Tuscan poet lamented, if they could but speak: 'and if die they must, they would rather die by the tusks of boars than by starvation or the sword'.[10] Petrarch's heart-wrenching appeal seems to reveal greater concern for dogs than for humans, and, assuredly, this was neither the first nor the last time that hunting hounds garnered greater consideration than did subjects. Petrarch also gives voice to sincere affection between human and canine, and to the familiar trope of the loyalty of man's best friend.

The most familiar canine courtier of the dog-eat-dog world of the Renaissance court is no doubt Rubino (Ruby), who contentedly relaxes under Ludovico Gonzaga's chair in Andrea Mantegna's frescoes

29 Rubino, detail from Andrea Mantegna, *The Court of Gonzaga* (illus. 30).

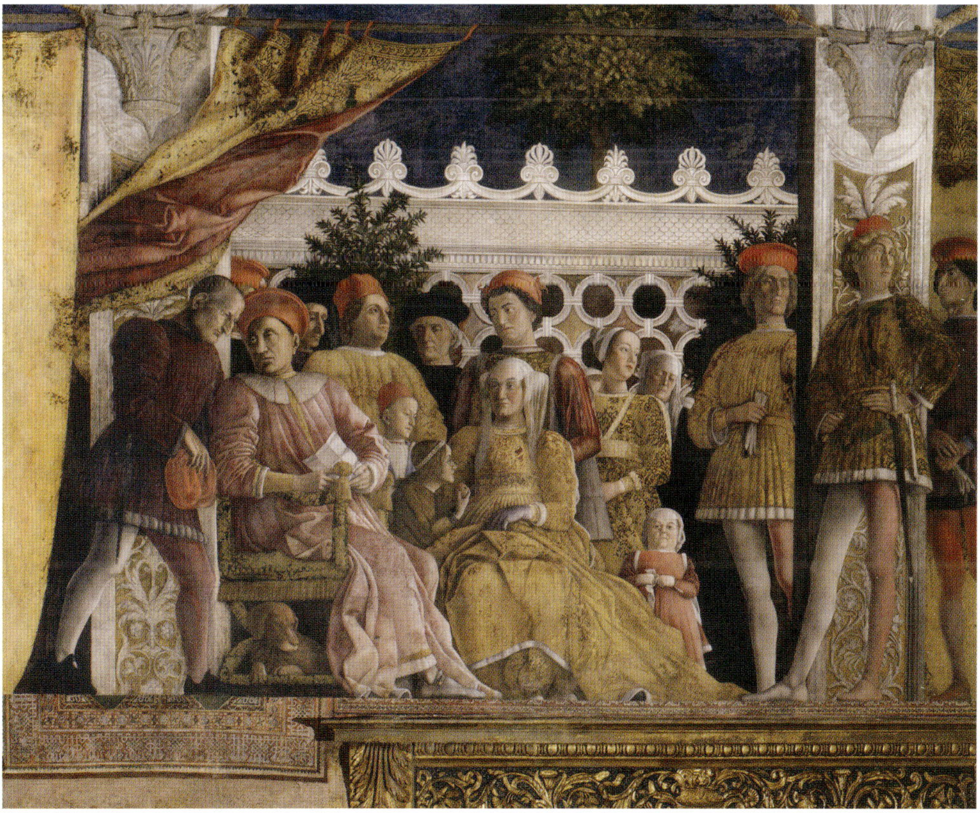

30 Ludovico Gonzaga with Rubino and other courtiers and family members, from
Andrea Mantegna, *The Court of Gonzaga*, 1465–74, fresco, north wall, Camera Picta,
Castello di San Giorgio, Mantua.

31 Two greyhounds and a scent hound at Borso d'Este's feet, detail from Francesco del Cossa, *April* (illus. 32).

32 Borso d'Este's court, from Francesco del Cossa, *April*, late 1460s, fresco, east wall, Salone dei Mesi, Palazzo Schifanoia, Ferrara.

in the Camera Picta, his paws casually resting on the chair's base, with one slung over it (illus. 29 and 30). Rubino – a *bracco*, or pointer – is allowed a physical vicinity to his prince that would make even the most confident courtier jealous. Indeed, adored animals were afforded unparalleled access within palaces. The Medici possessed 'dog-door' curtains adorned with their coat of arms, and Ercole d'Este had apertures cut into doors so that his cats could come and go.[11] Rubino also roamed freely. After one escape, he returned to the Gonzaga castle soaking wet and anxiously 'wandering from room to room, searching for' Ludovico, who was equally desperate for the hound to turn up. When Rubino died five years later, Ludovico ordered a tombstone and coffin.[12]

Princes' dogs were often branded. Seared flesh marked aristocratic ownership. In 1442, the goldsmith Amadio da Milano fashioned a copper iron in the shape of a greyhound's head for 'branding the dogs of the illustrious' Leonello d'Este.[13] Hunting dogs approach Leonello's brother Borso in the frescoes of Palazzo Schifanoia's Salone dei Mesi. A scenthound lounges comfortably at Borso's feet amid a crowd of courtiers in *April* (illus. 31 and 32). Two sleek, elegant greyhounds stand in front of their lord, facing him – one's white, curly tail is visible among the forest of human and canine legs. A dialogue celebrating dogs and horses, composed in the 1460s by Battista Guarino for the Este courtier Teofilo Calcagnini, asserts that 'wherever he went', Borso had 'two dogs beside him', on account of his lordliness. Guarino also proclaims the dignity of dogs, who as 'noble companions' are worthy of sharing the prince's chamber, in a quote calling Rubino to mind.[14] In *June*, *August* and *September*, four dogs, typically paired, amble around the mounted Borso and his men. Though it is difficult to make out every animal because of the frescoes' degraded condition, most seem to be hounds and a few have their muzzles set to the ground to track a scent. Beyond the court scene in *March*, in the far distance, Borso leads about a dozen men on horseback, at least four of whom have falcons perched on their wrists (illus. 33 and 34). All were once dressed in cloth of gold or silver, though the metallic frescoes have tarnished and deteriorated. This horizontal scene is a bit awkwardly wedged in between the court below and farmers tending vines behind, so the coursing greyhounds, dramatically chasing two hares, follow Borso's pack of hunters. The lone scenthound, with nose to the ground, seems to be leading the cortège off a cliff.

Renaissance nobles formed intense, tactile and affective relationships with their dogs, including hunting bloodhounds, greyhounds, shepherds and mastiffs. They also cherished silky, devoted lapdogs: spaniels, griffons and bichons such as the Maltese and Bolognese. The Scottish king James III supplied Galeazzo Maria Sforza four terriers and three greyhounds in 1473. Four decades later, Isabella d'Este and her ladies mourned the tragic death of her playfully nipping lapdog Aura, who suffered a high fall while scrapping with her rival Mamia. Elegies immortalizing Aura and paying tribute to Isabella's grief soon arrived in Mantua, penned by poets across the peninsula. Isabella also arranged a funeral for her cat Martino, with other pets in attendance and a sermon delivered by Mario Equicola.

In 1512, Isabella's twelve-year-old son Federico Gonzaga sent to her, from Rome, a rare, imported 'Indian' cat who spent much of the rest of its short life in Isabella's capacious sleeve.[15] Nearly two decades later, Titian painted Federico, now marquis of Mantua and decidedly a man, no longer a boy. Federico strokes a small, fluffy dog who dutifully and charmingly paws at her master, while his other hand braces the sword girded at his waist (illus. 35). A crimson codpiece – another symbol of the prince's virility – pokes out from his scintillating blue velvet garment. The depiction of Federico affectionately petting his dog provided Titian the opportunity to show off the lord's rings and the creature's soft fur. Federico's fingers sink into her silky coat. She may be Viola, who died giving birth, or perhaps another of the Gonzaga dogs immortalized in both tombs and epitaphs.[16] Yet, opposite this furry pup, the sword at the ready by Federico's side reminds us that as disarming and elegant as he seems, he is no less virile or confident. In Titian's portrait, sumptuous textiles, a menacing weapon and a faithful lapdog in concert fashion Federico Gonzaga's courtly masculinity.

Regal Raptors

Gifts of animals solidified political allegiance. The four falcons that Bona of Savoy sent to Lorenzo de' Medici mere weeks after her husband Galeazzo's assassination helped secure Florentine support for the vulnerable Sforza regime. Lorenzo's heartfelt response suggests that the desired results were achieved. A year later, when the exiled Ludovico Sforza sought the help of Ercole d'Este – whose

33 Borso d'Este and his mounted courtiers in the hunt, detail from Francesco del Cossa, *March* (illus. 34).

34 Borso d'Este and men following a scent hound, with two greyhounds chasing hares and workers tending vines, from Francesco del Cossa, *March* (illus. 2).

35 Titian, *Federico Gonzaga and Dog*, 1529, oil on panel.

young daughter, Beatrice, Ludovico would eventually marry – Ercole considered Galeazzo's death 'still too fresh' to approach Bona on Ludovico's behalf. To stress that their friendship was nevertheless strong, Ercole enthusiastically acceded to Ludovico's request for a falcon. Ercole's brother Sigismondo affirmed that the bird was a 'clever falcon' and that Ercole took much pleasure in giving it to Ludovico.[17] Not only aristocratic allies, but common vassals and subordinate communities also presented hunting animals to lords. The Sforza demanded that subject towns provide annual tributes of a hawk and a pair of scenthounds. Fines were steep when animals were not forthcoming, or when they were not sufficiently beautiful and well trained.[18]

The most venerated and culturally resonant hunting birds were raptors. Granting them marked favour and recognition. Of course, their privation signalled the opposite. When Galeazzo Maria Sforza moved against his feudatory Pietro dal Verme, the confiscation of hawks and dogs (specifically greyhounds and scenthounds) unmistakably announced Pietro's fall from power.[19] Princes sometimes showed greater regard for the well-being of these animals than for the humans they governed – at least for hunting birds deemed aristocratic, if not so much for fowl raised as poultry, chickens and the like, which were considered as common as peasants were. Falcons and hawks were esteemed vassals imputed personhood and individuality and were thus often named. Birds associated with husbandry were more akin to undifferentiated commodities.[20] Renaissance social hierarchies ordered not just humans but all members of the animal kingdom.

Birds of prey embodied aristocratic values. Their possession and display marked nobility and courtliness. For instance, a poet celebrated the memory of Galeazzo Maria Sforza by invoking his 'sparrowhawks, goshawks, peregrines and falcons', in addition to his 'worthy' horses and hunting dogs (again, both scenthounds and greyhounds, 'bracchi' and 'lipereri').[21] There was a staggering variety of practices to hunt birds, or hunt with them, including the use of nets, traps, projectiles and lime. Vittore Carpaccio's *Fishing and Fowling on the Lagoon* (illus. 36) in the Getty Museum may represent the most remarkable. Extravagantly dressed Venetian archers in boats – two of which are steered by Black oarsmen – take aim at waterfowl, ready to stun the birds with terracotta pellets rather than bloody them with arrows (thus keeping their plumage intact). Indeed, arrows are nowhere to be seen in Carpaccio's panel. This is a scene both of hunting birds and of fishing with them, as the jaunty archers could also launch the clay balls to control and manoeuvre cormorants trained to return to the boat and disgorge fish gathered during dives.[22]

Lords hunted waterfowl with falcons, and for this reason aviaries at the Gonzaga hunting park or *barco* at Marmirolo were stocked with 85 herons and 140 ducks in 1496. The dynasty's palace at Gonzaga was a prime location because of neighbouring marshes. Irrigation works

36 Vittore Carpaccio, *Fishing and Fowling on the Lagoon*, *c.* 1490–95, oil on panel.

made the area more attractive for aquatic fowl. Not surprisingly, scenes of this sort of hunt populate Renaissance frescoes. In the far left of *March* within Schifanoia's Salone dei Mesi, a falconer throttles the neck of a duck as his falcon looks down at its prey and a dog wades nearby (illus. 37). This is the confused and outraged duck that so struck George, the young protagonist of Ali Smith's gorgeous and heartbreaking 2014 novel *How to Be Both*. For George, the fate of Schifanoia's duck signifies the cruelty of everyday life.[23] We see the savagery of hunting throughout the frescoes. In *April* and *May*,

37 Falconer, falcon, ducks and dog, detail from Francesco del Cossa, *March* (illus. 2).

falcons attack cranes or herons in mid-air (illus. 38). Falcons adorn or alight from the wrists of Borso d'Este and his courtiers as they ride in *March*, *June*, *July*, *August* and *September*. In *April*, a youth gently caressing a hooded falcon is seated at the fresco's edge, with his legs dangling over it, conspicuously breaking the fiction of the painted room (illus. 32).

The knowledge, expertise and service of falconers was greatly esteemed in Renaissance courts (and, as Sarah Cockram has shown, the same was true of other animal handlers, including those who raised and trained horses, dogs and cheetahs). The physician Michele Savonarola advised Borso d'Este to ensure that his falconers avoided eating onions, which could impair eyesight.[24] A well-disciplined falcon manifested the lord's prowess and nobility by successfully attacking larger birds, typically herons, ducks and cranes. To convince a smaller bird to ignore its instincts and assault a crane or heron – who fought back and thus presented formidable danger for falcons – was no easy feat, and it validated masculine command. A falcon was conditioned to lose its fear of larger birds after feeding on chicken meat secured to the body of a dead heron or crane. The raptor would then be encouraged to attack birds mutilated with bent legs or broken beaks (and a Medici inventory included 'tools . . . to cut the beaks of birds') and would progressively graduate to incrementally less-maimed fowl, until it had developed a taste for them and would confidently take down able-bodied prey.[25]

This was a nasty business. Acclimatizing birds to human companionship often required that their eyes be seeled – sewn shut – for long periods, or that they be made to wear canvas or cloth straightjackets to keep from injuring themselves, until they became more docile or better habituated to their keepers. Training and housing birds not only demanded patient schooling by skilled falconers, but likewise the expenditure of considerable material resources.[26] Falcons' perches, cages, lures, bells and hoods might be gilded or bejewelled. So too were jesses (tethers) or vervels, the rings put on the birds' leg to help identify and secure them. Hoods, vervels and bells were often marked with seigneurial insignia, both to provide appropriately magnificent adornment and to identify errant birds. For instance, Gherardo di Andrea da Vicenza painted birdcage covers with Borso d'Este's emblems, and Sigismondo Malatesta's posthumous inventory recorded silk jesses decorated with pearls. Giovanni Trullo painted falcon perches in Ferrara; Galeazzo Maria Sforza's perches were adorned with velvet embroidered with gold and silver thread. In 1488, the Ferrarese ambassador in Milan raved about a falcon sporting 'very well-worked' bells and a hood outfitted with 'a few pearls, with a large one on top'.[27]

A gilded leather falcon hood – *cappuccio* or *cappelletto* – in the collection of Mantua's Palazzo Ducale seems to date to the fifteenth century. It soothed the dynasty's raptors, one of whom may have been the lanner or peregrine falcon represented in a stunning ink and

38 Raptor attacking a heron, detail from Francesco del Cossa, *April* (illus. 32).

39 Pisanello, *Falcon with Hood and Bell, Perched on a Gloved Hand*, c. 1440s, watercolour, pen, brown ink and brown wash over black chalk on paper.

40 Falcon hood, Northern Italy, *c.* 1500, gilded and punched leather and paint.

watercolour image associated with Pisanello (illus. 39). Two embossed leather and gilded *cappelletti* – dated circa 1500 and now in the Imperial Armoury in Vienna – can be associated, through their painted insignia, with the Emperor Maximilian and Empress Bianca Maria Sforza (illus. 40).[28]

Bells for falcons were sought-after luxury goods. One is depicted almost in three dimensions, built up of mordant gilding over pastiglia, attached to the leg of a falcon perched on its handler's leather glove just behind the youngest king in Gentile da Fabriano's *Adoration of the Magi* (illus. 41 and 42). In Ferrara, court silversmiths produced bells, which were, like the birds themselves, sent as diplomatic gifts.[29] Falconry's furnishings comprised a much-desired material culture exchanged between lords, and one to which we must be carefully attuned. For instance, most falcons depicted in Schifanoia's frescoes wear hoods. Contemporary viewers understood that those without *cappucci* were not only well trained but were, in that moment, primed for the hunt.

Because the skittish animals required quiet solitude, princely residences were outfitted with mews (the *falconaia* or *muda*), where birds were confined when moulting. Galeazzo Maria Sforza had the

41 Gentile da Fabriano,
Adoration of the Magi, 1423,
tempera, gold and silver
on panel.

42 Pastiglia falcon bell of
bird perched on the wrist
of the falconer immediately
behind the youngest Magus,
detail from Gentile da
Fabriano, *Adoration of
the Magi* (illus. 41).

43 Anonymous Lombard illuminator, 'Hunting scene with falcons and dogs', illuminated page from *Treatises on Falconry and Hunting*, 1459.

walls of a room housing his falcons in Milan lined with green velvet embroidered with Sforza arms.[30] Falconry treatises were immensely popular at court, and a sumptuous, brocaded case for a collection of medieval texts on hunting and falconry compiled for Francesco Sforza survives in Chantilly's Musée Condé. The codex opens with a full-page illumination (illus. 43) depicting noble hunters gazing skyward at a radiant falcon diving towards a larger heron. (And, not surprisingly, we recognize two pairs of scenthounds surrounding the pond full of aquatic birds, with the sleeker greyhound leashed near the hunters and patiently waiting to be set loose.) The young woman sitting sidesaddle may recall Ippolita Maria Sforza, a precocious falconer, as we will see below.[31] An illumination from a manuscript commissioned in Naples by King Alfonso or his son Ferrante reveals the mess of falcons' mews (illus. 44). This codex contains a Latin translation of the venerable Arabic book on falconry attributed to Moamyn, who was perhaps the ninth-century Abbasid physician Hunayn ibn Ishaq. Splattered about on both the floor and back wall are the nasty droppings of five hooded and tethered falcons. The image certainly gives one pause about the lived-in condition of Galeazzo's mews covered in plush velvet.

In 1476, Galeazzo sent a falconer known as 'il Bianco' to Moscow to request prized peregrines from Grand Prince Ivan III (The Great) Vasilyevich.[32] Two years prior, Sforza had dispatched another falconer

44 Master of the Offices (attr.), 'Five falcons in mews', illumination from Moamyn, *De scientia venandi per aves*, c. 1450–75.

to Norway and Denmark to meet up with a Milanese horse trader who had been in Ireland and France. Their mission in Denmark was severely complicated, however, by a prolonged and ultimately unsuccessful attempt to retrieve money that King Christian I owed Galeazzo. From Christian's castle of Gottorf (in Schleswig, Germany, but at the time in Danish territory), they wrote home marvelling at this 'strange country'. The wind and rain were strong enough to kill someone not accustomed to such weather. In June and July, it remained light enough to read and write the whole night through.[33]

Indeed, Renaissance emissaries travelled far and wide for birds, horses and hounds. Giuniano Maio praised his Neapolitan prince's dogs 'selected from different breeds and from foreign countries, [and] the falcons and other birds of prey imported from various parts of the world'. After the death of a dog sent to Milan by King Edward IV, Galeazzo Maria Sforza dispatched a courtier to England for a suitable replacement. According to Pier Candido Decembrio, Filippo Maria Visconti acquired various breeds of dogs from Britain, and 'even further away, with great expense, and not without having first conveyed rich gifts to the kings of those lands'. Filippo's dogs faithfully followed him around, eating cheese from his hand.[34] Visconti procured hunting birds from England, Poland, Hungary and Turkey, and an agent of his grandson Ludovico Sforza sought in Venice falcons arriving from Alexandria and Beirut. A man known in Milan as Michele Greco – one of several Greek falconers employed by the Sforza – furnished Ludovico birds of prey bought in Crete. Cypriot and Dalmatian nobles, and Milanese merchants in Tunisia, also presented hunting birds to Ludovico.[35]

Horses, Men and Horsemanship

We have seen Borso d'Este's instructions to his envoys travelling to Ifriqiya Tunis for Barbary stallions. His predecessor Leonello had dispatched hawks and a falcon to Caliph Uthman, looking to exchange raptors for racehorses. Borso and Ercole d'Este's agents (including the lutenist Pietrobono dal Chitarrino) also journeyed to Hungary, Germany, France, Spain, England and Ireland in search of superior horses. Irish horses were decidedly popular with Italian lords and were obtained via England by the Sforza and Gonzaga. Italian princes also granted equine diplomatic gifts to distant rulers. In 1466, Borso d'Este shipped two stallions to King Edward IV of England, along with sumptuously brocaded bards.[36]

Lords across Italy coveted war horses (coursers) from the Kingdom of Naples, where their exportation required his majesty's permission. Galeazzo Maria Sforza negotiated special concessions with King Ferrante and moved horses with the help of the Medici bank. According to an ambassador, Ferrante considered 'a pair of beautiful and good stallions' among the 'worthy gifts one prince could grant to another'. Neapolitan coursers were sent as gifts to the kings of England and France, and to the duke of Burgundy. Lords also gave away and received horses as they moved. When Borso passed through Perugia on his way to Rome in March 1471, the town's government presented him four coursers: two barded in opulent gold brocade and two in iridescent crimson velvet.[37]

The animals with which lords and their courts travelled and hunted communicated noble virility and authority. Radiant coverings, trappings, bells and collars shimmered and rattled. These beasts visually and aurally called attention to the cortège moving through space, as did the music that often accompanied them. The vast gold- and silver-brocaded bards of horses and mules provided bewildering displays of seigneurial splendour. For a Florentine observer, the young Galeazzo Maria Sforza's train of fifty mules manifested his 'great magnificence' in 1459. Twelve years later, Galeazzo's majestic cavalcade in Florence sported velvet barding, brocaded crimson saddlecloths and gold and silver fittings. The lord's herds of mules were draped in murrey and white damask – Sforza colours in figured silk.[38]

These beasts of burden required great expanses of fabric to cover. One mule cloak decorated with Medici arms, for instance, seems to have been reused as a door curtain in the dynasty's palace.[39] In the 1460s, lavish mule mantles brocaded with gold and silver ducal arms were produced in Ferrara and were, along with Sicilian mules, presented to Caliph Uthman of Tunisia. Most of the mules accompanying Borso d'Este's retinue from Ferrara to Rome in 1471 wore cloth covers dyed the Este colours of green, red and white. Those carrying Borso's personal belongings, however, paraded silver bells and crimson velvet embroidered with dynastic insignia. One chronicler counted 95 of the former and thirty of the latter. These textiles astounded viewers up and down the peninsula. A Perugian chronicler marvelled at Borso's 'great triumph and pomp' and his scores of crimson velvet mule covers.[40]

Horses, and not only their radiant array, embodied class distinctions and masculine prowess. This was the case particularly for pure-bred or particularly strong and swift stallions, which were kept at considerable expense given the labour and materials needed to feed, groom, shoe and tack the animals, and to manage their breeding. Treatises on the care of horses were composed and copied for princes, were inventoried in their libraries and may have been utilized by their farriers, grooms and stablemen. Leon Battista Alberti dedicated his 1443 treatise *De equo animante* (On the Living Horse) to Leonello d'Este.[41] Among that dynasty's other equine manuals is a mid-fifteenth-century manuscript now in Modena profusely and charmingly illustrated with pen drawings (illus. 45).[42] Horses were often on the minds of lords, who bonded with peers through shared stories and experiences in Renaissance Italy's elite homosocial spaces. At celebrations for Gian Galeazzo Sforza's wedding in 1489, Piero de' Medici was seated between the groom and Ludovico Sforza. Piero straight away hit it off with his Milanese hosts by 'discussing horses and other enjoyable matters', as the Florentine ambassador reported back to the teenager's father, Lorenzo the Magnificent.[43]

Courtiers' worth might be measured by the number of horses the lord would stable for their use. Guidelines composed in 1468 for the reception of ambassadors in Milan repeatedly advised that attention be paid both to visitors' 'quality' and 'condition' and to the number of their horses. Depending on the breed, horses served in battle, at jousts and races, during hunts, in fields, for travel, to pull carts and carriages, for couriers (*cavallari*), as pack animals and for myriad other purposes. One Este horse made daily trips to pick up butter and ricotta from the ducal farm at Stienta.[44]

Lords competed with one another through stallions charging down civic streets. Grand prize at these horse races was typically a brocaded *palio* (a stretch of lavish silk cloth, often brocaded velvet), and for this reason, the sprints are known today as the *palio*.[45] Other suitable trophies included noble animals and luxury garments. At a Ferrarese race in 1468 won by a horse belonging to Costanzo Sforza (the boy in illus. 12, less than a decade later), first prize was a valuable steed, second was two hounds and a hawk, and third was a *giornea*, a fashionable, masculine tunic. An inventory from 1440 lists the 25 banners, many of brocaded silk, won by Este horses in races held throughout Italy in that year alone. Leonello d'Este's horse Spiritello triumphed

45 Northern Italian illuminator (attr.), 'Afflicted horse cared for by a groom',
page from Bonifacio di Calabria, *Practica de' morbi naturali et accidentali, segni e cure de' cavalli*, early to mid-15th century.

twice in Florence, including in the race celebrating the town's patron John the Baptist. Lords invested large sums not only in horses but in the material culture of these spectacles. In Ferrara in 1461, Gherardo di Andrea da Vicenza was paid to paint six whip handles wielded by jockeys, who were dressed in expensive silk doublets and tunics and wore special racing spurs ('speroni da barbari'). Borso d'Este's courtier Teofilo Calcagnini, for instance, paid to have six doublets for jockeys

embellished with brocade. Though horses ran relatively unadorned and were generally ridden bareback, mantles and bards were also produced in Ferrara specifically for racing stallions.[46] We should imagine that these horses, before and perhaps after their sprints, may have been as radiantly arrayed as those on display in the jousts discussed in Chapter One.

Like jousts, races were dangerous for both horse and rider. Jockeys suffered broken bones during spills. Spectators also hazarded life and limb. In 1496, Isabella d'Este, a dedicated fan of horse racing, recounted that a horse slammed into the crowd cheering on the Mantuan *palio* for the feast of St Peter. A wool carder 'fell face-forward on the ground, hurting himself terribly, not without mortal danger to himself'.[47] On a harrowing *cassone* panel depicting the Florentine *palio* of St John the Baptist (illus. 46 and 47), a man in black in the right foreground gestures in horror and anguish as a jockey tumbles with his injured mount. The horse lies perilously splayed against the pavement, just below two still-upright riders who have turned their whips on one another. The raucous crowd includes lads who climbed rafters for a better view. Other youths hurl objects at the racers, and a small, agitated dog amusingly hustles alongside the frontrunners, no doubt barking at the stampeding beasts. The horses rush towards the finish line where we see, among the many spectators, two men hoisting up the winner's reward, the large, cloth-of-gold *palio*. On the painting's companion

46 Giovanni Toscani, *The Race of the Palio in Florence on the Feast of St John the Baptist*, *c.* 1418, *cassone* panel, tempera and gold on wood.

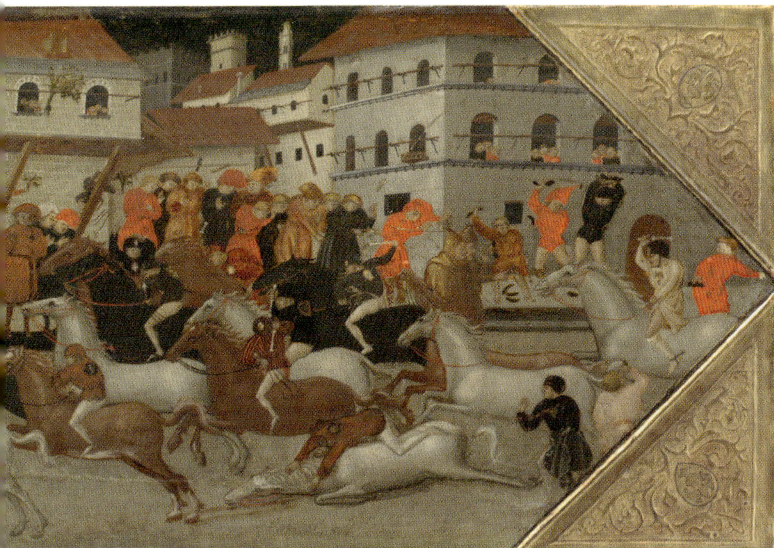

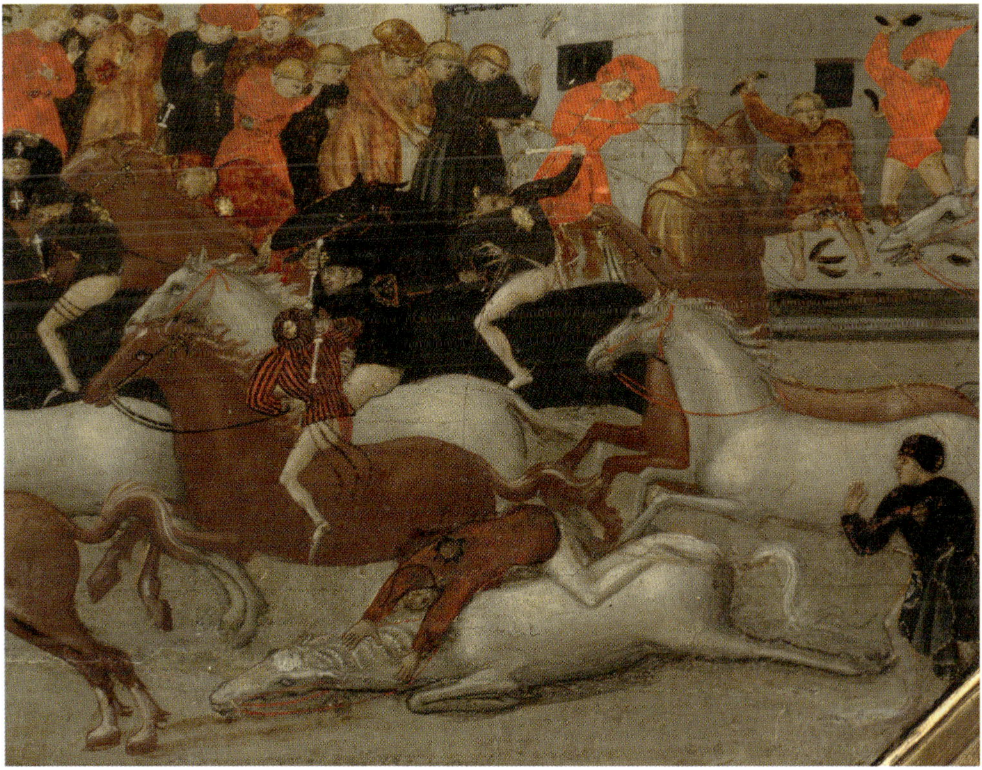

47 Tumbling horse, fighting jockeys and raucous spectators, detail from Giovanni Toscani, *The Race of the Palio in Florence* (illus. 46).

48 Giovanni Toscani, *Procession of Banners in Piazza del Duomo in Florence*, *c.* 1418, *cassone* panel, tempera and gold on wood.

panel (illus. 48), the lavish textile is paraded with many other opulent banners towards Florence's Baptistery, next to which we see a charlatan snake-handler (*sanpaolaro*) hawking his wares and waving around a serpent.[48]

The Este raced horses throughout their territory, for example on a lengthy and rather peculiar spiral-shaped track for stallions at the villa of Belfiore. The best known race, however, was a straight run down Ferrara's Via Grande, which the town government paid to have spread with sand, on the feast of St George. This *palio* was won by horses owned by the Bentivoglio, della Mirandola, Este and Gonzaga dynasties in the late fifteenth century.[49] During Borso d'Este's reign, grand prize on St George's Day was a stretch of fur-lined cloth of gold suspended from a pole supporting a shield and leather crest (*cimiero*) in the form of Borso's emblem of a unicorn under a date palm. For Leonello, the *cimiero* was surmounted by the blindfolded lynx familiar from his medals. The *palio*'s crest and shield were painted and adorned with gold and silver – by Cosmè Tura, in fact, in 1452.[50]

This elaborate, golden prize went to the winner of the first and most important race of the day, that of the *barberi* (what were considered Barbary or Arabian horses), which was followed by three further races: of asses; men (generally pimps, soldiers or members of another marginalized group); and women (often sex workers, though Ercole d'Este attempted to reform this in the mid-1470s by decreeing

49 The Race of the Palio of St George in Ferrara, from Francesco del Cossa, *April*, late 1460s, fresco, east wall, Salone dei Mesi, Palazzo Schifanoia, Ferrara.

that only 'honest and proper young girls' should participate). Trophies for the undercard were made of less opulent fabrics than were those for the Barbary race, though they were dyed red, white or green, the Este colours.[51] These four races – or, more precisely, their stretch runs – are conflated into one scene in Francesco del Cossa's representation from *April* (illus. 49), the month in which the feast of St George falls, in the frescoes of Palazzo Schifanoia's Salone dei Mesi. Seven mounted Barbary stallions in the lead gallop swiftly beyond the scene's confines. They are followed by four grey donkeys likewise ridden bareback, and then five semi-naked men and women running on foot.

Deanna Shemek has masterfully interpreted this image, and the races themselves, as political tools exploiting a 'whimsical or even parodic repetition' of the horse race to reaffirm 'social hierarchy in Ferrara . . . encompass[ing] the moral, political, and sexual domains'.[52] Indeed, the viewer is struck by the contrast between the charging *barberi* and the scantily and scandalously clad runners bringing up the rear. All five bare their legs, but visual attention is particularly drawn to the lumbering, shirtless man attired only in underwear and to the woman following him, with genitals exposed under her shift, seemingly framed and accentuated by the arch immediately behind her. Decorous, well-dressed men and women survey the races overhead: women from windows and balconies and men in more public spaces just above the fray, including seated civic officials in long robes. Francesco del Cossa's efficient economy of visual narrative at Schifanoia – four races in one, with spectators depicted above – informs the viewer about the day's entire racecard. The image efficaciously reinforces social division and sustains an image of courtliness and civic respectability through pointed juxtapositions of valiant steeds with galumphing asses and virtuous ladies with sex workers.

A chronicler records that in 1479 a group of noble women attended the races of 'men, women and asses' and then dined at Schifanoia. Eleonora of Aragon, Ginevra Sforza and Bianca d'Este must have inspected *April's* frescoes to relive the day's excitement and to relish their prime viewing location and privileged status among the crowd. On the palace's walls, they would have seen Eleonora's late brother-in-law Borso mounted on a white horse and, arrayed in costly brocades, significantly aligned with the *barberi* race that he intently watches, backed by a marble statue of St Sebastian from a church facade. Borso, in fact, had years before explained to a ducal official that he would rather starve himself than let his horses be deprived of food (and his *barberi* took home the *palio* in Florence's race for the feast of St John the Baptist in 1451 and 1459).[53] The Ferrarese *palio* of St George was so closely associated with Borso that in 1471 it was postponed for a month to allow for his triumphant return from Rome, now as the town's duke.[54] Indeed, as Christian Jaser has argued, Barbary horses served as proxies for Renaissance lords, dynamically speeding through urban space, enlivening it with their 'equine kinetic energy', and redounding honour on their noble owners, all of which resounded within the 'echo chamber' produced by narrow streets and spiritedly cheering crowds (illus. 46).[55]

The Gonzaga stables dominated Renaissance *palio* races. Their stallions won Ferrara's St George's Day race ten times between 1480 and 1502.[56] To acquire pure-bred Arabian and Barbary horses, agents of the dynasty travelled to Sicily, Naples, Spain, North Africa and Constantinople. Gifts of horses and access to the Gonzaga breeding programme mobilized crucial diplomatic networks. In 1488, Francesco Gonzaga's wedding present to his new brother-in-law Guidobaldo da Montefeltro included jousting armour and a stallion. Thanking her brother, the bride Elisabetta Gonzaga recognized in the horse, 'the great love that you carry for me'. Francesco also forged intimate relations with the Ottoman Sultan Bayezid II through the exchange of horses. King Henry VIII of England received Gonzaga steeds as well.[57]

Giulio Romano celebrated Gonzaga horses in portraits in the Sala dei Cavalli of the Palazzo Te (illus. 50), a complex that housed a breeding stud. Other villas and palaces were likewise outfitted with magnificent rooms dedicated to images of Barbary horses painted by Romano, Lorenzo Leonbruno and others: the Camara da li Cavalli at Gonzaga; the Sala da li Barbari at Marmirolo (also decorated with life-sized portraits of two jockeys); and a chamber in the Palazzo San Sebastiano in Mantua furnished with representations of 'belli cavali' and 'belli cani'. Beautiful horses and dogs still grace the walls of Andrea Mantegna's Camera Picta (illus. 51).[58] We are meant to admire the powerful courser decked in radiant studs and trappings, including ornately wrought gilded stirrups, attended by (counting the legs and motley *calze* under the horse) three handlers, though only one is clearly visible. Close looking reveals at least part of one of the hidden groom's tunics, overlapping with but a slightly different shade of blue than that of his more conspicuous colleague. To the immediate right,

50 Two horses and the god Jupiter, from Giulio Romano, Sala dei Cavalli, 1525–7, fresco, south wall, Palazzo Te, Mantua.

51 Gonzaga dogs, a horse and their handlers, from Andrea Mantegna, Camera Picta, 1465–74, fresco, west wall, Castello di San Giorgio, Mantua.

two *alani* or Alaunt hunting dogs are masterfully controlled by the taut leash of a *canatero* (and Sforza kennelmen were also provided splendid tunics, doublets and stockings in dynastic colours). Opposite the adjacent, fictive pilaster, two additional handlers manage three dogs (it is difficult here to distinguish between sighthounds and scenthounds, though one seems to smell the air).[59]

Hunting and Noble Masculinity

It was imperative for lords to demonstrate dexterous horsemanship and hunting prowess. As Giuniano Maio advised King Ferrante of Aragon in his treatise *De Maiestate* (On Majesty), the 'first type of magnificence is when, seated majestically on a horse, you are the most stalwart prince, as well as the most powerful rider among all those who handle horses'. Maio's second expression of magnificence is hunting, 'a worthy training for a noble knight and for a magnanimous and excellent king ... [through which] the health and fitness of your body is preserved'.[60] Horses conspicuously established class distinctions by separating those mounted above from those on foot below. Command of a horse was essential. Sforza legend tells that the dynasty's founder Muzio Attendolo rode unbroken horses to flaunt his virility and military prowess. His son Francesco, late in life, was praised by Pope Pius II for riding his horse 'like a young man'. Consequences could be dire when a lord failed to control his horse, as was the case for Malatesta Novello, taken prisoner when his mount bolted straight into the enemy ranks.[61]

Hunts put lords on display, typically on horseback. At age twelve, Ludovico Sforza recounted to his father Francesco a harrowing deer hunt in Pavia's hunting park or *barco*, which stretched 8 kilometres (5 mi.) north to the Certosa and was the site of the disastrous Battle of Pavia in 1525. Winds howled; barking dogs escaped their leashes; arrows and lances flew all around.[62] Ludovico missed with the *stambecchina* (a hunting lance or bolt, here seemingly shot from a crossbow) that his father had given him and that he hurriedly let loose at a deer. He struck the animal with an arrow, and it ultimately succumbed to 'many wounds' inflicted by Ludovico's hounds and men. The deer was sent to Francesco with the letter, so that, in the boy's own words, his father would 'understand all my progress and delight' (in hunting). Spoils were commonly granted to the prince's relatives and courtiers not only to provide sustenance but likewise to demonstrate seigneurial hunting prowess and liberality. The distribution of spoils also communicated status at court, with quarry allocated according to the recipients' rank. Both young Ludovico's dramatic yet triumphant tale and the deer's carcass served as proof that he was well on his way to becoming a proper lord.

During his brother Galeazzo's reign, Ludovico needed express permission to hunt in Milan's ducal park, as a document recording its conferral attests. Indeed, lords carefully and jealously protected hunting rights. They enforced harsh penalties against those deemed poachers, exercising economic and social privileges and seeking to maintain strict class distinctions, even though boar and deer threatened subjects' agricultural production, and thus livelihood, and even if hunters acted out of necessity.[63] Bernabò Visconti purportedly had a subject's hand cut off for merely dreaming that he had hunted a boar, and Galeazzo Maria Sforza was reputed to have killed one of his by commanding him to eat an illicitly captured hare raw, fur and all. Days before his assassination, after losing one of his most loyal hunting dogs, Galeazzo decreed that anyone who stole a dog – any dog at all – could suffer the confiscation of their goods.

The administration of hunting lands and rights served the Sforza as a vigorous yet malleable means to consolidate power; to expand, unite and dominate their territory; and to surveil both individuals and subject towns.[64] Indeed, the staggering expanse of land occupied by *barchi* manifests and materializes, in a physical way, the vigorous links between hunting and authority. The Sforza stocked parks at Milan, Vigevano, Cusago and Pavia. Ducal expenses in 1476 included the construction of a *barco* at Villanova and the purchase of deer and boar to fill the dynasty's parks.[65] Borso and Ercole d'Este invested heavily in hunting reserves as well.[66] Sperandio Savelli of Mantua sculpted and possibly painted two marble portraits of Ercole for placement over the entrance to Ferrara's *barco*. A profile bust in the collection of Ferrara's Palazzina di Marfisa d'Este, and a similar relief in the Louvre (distinct in that it is backed by a marble ground and frame), seem to be these portal portraits. In the sculpture now in Ferrara, Ercole sports jousting armour with plates curving up at each shoulder to deflect lance blows. Sperandio carved numerous round studs in the stone, representing the bolts securing metal lames in place. Indeed, all sorts of metals are simulated in marble. Ercole's lance rest is visible, though

52 Sperandio Savelli,
Ercole d'Este, c. 1475,
marble.

damaged. Intricately carved and interlaced mail protects his neck
(illus. 52).[67]

Ercole d'Este also hunted with cheetahs and, when Ludovico
Sforza visited Ferrara, had hurdles set up for the fleet-footed felines
to leap. Cheetahs – which were generally referred to as hunting leopards in contemporary sources – came to Italy from Africa, where they
roamed much more widely than today, via Tunisian, Cypriot, Maltese
or Egyptian trade. Cheetahs are also native to Iran, and some reached
Lisbon from the Kingdom of Hormuz. Niccolò III d'Este was presented a cheetah when he departed Cyprus on pilgrimage to Jerusalem
in 1413. Pier Candido Decembrio relates that Filippo Maria Visconti
sought the cats from throughout 'the Orient' – his father Gian
Galeazzo had been gifted some from the Mamluk Sultan Barquq.
Ercole d'Este and Galeazzo Maria Sforza looked to Venice for their
cheetahs.[68]

Languid cheetahs sport collars in drawings by artists including Pisanello and Giovannino de' Grassi (and their followers) (illus. 53), and a leashed cat is poised at the ready in the upper margin of folio 86r of the Sforza hunting and falconry manuscript in Chantilly mentioned above. Rooms known as 'of the leopards' (that is, of the cheetahs) graced the palaces of the Gonzaga, Visconti and Sforza dynasties, whose lords hunted with the cats. Handlers (*parderi*) trained cheetahs to ride horseback and from there to launch themselves dramatically headlong into the chase. They sat at the ready upon a crupper, cushion

53 Anonymous Lombard artist, *Two Cheetahs*, c. 1400, brush drawing in watercolour and bodycolour, on vellum (formerly from a sketchbook).

or riding carpet, as in Benozzo Gozzoli's frescoes in the Medici Palace's Chapel of the Magi (illus. 54). In the royal train in the far distance of Gentile da Fabriano's *Adoration of the Magi*, in the upper centre of the painting, two cheetahs ride on carpets on the backs of horses immediately preceding the magi. The cat facing left sits calmly, while its companion is more tensely perched, up on all fours and intently watching a bounding deer, set to pounce (illus. 55 – though see illus. 41 to spy the deer). Below, amidst the retinue that has now reached Christ, a cheetah with a gilded collar bares its teeth and seems to growl at a

54 Two cheetahs among the followers of the Magi, from Benozzo Gozzoli, *Journey of the Magi*, 1459, fresco, west wall, Cappella dei Magi, Palazzo Medici-Riccardi, Florence.

55 Train of the Magi with two cheetahs riding horses on hunting carpets, detail from Gentile da Fabriano, *Adoration of the Magi* (illus. 41).

horse, while a second cat just above looks up, with a bit of puzzlement, towards a raptor taking a bird in mid-air (illus. 56).

The teenaged Galeazzo Maria Sforza – writing in 1457 from the Este villa of Belfiore, where, he said, there was hunting 'without equal' – described mornings spent hunting with Borso's cheetahs. Decades later, Giovanni Sabadino degli Arienti praised Belfiore's frescoed scenes of cheetah hunts. Borso gifted two cheetahs to Francesco Sforza, who gave his wife Bianca three. Two *parderi* – Bassano dalli Leoni and Antonio Parpalione – entered the court's service at about this time. These men's surnames suggest that they came from a line of keepers of big cats. That the profession was passed down from generation to generation may be confirmed by the *pardero* Giovanni Parpalione, who cared for three Sforza cheetahs in 1477.[69]

Ferrarese cheetahs were renowned throughout Europe. In 1479, Ercole d'Este provided the grateful French king Louis XI a crimson riding carpet and the 'most beautiful' cheetah the monarch had ever seen – along with, indispensably, the expertise and advice of the

56 Two cheetahs among the followers of the Magi, detail from Gentile da Fabriano, *Adoration of the Magi* (illus. 41).

Este *pardero* Battista da Bataino (or Battaglino), who delivered the cat. Louis's grandson Louis XII likewise hunted with Italian cheetahs, including those seized from Ludovico Sforza following his regime's collapse in 1499. At a hunt a decade later, the king was astonished by a Ferrarese cheetah – a gift from Cardinal Ippolito d'Este – who took down a deer with its paws, unable to use its jaws because it refused to let go of a hare captured moments earlier. For Ippolito's brother Duke Alfonso, Titian painted a pair of cheetahs leading Bacchus's chariot and raucous crew. One disarmingly glances at the other as they arrive

57 Titian, *Bacchus and Ariadne*, 1520–23, oil on canvas.

upon the despondent Ariadne, who has just been abandoned by Theseus on Naxos (illus. 57).[70]

Yet the undisputed king of Renaissance cats was the lion. Captive lions could be seen throughout Italy, from Naples to Venice, from Perugia to Milan. Leonardo da Vinci's notes mention a lion just outside the Sforza castle in Pavia, and also the birth of a cub in the ducal *barco* there. When Emperor Frederick III visited Naples in 1452, King Alfonso paraded four of the royal menagerie's lions through town, along with a number of ostriches, camels and lynxes.[71] Lions were often resonant civic symbols. Florence's lions were housed near the town hall (hence today's Via dei Leoni to the rear). They were moved north, near San Marco, in the ducal sixteenth century.[72] Lions were frequently requested and offered as diplomatic gifts. In 1488, Sigismondo d'Este granted Francesco Gonzaga a young and 'rather tame' lion to breed with a Gonzaga lioness. Four years later, Ludovico Sforza sent Francesco lions and – because of their 'ferocità' – their keeper. In 1474, a Venetian offered Galeazzo Maria Sforza a 'most delightful' lioness with a 'proud and fearsome' manner, though she was as 'humane and acquiescent with people as a hound'.[73]

In 1458, a chronicler recorded in matter of fact but chilling language that an eleven-year-old girl was eaten alive by one of Borso d'Este's lions: 'uno leone ... mangiò una puta viva ... quasi tuta'. Following the arrival in Florence of Lorenzo de' Medici's giraffe (a gift from the Mamluk Sultan Qaitbay), a formerly tame lion, agitated by its new neighbour, killed a boy of the Giuntini family, notwithstanding the desperate intervention of the cat's keeper.[74] Of course, indigenous animals such as bears and wolves also menaced lives and livelihoods in Renaissance Italy. Fears of savage predators are visualized and simultaneously mitigated in the miraculous truce brokered by St Francis of Assisi between the citizens of Gubbio and a wolf who had preyed upon them. In a panel by the Sienese painter Sassetta (illus. 58), human body parts gruesomely strewn about are the only remnants of the beast's victims. As the town watches – men crowded at the gate and women peering out from above, shielded by the crenellated walls – Francis and the wolf shake to ratify their pact. Francis turns and gestures to his right, and the wolf stares in the same direction; both guide the viewer to a seated notary who records the public promise of peace lawfully sealed by hand joined to paw. For a moment, human society and the animal kingdom are in accord. Yet for much of the Renaissance, we were hardly so humane.

Indeed, hunts took place not only in forests and marshes but in civic *piazze*, where lions slaughtered dogs, bulls and boars in public spectacles – or were meant to. Florentines were embarrassed when a bull drove lions back into their stalls 'as if they were sheep', at a hunt arranged for Ippolita Maria Sforza in 1465. A noteworthy hunt six years prior had marked the visits of Pope Pius II and Ippolita's brother, the teenaged Count Galeazzo. Tall fences and ample seating were erected in the Piazza della Signoria. Various beasts were let into the makeshift arena, including aggressive mastiffs who terrorized the other animals. Finally, four roaring lions entered as the audience watched with bated breath. One set upon a horse and, as a poet described, tore into its flank a 'gaping hole that could have held a hoard of buried treasure'.[75]

The lions strolled the piazza, but soon lay down, either too well fed or perhaps cowed by the ruckus. Animals wandered at will, and the lions could not be goaded to attack, though they were poked and roused by men hidden within mobile wooden machines: a large sphere something like a human-sized hamster ball and an enormous 'giraffe' covered in a pelt over the frame (and similar tortoise- and porcupine-shaped vehicles would be deployed at a lion hunt in Florence 55 years later). Though, a poet tells us, you 'can be sure that the giraffe and ball/ went over to torment him', even the fiercest lion, because of 'divine instruction', became docile and allowed the crowd to approach and pet him. They felt the lion's fur and feet, and the happy cat offered its tongue 'to lick/ them all, and wagged its tail in great delight'. Scholars have labelled this hunt a failure, yet contemporary Florentines discerned an augury of 'faithful friendship' between Milan and Florence, between Sforza and Medici.[76] Perhaps one of these lions was that whom the Hafsid Caliph Uthman presented to Francesco Sforza in 1452 (and Uthman would provide two lions and two ostriches to Borso d'Este in 1463, the year before the gift-giving gambit with which we started this chapter). Francesco Sforza soon sent the cat to Florence as a diplomatic gift. It had been too much for its handler in Pavia to manage, as we know from a despairing letter he wrote to the ducal chancellor Cicco Simonetta, complaining that the lion had damaged the door of its chamber. Though the keeper had put 'great effort' into 'governing' the animal, he feared that danger was unavoidable, as 'powerful' as it was.[77]

Nature was indeed 'possente', as the Pavian lion handler had characterized this beast. Accordingly, Renaissance lords advertised prowess in the hunt in order to evoke aptitude in war.[78] Frescoes depicting the hunt broadcast the noble, homosocial networks that the activity engendered. Falconry and hunting parties were depicted at Belfiore and other Este villas and palaces, and a number survive in vignettes and cavalcades within Schifanoia's Salone dei Mesi. Scenes of falconry and hunting were intended to occupy substantial wall space as part of the frescoes that Galeazzo Maria Sforza planned for his castles. At the Milanese Castello Sforzesco, the duke was to be surrounded by family members, courtiers, horses and dogs. Galeazzo would be shown on horseback and wielding a sword ('with sword in hand, to wound a deer'), or with a lance. The Pavian frescoes portrayed a deer hunt, and in the loggia outside an entrance to the duke's apartments, the stable master was represented holding Galeazzo's horses at the ready. Privileged viewers also contemplated scenes of falconry involving Galeazzo, Bona of Savoy and the falconer Pietro da Birago. Sforza, moreover, requested that a portrait be painted based on a fresco of his great-grandfather Gian Galeazzo Visconti's horse, with particular attention paid to its saddle and trappings. Visconti frescoes from the castle included hunting scenes representing, once again, both greyhounds and bloodhounds.[79]

Expertise and the willingness to lend animals or assist in obtaining them were highly valued within aristocratic, homosocial networks. In 1478, Lorenzo de' Medici looked to the Ordelaffi of Forlì for a jousting mount. He eventually managed, through the Martinengo dynasty, to secure the use of Frison, the *condottiere* Bartolomeo Colleoni's trusted horse who had outlived his owner. The Medici frequently relied on Milanese lords to provide the noble beasts essential for their spectacles. In 1454, for example, they requested the best horse that the Sforza could afford to loan, plus two 'most valiant' warriors, for jousts celebrating Pier Francesco de' Medici's marriage.[80]

Months before the 1475 joust in which he would star, Giuliano de' Medici hoped that Galeazzo Maria Sforza would lend gallant horses. Relations between the two dynasties were becoming increasingly frayed, however, and they further unravelled when – in the midst of tense, sniping correspondence full of excuses, evasions and bruised egos – Galeazzo refused to provide any horses. Sforza explained that he had 'opened our stalls' to the Medici envoy who selected only one horse, which was, unfortunately for Giuliano, 'as dear to us [Galeazzo] as our right eye'. He likewise denied an appeal for jousters, ostensibly because the best men were his father's courtiers who were by now elderly or deceased, and because young knights would bring insufficient honour. Giuliano was having none of Galeazzo's excuses and pitifully complained that Sforza horses and knights had accompanied his father, uncle and brother in jousts, but that he would have to appear 'alone, deprived and nude'. Galeazzo eventually agreed to send four trumpeters, though he delayed their departure from Milan until the last possible moment, no doubt to make Giuliano sweat it out. Of course, Giuliano was neither nude nor deprived at his joust. He had inquired about horses with a dozen or so lords, including Federico da Montefeltro, Costanzo Sforza, Marco Pio of Carpi, Sigismondo d'Este and Roberto Sanseverino. He ultimately rode Orso (Bear),

58 Sassetta, *The Wolf of Gubbio*, c. 1440, tempera on poplar wood.

borrowed from King Ferrante of Aragon. Moreover, Giuliano showed off splendid garments and weapons, plus a silk garland adorned with two white feathers, pearls, a balas and a diamond. Giuliano also successfully acquired prized Milanese armour for the occasion, arranged through the Medici Bank's branch in Milan.[81]

Familiarity with optimal hunting grounds was also privileged knowledge to be marshalled strategically. Lorenzo de' Medici located for Ludovico Sforza – during a time of plague, echoing Boccaccio's *Decameron* – a villa in a well-provisioned location, 'apt for hunting'. In preparation for his trip to Florence in 1471, Ludovico's brother Galeazzo had written to a Florentine official in Pontremoli, in mountainous northwest Tuscany, requesting that he direct the lord to the best site for hunting boar. Sforza princes also tracked wolves and bears (specifically the brown bear, *Ursus arctos*). In November 1474, Galeazzo, with 'his brothers and many other courtiers', slew a 'grossissimo' bear and two chamois. Two years later, a dog perished and three men were seriously injured when Galeazzo took yet another 'grossissimo urso'. This bear seems to have been displayed atop the Castello Sforzesco's ravelins, menacing Milan's citizens and manifesting their lord's noble virility. A decade and a half later, Ludovico Sforza parcelled out as gifts parts of a bear that he hunted.[82]

Elite Renaissance men hunted when they travelled, and when conducting business and diplomacy. (We might think of hunting *barchi* as fifteenth-century Italy's golf courses – generally, though not exclusively, homosocial sites of male power, privilege and leisure.) A detailed account of Ludovico Gonzaga's approximately week-long visit with Borso d'Este in the Ferrarese countryside in 1458 reveals that the two lords hunted almost every evening and additionally while moving between estates. A few decades later, in 1493, Ludovico Sforza remained in Ferrara's hinterlands hunting and examining fortifications with Ercole d'Este, while his wife Beatrice (Ercole's daughter) was in Venice.[83] The following year, Ludovico had his nephew Gian Galeazzo poisoned, cementing control over Milan. Gian Galeazzo was a devotee of both tourneys and hunting – for instance, on the same day in August 1492, he attended an impressive display of combat between two of Ludovico's men in Pavia, and after he ended the duel, headed over to the ducal *barco* where he took four deer.[84] On his deathbed two years later, at age 25, Gian Galeazzo repeatedly demanded that his favourite hounds and horses be brought to his chamber. One can only imagine the tearful farewell that Gian Galeazzo bid his faithful beasts, assembled as an audience for their lord.[85]

'Fare le cose de homo': Becoming Men

Gian Galeazzo Sforza, son of the inveterate hunter Galeazzo, followed in his father's footsteps. Doing so was crucial. Failure to conform to ideals of courtly masculinity were met with shame if not downright condemnation. In the mid-1520s, the fifteen-year-old Ippolito de' Medici requested 'with as much desire as is possible and [with] extreme longing' that the Gonzaga ambassador have a kitten (*gattino*) sent to him from Mantua (and these are the envoy's words, so we can only imagine how woefully Ippolito pleaded).[86] For Renaissance princes, hunting dogs were culturally coded as more masculine than cats. Ippolito had already received hounds from the Gonzaga, and they were searching for a suitable horse. Yet Ippolito would not temper his appeals for a kitten, even though the ambassador did his best to ignore the entreaties to please Ottaviano de' Medici, who was closely involved in the teenager's upbringing. As the art historian Guido Rebecchini has suggested, Ottaviano was embarrassed by Ippolito's lack of interest in properly adult and, I would add, normatively masculine activities and animals. Ottaviano, in fact, seems to have commissioned from Pontormo a portrait of Ippolito with a large dog named Rodon. The painting was mentioned by Vasari but is now lost, though a drawing in the Uffizi's Gabinetto dei Disegni of a wide-eyed boy overwhelmed by his mantle and flanked by a barely visible dog has been connected to Pontormo's portrait.[87] One suspects that Ottaviano would not have allowed a portrayal of Ippolito with the kitten he had so ardently wished for. The Medici demanded much of the boy, above all else that he comport himself as a man.

Young princes fully grasped, and grasped at, these ideals and expectations. As a boy, Galeazzo Maria Sforza was eager to please his father. No doubt encouraged by his tutors, the eight-year-old promised to 'tire himself' in striving to live up to Francesco's 'Herculean deeds'. Galeazzo found inspiration in his father's gift of a 'most beautiful and excellent' *ronzino* (rouncey). He also implored Francesco not to 'leave me lacking horses, dogs, birds or anything else that would bring me pleasure'. The lad had already sent his father two dog collars as tokens of affection and gratitude. At age twelve, Galeazzo once again declared his skill and joy in hunting. Galeazzo implicitly acknowledged that hunting helped prepare for battle, when he described for his father the 'war' that he and his hawk had 'waged against the quails' – assisted by his younger sister Ippolita and her 'brave squad'.[88] Ippolita was a fierce hunter, who that same week informed her father that she had caught several quails herself and had chosen hunting over dancing. She sent Francesco some quails 'with my name tied to their feet', so that he could distinguish the ones she had snared. A few weeks later, Ippolita expressed disappointment and hurt that Francesco nevertheless mocked her hunting in a letter to her mother. Francesco attempted to mollify his daughter, by reassuring her that for 'being young and new in the pursuit, you comported yourself very well'.[89] Francesco Sforza clearly thought that hunting was for boys.

These ideals were deeply ingrained in little lords. Galeazzo's illegitimate brother Polidoro – who spent his youth in Parma, separated from the Sforza court – professed his love for hawking, riding horses and his vocation as a soldier, when he requested brocaded doublets from his father. Polidoro perfectly understood which animals made him a man in his father's eyes, as did Giovanni Gonzaga, who, in 1482 at age eight, tried to convince his father (Federico i Gonzaga) to give him a new horse. Giovanni asserted that he only wanted to please *papà* and become a 'man of arms'. A similar education began even earlier for Federico ii Gonzaga (Giovanni's nephew), who, before his first birthday, received 'little horses, dogs, deer and various other sorts of animals made of stone and brought from Venice, which are the best toys in the world for a boy'.[90] These small playthings call to mind carved and cast jousting knights, including bronze toys that rolled on wheels and could be pulled with strings (illus. 59). Combatants could be dismounted by their opponent's lance, which may also be the case for similar toys depicted atop a table near the convalescing, three-year-old Matthäus Schwarz in an image from his remarkable *Little Book of Clothes* (*Klaidungsbüchlein*) (illus. 60).[91] Young Federico ii Gonzaga also recognized the gendered valences of weapons; just two-and-a-half years old, he delighted his mother Isabella d'Este when, after she handed to him the sword that the merchants of Mantua had presented to her, he responded – as Isabella recounted to the boy's father – 'all by himself and without any reminders from anyone . . . "Many thanks, we will save it for our lord Pa."' Before long, the precocious Federico's education in hunting and horse breeding was well underway. His father Francesco led the three-year-old around the stables of the dynasty's stud farm at Gonzaga, pointing out the mares pregnant with 'little Barbary foals'. A year later, Federico dispatched a cockerel with a miniature bow and arrow and, the next day, the boy proudly informed his mother that he had vanquished a goose.[92]

Galeazzo Maria Sforza's parents came to believe that the lad's obsession with hunting distracted from critical matters. Ideal masculinity – even for lords – required the exercise of restraint, or at least its appropriate display, if not its sincere or all-encompassing practice. At age nine, in 1453, Galeazzo informed his father that his mother had insisted that he first study, and only in his spare time turn to the 'pleasure and solace of hawking and hunting'. Three years later, when recounting to his father the 'war' against the quails, Galeazzo rather unconvincingly protested that he preferred 'books and studies'. Francesco remained worried the following year (1457), when Galeazzo neglected his duties while visiting Ferrara, no thanks to Borso d'Este.

Misgivings about his son and heir's priorities only intensified. Renaissance princes were expected to grow up fast, and, for Francesco, Galeazzo was not doing so quickly enough. In 1463, Francesco explained to the Mantuan ambassador that Galeazzo was forbidden to visit the Gonzaga court because he needed to 'leave birds behind and devote himself and attend to important things, in order to learn the style and practice of ruling and governing'.[93] Three years later, and mere weeks before his death, Francesco pointedly admonished his 22-year-old son to turn his 'soul and mind' to soldiering and warfare and to 'leave

59 Toy figures of jousting knights, *c.* 1505, cast bronze with traces of paint.

60 Narziß Renner, 'In August 1500, I suffered badly from chicken pox,' illuminated page from Matthäus Schwarz, *Klaidungsbüchlein* (1522–35).

behind boyish things and do manly things [*ussire da le cose de pucti et fare le cose de homo*]'. Francesco had cause for concern, for in recent correspondence – from France, where he assisted King Louis XI's alliance of noblemen – Galeazzo confessed the 'pleasure' he took in falconry and carried on about the birds and dogs that the king had given him.[94] Galeazzo strove to please his father until the very end.

According to Bernardino Corio, on Christmas 1476 – the day before he would be assassinated – Galeazzo told the assembled crowd of family members and courtiers that he wished his father were still alive to see how splendid and magnificent his court had become.[95]

When Francesco counselled Galeazzo to apply himself to 'cose de homo', in this instance he referred to the violence of soldiering. Other 'manly things' expected of Renaissance lords, however, included seducing women and siring heirs. In this respect, Galeazzo assuredly demonstrated his manhood. Galeazzo had fathered his first illegitimate child, Carlo, by the age of fourteen, and three additional acknowledged bastards by the age of 21.[96] Galeazzo assumed the position of dynastic patriarch in other ways as well – his younger brother Ludovico, for instance, addressed him in a letter as 'most illustrious prince and most excellent lord, brother and father' two months after Francesco's death.[97] For men and boys incessantly exposed to courtly texts, spectacles and images such as the *Rape of the Sabine Women* (illus. 25) in Ludovico's grammar – with Romans and Sabines dressed as fifteenth-century princes and damsels – it seemed entirely natural that erotic imagery visualizing coercive seduction and domination would constitute noble virility and power. As the next two chapters show, not only the lord's military and courtly prowess communicated through jousting, hunting and hawking, but equally his sexual prowess and allure, displayed through mistresses, were essential for making the Renaissance man.

3

Courtly Mistresses: Representation and Power

We now turn from chivalric spectacle to courtly love, and from demonstrations of masculine valour exhibited in jousts and hunts to equally resonant declarations of manliness displayed in art celebrating the women whom lords seduced. Noble men asserted virility, political authority and sexual prowess by advertising their mistresses. Indeed, Renaissance rule rested upon an erotics of power conveyed through images of love, seduction and domination.[1] Princes and mistresses were commemorated as heroic knights and chivalric damsels. Unlike earlier, more chaste ideals of courtly love, however, in fifteenth-century Italy the lord and his *inamorata* were linked through adultery and sex. For *signori*, not just adulterous sex but its attendant violence also constituted normative masculinity. Men inflicted violence upon hunted animals, noble adversaries and disloyal (and loyal) subjects – and equally on wives, lovers, sisters and daughters. Much was at stake when it came to the prince's virility and honour (not to mention related questions of paternity, and maternity). Even aristocratic women could find themselves victims, or somehow caught in the margins, with devastating consequences.

This exploration of lords and their mistresses allows us to shift attention to the interdependent, inter-relational nature of gendered configurations of patriarchal authority visualized through images of noble men and women. Put another way, constructions and ideals of masculinity can be found in portraits of men and women alike. We focus our analytic gaze on three mistresses and on their representations in an array of media. Bianca Pellegrini and Lucia Marliani take centre stage in this chapter, while Cecilia Gallerani, Ludovico Sforza's lover who was painted by Leonardo da Vinci, is given full attention in the next. Lucia Marliani, the best rewarded mistress of Milan's duke Galeazzo Maria Sforza, lived in courtly splendour and exercised considerable power as the countess of Melzo. Bianca Pellegrini, mistress of Pier Maria Rossi of Parma, inspired a multivalent campaign of imagery celebrating the 'fair pilgrim' or *bianca pellegrina*, through which Rossi activated dynastic histories and devotions engaging traditions of knighthood, crusade and pilgrimage. These women served as important instruments in political strategies and bolstered the prince's authority by amplifying his virility. They also accrued substantial wealth and prestige. Mistresses operated not just to their own benefit, but to that of their families (and sometimes their husband's families as well). These women were dynamic actors, hardly mere objects or passive partners.[2]

Renaissance Lords and Mistresses

By advertising mistresses in poetry, painting and medals, lords deployed adulterous relations to claim 'an independent position *vis-à-vis* the web of marital and political alliances'.[3] If wives were chosen for princes, mistresses afforded the opportunity not only to enjoy sexual pleasure, but equally to display virility and autonomy and to forge extensive networks of power. *Signori* publicized mistresses through medals and other artistic media, and through gifts of opulent clothing and grants of land. In 1475, courtiers and lords from Milan, Parma and Piacenza witnessed Galeazzo Maria Sforza's investiture of feudal titles and territory to his lover Lucia Marliani. The documents incorporated amorous language (one mentions Galeazzo's 'immense ardor' for Lucia), and they cursed anyone, his wife Bona of Savoy and future heirs in particular, who might interfere with donations to Lucia: 'we call on omnipotent God so that in vengeance for us, if one acts against this as described above, He may damn by the curse with which Dathan was cursed, and Abyron, whom the earth would not bear, but swallowed alive; and so Judas Iscariot.'[4] Indeed, Galeazzo understood better than most the need to protect gifts to mistresses by any means necessary, for he had confiscated both moveable goods and real estate from his father's lover Elisabetta da Robecco. Following Francesco Sforza's death, Galeazzo forced Elisabetta to return expensive jewels and a palace (a building that would be subsequently bestowed upon Federico da Montefeltro and then Lorenzo de' Medici). According to an ambassador, Elisabetta was made so desperate by Galeazzo's demands that she contemplated suicide. The duke threatened to lock her away if she and her husband did not relinquish the *palazzo*.[5]

Adulterous sex was a formative, almost essential component of noble masculinity and sexuality. This male prerogative provided sexual pleasure and cemented bonds between aristocratic dynasties, thus amplifying broader networks of alliances. Indeed, lords tenaciously protected the privileges afforded by extramarital relationships because they efficaciously bolstered rule. Though the prominent fourteenth-century jurist Baldo degli Ubaldi found Bernabò Visconti's donations to his mistress 'repugnant', he admitted that too strong a legal protest

61 Bonifacio Bembo and workshop, *Bianca Pellegrini Crowns Her Knight Pier Maria Rossi*, c. 1460, fresco, west lunette, Camera d'Oro, Torrechiara Castle.

would be met with such fierce resistance as to 'be pointless; to wear myself out just for the sake of provoking indignation would be completely insane'.[6] As Helen Ettlinger has persuasively shown, adultery did not flout the system in fifteenth-century Italian courts. It was the system.[7]

The frescoes of Torrechiara Castle's Camera d'Oro depict the mistress Bianca Pellegrini ennobling Count Pier Maria Rossi and thus reinforcing his authority (illus. 27, 61). These scenes proclaim that power comes from Bianca, and indeed, women represented in the visual imagery of courtly love seem, at first glance, elevated. Yet such representations idealize and mystify gendered hierarchies, and men more so than women were entitled to desire and to act. Paintings of mistresses, in fact, reveal much about the desires and expectations of lords. Within the conventions of what we now call courtly love, women inspired men to great deeds, whereas men rivalled one another over their devotion. All the same, certain mistresses were effective actors who gained financial and political power through their status and visual representation.[8] Like all members of Renaissance society, these women were bound by and complicit in prevailing power structures, yet they could use their relative privilege to generate room to manoeuvre.

In Renaissance Italy, status and class structured sexual relations – noble and otherwise. The adulterous lord was generally of a higher class than his female lover, and the hierarchy of mistresses was ordered by social rank. The women who were best rewarded and most visible in art came from the nobility or elite merchant classes. These included Cecilia Gallerani, Bianca Pellegrini, Lucia Marliani and Isotta degli Atti (Sigismondo Malatesta's beloved who was celebrated in a multimedia campaign) (illus. 62). It is hardly coincidental that in his influential *Art of Courtly Love*, Andreas Capellanus discussed adultery chiefly in the dialogue, 'A man of the higher nobility speaks with a woman of the simple nobility.'[9] Yet *signori* enjoyed and exploited masculine privileges afforded by their status through coercive, often abusive, sexual relations with social inferiors of all sorts: servants, enslaved persons and common subjects, who remain much less visible to historians.

The elite participants in these networks of adultery were well rewarded. Husbands of mistresses were granted political appointments, and unmarried female lovers were often (eventually) compensated with marriage to a noble husband. Mistresses' parents, husbands and brothers received land, benefices and cash, and sisters were provided dowries, relieving families of an imposing financial burden. Though he wrote decades after the fact, Paolo Giovio was not far off the mark when he commented that during Galeazzo Maria Sforza's reign, sexual relations with the prince were not shameful and that only the 'stupid' considered the husbands of his mistresses to be cuckolds. Instead, these men with 'their gilded horns' acquired significant prestige.[10] So too did mistresses who exercised remarkable agency within courtly networks, attaining financial and political prominence for themselves and their families. The cultural forms of Renaissance adultery provided systems of commerce and exchange that were significantly more complex than the traditional model of courtly love allows.

Until recent decades, however, scholars have acknowledged the presence of mistresses and illegitimate children in Italian Renaissance courts with disdain. The nineteenth-century historians Alessandro Luzio and Rodolfo Renier reckoned the ubiquity of mistresses a 'symptom of profound corruption'. In an anti-aristocratic vein, Luigi Napoleone Cittadella harshly criticized the Este for maintaining mistresses but simultaneously punishing such practices among their citizens. Artistic representations of mistresses have occasioned similar indignation. In the mid-nineteenth century, Alexis-François Rio claimed that Leonardo da Vinci broke down on his deathbed, cried 'bitter tears' and reprimanded himself for having painted Cecilia Gallerani. In the late twentieth century, James Beck asserted that

62 Matteo de' Pasti, *Isotta degli Atti* (obverse), *c.* 1450, bronze.

associating Ludovico Sforza with Leonardo's portrait of Cecilia would have 'caused embarrassment' for contemporary viewers.[11]

Lords and their subjects, however, understood the importance and utility of mistresses. The public artistic campaigns celebrating mistresses, and the investitures rewarding them, suggest that these affairs were emphatically not hidden indiscretions. In 1472, Ercole d'Este commissioned Cosmè Tura to paint a portrait of himself with his illegitimate daughter Lucrezia, born to his lover Lodovica Condomieri. Tura's canvas was sent to Naples in advance of Ercole's wedding to Eleonora of Aragon. The new bride and her dynasty were not expected to be scandalized by the image, but instead reassuringly convinced of Ercole's lordly virility and potency. Eleonora, in fact, was involved in the commission, six years later, of an additional portrait of young Lucrezia painted by Tura, though the intended audience was in this instance the family of the girl's *promesso sposo*, Annibale II Bentivoglio.[12] Neither portrait seems to survive, but we still see Lucrezia prominently depicted with her father and his new wife in an Este genealogical manuscript illuminated a year or two after their nuptials (illus. 93).

The Fair Pilgrim of Torrechiara: Bianca Pellegrini, *bianca pellegrina*

In the frescoed vaults of Torrechiara Castle's Camera d'Oro, Bianca Pellegrini wanders her *signore*'s territory in the guise of a pilgrim (*pellegrina*), a pun on her aristocratic family name (illus. 63). In the lunettes' rituals of courtly love, as we saw in Chapter One, this mistress ennobles Pier Maria Rossi. The golden chamber's protagonists are based on, but not entirely encompassed by, Pier Maria Rossi and Bianca Pellegrini. Portraits, after all, negotiate cultural ideals and particular appearances. Bianca Pellegrini is visualized not merely as herself but as a multivalent, efficacious figure whom I call the fair or white pilgrim, the *bianca pellegrina*: mistress, chivalric damsel, devout pilgrim and vigilant peregrine falcon. The *bianca pellegrina*, moreover, activated the Rossi dynasty's crusading and pilgrimage traditions and devotions, and in so doing visualized Pier Maria's authority. This imagery was represented over a wide geographical expanse far beyond Torrechiara's walls, for varied audiences, and in a variety of materials and media: frescoes, medals, bronze bells, manuscript illuminations, terracotta reliefs and intarsia.[13] Visible on the exterior and throughout the interior of castles and churches, these images were insistently publicized to construct a multivalent Bianca. They were not, however, straightforward or secret indications of Pier Maria's authentic love.

The geographical spread of the *bianca pellegrina*'s imagery – and the many audiences to whom it was addressed – suggest that many of Rossi's subjects and peers would have known of his mistress, though not all would have been familiar with even the basic information about Bianca now available to historians (that she was the daughter of Andrea de' Pellegrini of Como, the wife of the Milanese noble-man Melchiorre d'Arluno, and the mother of two children, Ottaviano and Francesca, fathered by her husband).[14] They saw a pilgrim and, depending on their privilege or access to knowledge, might have known her name. Even though – or perhaps precisely because – the play on Bianca's name is so readily accessible, fifteenth-century liter-ary sources refrain from identifying her directly. In *terza rima* verses celebrating the Rossi dynasty and the Camera d'Oro, the Piacentine poet Gerardo Rustici refers to the 'damsel' and 'pilgrim'. The human-ist and Rossi apologist Jacopo Caviceo mentions the 'Milanese woman with whom he [Pier Maria] was madly in love'.[15] Though Gian-francesco Enzola's medals identify Bianca Pellegrini by name, their inscriptions insist on the mistress's mediated identity through invok-ing the 'simulacrum' of her chivalric and peregrine imagery. The *bianca pellegrina*, the fair pilgrim of the Camera d'Oro, is assuredly Bianca Pellegrini, though she is not only or merely her.[16]

The earliest imagery associated with Bianca Pellegrini dates to the mid-1450s. Two medals cast by Gianfrancesco Enzola celebrate the Camera d'Oro's *bianca pellegrina*, spreading the fame of the room and of Rossi's devout mistress through examples of an intimate yet inher-ently publicizing medium that travelled among peers who carefully scrutinized these handheld, tactile objects. The centrality of the *bianca pellegrina* to Rossi's artistic enterprise is indicated by the fact that only one of the five known medal types associated with his patronage – Enzola's 1471 medal now in the collection of the Victoria & Albert Museum, depicting Pier Maria's profile on the obverse and an image of a mounted warrior on the reverse – neither pictures Bianca nor visualizes peregrine iconography.[17]

Gianfrancesco Enzola's medal of 1457 (illus. 64) represents the 'simulacrum' of 'Divine Bianca' opposite a castle flanked by pilgrims' staffs and surmounted by a bird of prey. This pilgrim's castle also

63 Bonifacio Bembo and workshop, *Bianca Pellegrini Traverses Rossi Territory*, c. 1460, fresco, ceiling, Camera d'Oro, Torrechiara Castle.

64 Gianfrancesco Enzola, *Bianca Pellegrini* (obverse) and *Pilgrim's Castle* (reverse), 1457, bronze.

appears on the Camera d'Oro's terracotta walls (illus. 65) and frescoed in the courtyard portico of Roccabianca Castle, where it was later overpainted and is thus now only faintly visible above its circular moat. The reverse of a medal in Naples in the early twentieth century and now seemingly lost exhibits a wandering pilgrim closely related, though not identical to the pilgrim of the Camera d'Oro's north vault (illus. 66 and 67).[18] The frescoed pilgrim uses her staff (*bordone*) as she strides, while the sculpted *pellegrina*, walking in the opposite direction, supports the staff over her shoulder and is accompanied by

65 Unknown artisans, *Pilgrim's Castle*, c. 1460, terracotta with traces of polychromy, lower walls, Camera d'Oro, Torrechiara Castle.

66 Gianfrancesco Enzola (attr.), *Bianca Pellegrini* (obverse) and *Pilgrim Wandering* (reverse), *c.* 1460.

67 Bianca Pellegrini with brooches and a wallet hanging off her staff, north vault, detail from Bonifacio Bembo and workshop, Camera d'Oro (illus. 63).

68 Bianca Pellegrini with emblems of pilgrimage and the M initial emblem of Pier Maria Rossi, south vault, detail from Bonifacio Bembo and workshop, Camera d'Oro (illus. 63).

a loyal dog. The medal reverse's inscription – LIZADRA ET PELEGRINA SOPRA TUTO (Elegant and Beautiful Above All) – inventively refers not only to Bianca's supreme beauty, which exceeds her rivals, but to the frescoes and their protagonist depicted on the ceiling, above all viewers. *Pellegrina* and *peregrina* were familiar poetic adjectives, meaning beautiful, elegant and refined. One word, then, identifies Bianca as a pilgrim, describes her as beautiful and refers to her family name and noble heritage. *Bianca* was likewise poetically suggestive, signalling purity and beauty – radiant and fair, and thus courtly and noble. The white scarves or cloths held or worn by Torrechiara's pilgrims recall Bianca's name as well. These are tokens of amorous devotion, and in the south vault one is embroidered with the emblem of Pier Maria's initials also represented on the Camera d'Oro's terracotta walls (illus. 68).[19]

Two emblems of pilgrimage, the crossed keys of Rome and the scallop shells of Santiago de Compostela, are pinned to the *bianca pellegrina*'s cape or mantle. She clutches the knotted, wooden staff that appears in the device of the pilgrim's castle and is mentioned in Gerardo Rustici's poetic invocation of the painted pilgrim 'with the staff [*bordone*] and her brown *borsete*'.[20] *Borsete* – small bags or wallets – were frequently carried by pilgrims. They hang from the *pellegrina*'s staffs in the north and west vaults and from those flanking the castle (illus. 65 and 67). Yet the *bianca pellegrina* is not austerely attired. Her lavish array manifests Rossi's wealth and the frescoes' glittering materiality. The adornment of the caps and veils implies scores of luminous pearls, though they are damaged (as are the pilgrim's fair faces, now tarnished black). The *bianca pellegrina*'s head coverings and extravagantly brocaded clothes were once splendid and sumptuous, particularly so when contrasted with pilgrims' customarily humble garb.

The *pellegrina*'s castle, depicted on Bianca's medals and on the Camera d'Oro's terracotta walls, is surmounted by a peregrine falcon and flanked by *bordoni* with hanging *borsete*. Viewers may have equated the castle with Roccabianca (White Fortress), promised to Bianca in Rossi's wills and depicted next to her in the final lunette of the Camera d'Oro's amorous progression (illus. 8). In the 1450s, the castle was constructed on a site known as Arzinoldo. Roccabianca then replaced the town's previous nomenclature consistently in investitures

69 Roccabianca Castle, built 1460s.

and other documents (illus. 69).[21] Though scholars dispute whether the castle's name refers to Rossi's mistress or to its whitewashed exterior, contemporary evidence argues for both possibilities. Circa 1490, Jacopo Caviceo claimed that Roccabianca was named for Bianca, though a bit later one of the town's elders reminisced that it had been called Roccabianca 'because the *rocca* was entirely white'. Traces of whitewash remain, yet castles were commonly named after women. Rolando Pallavicino built Cortemaggiore, near Piacenza, as Castel Lauro, in honour of his wife Laura Landi. Sigismondo Malatesta's *torrione Isotteo* in Senigallia echoed his mistress and then wife Isotta degli Atti.[22]

To name a castle could be a multivalent act – resolutely public and political. Roccabianca's whitewashed facade, of course, reiterated Bianca's noble radiance, and the intimation of a courtly love affair in its name must have also resonated. Roccabianca's double meaning need not be considered contradictory or explained away as Rossi's attempt to hide Bianca from his wife Antonia Torelli or from his subjects, as scholars have often done. Roccabianca imaginatively advertised both the lord's mistress and an ideally pure and candid courtly realm. The association between Roccabianca and Bianca Pellegrini is strengthened by the courtyard portico's monumental, though faded fresco depicting the pilgrim's castle. Varying audiences entered this relatively public space at a key site for Rossi territorial administration. Pier Maria's multimedia campaign exalting the *bianca pellegrina* was available beyond Torrechiara's golden chamber to many peers and subjects.

Atop Bianca's castle, a peregrine falcon surveys Rossi's territory, while in the moat below float ducks – aquatic fowl that falcons were trained to hunt. Italian lords were well attuned to falconry lore and practice. Falconry was equated with love's pursuit, and the bird served as a metaphor for both male and female lovers.[23] The nobility of the peregrine falcon, in particular, was renowned. Small, fierce and fast, it soars upwards of 300 kilometres per hour (200 mph) and was known as the *gentiles peregrinus* (noble peregrine). The 'pelegrin falcon zentile' symbolized an elevated poetic style in one of Gaspare Visconti's sonnets extolling Bramante at the Sforza court, and falcon-crazed lords and courtiers may have commended Bianca's peregrine knowing that female raptors (formels) are larger than males (tiercels) and were thought to be bolder, superior hunters. Peregrines were popular enough in Renaissance courts that certain falconers (*pelegrineri*) specialized in rearing and caring for the birds.[24] The *falco pellegrino*, yet another peregrine image poetically and wittily invoked within the Camera d'Oro, is perched regally over Bianca's castle, offering protection and surveillance while threatening prey below.

Aristocratic status fundamentally structured raptor lore. The most noble of birds were not falcons but rather eagles, as we see represented on the reverse of Pisanello's medal for the Neapolitan King Alfonso of Aragon. Alfonso's imperial eagle is perched above lesser birds of prey who acknowledge his authority and with whom he shares his quarry, as a demonstration of regal generosity (illus. 70).[25] In a story retold and adapted throughout Europe – and in Italy from the anonymous *Novellino* of the late thirteenth century, to Matteo Bandello in the sixteenth, to Gabriele D'Annunzio in the early twentieth – a falcon was hanged or decapitated for killing an eagle. Either a (human) king or emperor commands that the proud falcon be executed for having assassinated its lord, notwithstanding its courage and ferocity, and despite the fact that (or perhaps specifically because) courtiers had enthusiastically praised the less noble bird.[26]

In the Camera d'Oro's north lunette (illus. 8), Pier Maria is attired as a blond, beautiful and courtly knight, an ideal that was more than imaginary or nostalgic for the lord. The Rossi had long fostered legacies of pilgrimage and crusade. Bianca Pellegrini's imagery thus provided a potent symbol through which Pier Maria activated dynastic

70 Pisanello, *Eagle and Lesser Birds of Prey in a Rocky Landscape* (reverse of Alfonso of Aragon medal), 1449, lead alloy.

traditions and devotions. Two pilgrimages undertaken by Pier Maria's father, Pietro, shaped Rossi interventions in regional and international politics. These journeys initiated and then strengthened patterns of ecclesiastical patronage back home in Parma. Pietro Rossi and a group of Italian noblemen accompanied Niccolò III d'Este to Jerusalem in 1413. The pilgrimage was both a display of piety and of allegiance to the Este, who ruled Parma in the second decade of the fifteenth century. Pietro was knighted in the Church of the Holy Sepulchre, an honour that the Rossi advertised by fostering the cult of the Holy Sepulchre during and beyond his lifetime.[27]

On a similarly devotional and political expedition undertaken soon after the Visconti regained control of Parma in 1420, Pietro Rossi travelled to Santiago de Compostela, visiting various Spanish and Portuguese episcopal and royal courts. On both the outgoing and return legs of this pilgrimage to Compostela, Pietro visited the church of St-Antoine-l'Abbaye (St Anthony Abbot) near Vienne, where Gian Galeazzo Visconti's viscera were entombed.[28] The Rossi dynasty's ecclesiastical patronage in Parma orbited around peregrine and crusading devotions at the churches of San Sepolcro (Holy Sepulchre) and Sant'Antonio Abate (St Anthony Abbot). Pier Maria Rossi held rights over at least two chapels within San Sepolcro, and in 1463 Pier Maria and his wife Antonia Torelli bequeathed land in return for perpetual masses in their memory. In 1471, Rossi declared his 'devotione & amor' towards San Sepolcro and suggested architectural interventions where the church was 'ruined and desolate'. An inscription documenting the dedication of a chapel for Pier Maria's salvation in 1475 explicitly invokes his piety and magnificence.[29]

Sant'Antonio Abate in Parma, a church that his father Beltrando had helped build, soon became the site of Pietro Rossi's burial chapter dedicated to the Holy Cross, which was finished posthumously by his widow, Giovanna Cavalcabò. Devotion to the Holy Cross and to St Anthony Abbot developed into vital cults in the wake of Pietro's pilgrimages. For instance, the Holy Cross and the Holy Nail were given particular significance in two manuscripts patronized by generations of the Rossi.[30] Though Pietro's chapel of Santa Croce at Sant'Antonio Abate in Parma was destroyed in the eighteenth century, surviving inscriptions and a sixteenth-century description of the space help us to imagine it. Pietro Rossi, kneeling in prayer and dressed in sumptuous cloth of gold, directed his devotion towards a scene of the Last Judgment.[31] The azurite walls and the gold of Rossi's brocades would have contributed to a magnificently pious chapel, one materially akin to his son's Camera d'Oro at Torrechiara. This chapel's loss impoverishes not only our knowledge of mid-Quattrocento Lombard and Emilian painting, but equally the legacy of Giovanna Cavalcabò, a significant patron in her own right, who also directed work on her father's commemorative chapel at Sant'Agostino in Cremona.

Rossi ecclesiastical interventions in the heart of Parma engaged pilgrimage's dynamic political and chivalric resonances. In short, peregrine devotions bolstered the dynasty's power. Pietro was not the only Rossi pilgrim, however. His illegitimate son Rolando was a Knight of St John celebrated for fighting at Rhodes and a key player in Parmense politics. Rolando returned from crusading to besiege castles and assault enemies on behalf of his brother Pier Maria on numerous, well-timed occasions, abetted by his thugs Stramazzo (Brawler) and Colombaccio (Bad Bird).[32] Moreover, the best-known work of Pier Maria Rossi's adherent and biographer Jacopo Caviceo – *Il Peregrino* – tells the tale of a pilgrim wandering the Mediterranean in search of his lover. Though the text was published after Pier Maria's death and for the Ferrarese court (and though the genders are reversed from the Camera d'Oro), the narrative is clearly informed by Rossi's peregrine iconography. Indeed, the poet describes Torrechiara in abundant and reverent detail, as a majestic destination on the pilgrim's journey.[33] With Pier Maria's father a celebrated pilgrim and his brother Rolando a crusading warrior, the polyvalent *bianca pellegrina* embodied an ideal that was at once chivalric, devout, martial and pious. The allegorical imagery of this pilgrim – her castle, falcon and knights – efficaciously amplified Rossi seigneurial authority and virile masculinity, reverberating with his dynasty's peregrine cults, traditions and histories.

Negotiating Adultery: Sex, Power and Violence

Part and parcel of Pier Maria Rossi's identity as bellicose prince was the lordly prerogative of sex with his mistress, who inspired but also submitted to her *signore*. Gender and class shaped normative conventions surrounding adulterous love in practice and in cultural production. Adultery was negotiable, not absolute. It was customarily a crime of wives, and aristocratic men were not held to the same ideals of chastity as were women, both because of gendered power differentials and to ensure the paternity (and less imperatively the maternity) of heirs. Though he was the illegitimate son of a cardinal, 'il Cardinalino' Francesco Gonzaga had his wife, Taddea Forlani, imprisoned for adultery. The double standard may be best suggested by a legend surrounding the *condottiere* Niccolò Piccinino, the father of numerous bastards, who, returning home to a newborn son after a military campaign of eleven months, ordered his wife to be killed for her apparent infidelity.[34] The rest of the story, that Niccolò's mother informed him that he had been carried twelve months *in utero*, betrays contemporary anxieties around, and recognition of, the gendered contradictions of aristocratic adultery.

While adulterous love was encouraged at court and celebrated in art and poetry, women contravened its gender and class constraints only with great risk to their status and even life. The violence enacted in war, jousts and hunts – directed by lords against subjects, enemies and animals – was also inflicted upon wives and lovers. Numerous noble women were murdered or executed for adultery or its allegation. Agnese Visconti, wife of Francesco Gonzaga, was decapitated in 1391 after meeting her lover in a chamber that may have been frescoed with scenes depicting Lancelot and Guinevere's encounters, in an affair evoking Dante's tale of Paolo and Francesca. In 1418, an executioner beheaded Filippo Maria Visconti's first wife Beatrice di Tenda, who was accused of infidelity, in all likelihood unjustly, and seems to have confessed under torture. And in 1466, Penelope Orsini, mistress *and* cousin of Aldobrandino Orsini, was killed along with her young son by Aldobrandino's son Niccolò, after she had plotted to poison Niccolò's brother in a bid for control of Pitigliano, in southern Tuscany.[35] Women suffered imprisonment, corporeal punishment and so-called 'honour' killings at the hands of male relatives, who were typically exonerated. In 1483, Rodolfo Gonzaga brutally murdered his wife Antonia Malatesta – also known as Anna, the daughter of Sigismondo Malatesta and Isotta degli Atti – along with her lover, the Spanish dancing master Fernando Flores Cubillas.[36] Rodolfo went unpunished for this crime, though like many of his peers, he eventually met a violent end. Rodolfo perished in 1495 at the Battle of Fornovo.

Noble wives were defended by fathers and brothers, because chastity signalled family honour as much as male aggression and virility did. Alessandro Sforza, who we saw about to be struck by Cupid in Chapter One, repeatedly physically abused his second wife, Sveva da Montefeltro, whose brother Federico attempted to poison Alessandro in retaliation (or at least Alessandro believed that he did).[37] Federico da Montefeltro maintained his innocence and instead implicated his inveterate enemy Sigismondo Malatesta who sought control of Pesaro, which had been given by his kinsman Galeazzo Malatesta to Alessandro at the time of Sforza's first marriage (to Galeazzo's niece, Costanza da Varano). To escape her husband's abuse, Sveva withdrew to the convent of Corpus Christi in Pesaro. She became so renowned for piety that she, known as Serafina Sforza, was beatified in the eighteenth century.

Sigismondo Malatesta, for his part, deflected accusations that he had ordered the suffocation of his wife Polissena Sforza (Francesco's illegitimate daughter) by claiming that she had been unfaithful. Sigismondo may have imprisoned and starved Polissena's Franciscan confessor, who refused to back up his story that she had admitted adultery. Francesco Sforza believed that Polissena had been killed on Sigismondo's command so that he could marry his mistress Isotta (illus. 62). Sforza further alleged that the friar, who would 'never consent to say such a falsehood and wicked thing', was left to die in a dungeon.[38] Like this cleric, some men caught up in the politics and networks of adultery suffered cruel fates. Galeazzo Maria Sforza is reported to have ordered Pietrino da Castello's hands cut off after the courtier raised his lord's suspicions by conversing too familiarly with one of his lovers.[39] Women were sometimes protected, or at least their assailants were punished, because of the courtly favour that they or their families enjoyed. In 1493, the painter Baldassare d'Este's daughter Cassandra was raped by three youths from Reggio. Baldassare's half-brother Duke Ercole intervened, as did the poet Matteo Maria Boiardo (best known for his *Orlando Innamorato*, and an important civic official in Reggio). The perpetrators were tortured and fined a significant sum to furnish Cassandra's dowry.[40]

Noble kinsmen did not always protect wives from husbands who battered them. Networks of women offered an additional measure of security and intervention (though not in all cases, as we learn from Isabella d'Este pleading mercy for Bartolomeo Tromboncino, a musician who murdered his wife after finding her alone with another man, because, in Isabella's chilling words to her husband, 'he had legitimate

cause to kill his wife and since he is such a good and talented man').[41]
The Sforza *condottiere* Colella di Napoli informed his wife Elisabetta
Visconti that he abused her because of disputes with her brothers,
'out of spite' and disdain for them. Elisabetta confided in her distant
cousin Duchess Bianca Maria Visconti Sforza that Colella taunted
her and gave her precisely this explanation for his frequent brutality.
He fractured three of Elisabetta's ribs in one beating, and the following day, as she tells it, 'broke my body from head to toe'. Colella also
bashed Elisabetta's face black and blue and pulled out her hair with
his bare hands. Though she suffered a miscarriage because of her anguish and abuse, it seems that Elisabetta dared not provide her brothers
a full account, given her husband's threats. The duchess of Milan was
one person whose power Colella truly feared – indeed the only reason,
Elisabetta claimed, that he had not murdered her, given how often
he 'came at me with his hands around my neck'.[42]

Perhaps the most sensational noble affair in fifteenth-century Italy
is that of Ugo d'Este (Niccolò iii d'Este's eldest acknowledged son)
and his stepmother Parisina Malatesta (Niccolò's second wife). Their
story was adapted by writers from Matteo Bandello to Lord Byron
to Gabriele D'Annunzio.[43] Ugo was the son of Niccolò's mistress
Stella de' Tolomei, whose love was inflamed by Cupid sent by Jupiter,
according to Tito Vespasiano Strozzi's epic *Borsiad*.[44] Ugo would never
assume Ferrara's *signoria*, however, and was beheaded in 1425 for this
romance with his stepmother. Niccolò was advised of their relationship by a courtier in whom Parisina had confided, and he watched the
two lovers *in flagrante delicto* from a hole in the floor of her chamber
at the Este villa of Fossadalbero. Parisina, who was much closer in age
to her stepson than to her husband, was also put to death, as was the
courtier accused of facilitating the liaison (and two women from
Parisina's retinue, according to one source). Indeed, at the time of the
executions, Parisina was about twenty years old, Ugo a year younger
and Niccolò in his early forties. He had married the fourteen-year-
old Parisina at age 35.

This was a multifaceted transgression: Ugo at once betrayed his
father, committed incest and cuckolded his *signore*. A newly bound
manuscript of *Tristan and Isolde* interested Parisina in the years prior
to the affair, and one wonders what inspiration or admonition this
narrative provided. Further caution may have arisen from the fate
of her father's first wife, Rengarda Alidosi, daughter of the lord of

Imola, who had been repudiated by her husband for infidelity at the age of fifteen and consequently poisoned by her brothers in yet another merciless 'honour' killing.[45] Like other Italian aristocrats – readers of chivalric narratives – Parisina and Ugo were well aware of the benefits and privileges, but also the dangers, of adulterous love.

Before taking a noble mistress, or at least before their love could be celebrated in poetry or painting, princes generally sought, and sometimes bought, the consent of her husband and family. Galeazzo Maria Sforza and Ambrogio Raverti, the husband of Lucia Marliani (whom we will learn much more about soon), were in 'buona concordia' after Ambrogio was paid 4,000 ducats and appointed *podestà* of Como.[46] Similar agreements were made by other lords. For instance, Galeazzo had been informed by his ambassador in Naples, in 1472, about the young Giovannella Caracciolo, who had been led away in tears to the quarters of King Ferrante in the Castel Novo after arrangements had been made with her father. In the previous decade, Giovanni Antonio Parravicini was made *podestà* of Varese for two years just as his wife Elisabetta da Robecco became Francesco Sforza's favourite mistress. Francesco reassured a papal ambassador that even though he visited Elisabetta in her house, he did nothing without her and her husband's approval.[47]

Consequences were disastrous when the mistress's or wife's family disapproved of the lord's wandering eye. To have mistresses was (nearly) obligatory yet simultaneously fraught with danger. The prince had to manage these essential manifestations of seigneurial virility and prowess astutely, for their abuse or mishandling could threaten his rule. The motives of Galeazzo Maria Sforza's three assassins were manifold. Yet Carlo Visconti was, in part, provoked by the duke's coerced sexual relations with his sister, and Giovanni Andrea Lampugnani was infuriated because Galeazzo, he believed, had sent him to Genoa to have easier access to his wife.[48] Once again, analogous episodes abound. Condemnation was swift, and military action threatened, when rumour spread that Sigismondo Malatesta abused a Bavarian noblewoman passing through Venetian territory. In 1488, men loyal to Francesca Bentivoglio hid under her bed to ambush her husband Galeotto Manfredi, the lord of Faenza, whose philandering damaged Francesca's honour as she and her father perceived it.[49]

To be sure, adulterous relations caused jealousy and shame for women and their families, yet many endured or condoned their husbands' lovers. Bianca Maria Visconti Sforza tolerated her husband Francesco's mistresses until she feared that his sexual activity threatened his life, and by extension the Milanese state, because of his advanced age and chronic health issues. Francesco fathered at least 35 children, including five with his mistress Giovanna d'Acquapendente. He seduced young women well into his sixties, aided by witchcraft according to accusations levied by Pope Paul II.[50]

Lucia Marliani, the Contessa di Melzo e Gorgonzola

Francesco Sforza's son and heir Galeazzo likewise took full advantage of the patriarchal sexual privileges promised to men of his status. An ambassador joked that Galeazzo was inclined to lust in 'full perfection' and 'in all the fashions and forms that it can be done'. Sforza seduced, coerced and no doubt sexually abused and violated lovers, including men and boys. His own courtier Bernardino Corio affirmed that Galeazzo was 'not a little subject to Venus, and to his own filthy libido'; that he upset and harassed subjects with these affairs; and that when satisfied himself, Galeazzo passed women off to 'many of his men to be raped'.[51]

The most historically visible of Galeazzo's mistresses is Lucia Marliani, the countess of Melzo and Gorgonzola. Franca Leverotti's authoritative study sheds much light on Marliani, the 'most beautiful woman in Milan' according to the Gonzaga ambassador to the Sforza court. Galeazzo dressed Lucia 'like a queen', and thus conspicuously above her rank, in a variety of shimmering silks including gold-brocaded damasks. Galeazzo granted Marliani many other gifts during their three-year love affair: silk bed furnishings, table silver, ivory chair backs, saddles, a magnificent mule cover and many jewels, among them a gem-studded golden cross produced by the goldsmith Dionigi da Sesto, in addition to an expensive balas that Galeazzo acquired from Lorenzo de' Medici for his 'amorosa'.[52]

Galeazzo's pronouncement to Lorenzo that he would provide Lucia with 'every favour in the world' hardly seems to have been overstated. The lord's devotion is revealed by the careful attention that he paid to the manufacture and delivery of items arranged for her. On 1 April 1475, for instance, Galeazzo ordered for Lucia seventeen lavish garments of various silks – damask, satin and the light *terzanello* – six of which were brocaded. For four of the mantles, it was 'no big deal [*non ne faremo grande caso*]' whether they were adorned with either gold or silver brocade, but for the rest, it was imperative that Gottardo Panigarola, the court *spenditore* or spender, follow his lord's instructions 'without any variation whatsoever'. A week later Sforza inquired again about Lucia's gifts, and in particular about a white, gold-brocaded cloak to be worn on the feast of St George. He advised Gottardo to check the *guardaroba* to see if the fabric was in stock. The feast of St George was Milan's most magnificent public spectacle during Galeazzo's reign. His splendidly attired court and army paraded from the Castello Sforzesco to the Duomo, for the benediction of civic banners. As the celebrations approached in 1475, Galeazzo sent multiple reminders to Gottardo: 'once again we repeat and we say to you' to make sure that Lucia's clothing was magnificently furnished and finished on time.

Galeazzo requested for Lucia two decks of *triumphi* or trump playing cards ('well made so that they are beautiful') and a velvet cushion so that she could comfortably watch games of *palla*. The duke was happy to spread the wealth, particularly if that meant he could have Lucia all to himself. Her husband, Ambrogio Raverti – he of

71 Unknown artist, emblems of Galeazzo Maria Sforza (above) and Lucia Marliani (in the initial), illuminations from *Donationes, concessiones et privilegia facta Magnificae dominae Luciae Comitissae Meltii per dominum ducem Mediolani*, 1474.

the 'gilded horns', who had married Marliani with a large dowry in 1473, the year before she had come to Galeazzo's attention – was given 4,000 ducats and the prestigious position of *podestà* of Como, which also required that he reside away from Lucia. To make certain that future offspring would be potential ducal heirs, Lucia agreed in writing not to 'couple carnally' with her husband without Galeazzo's explicit, written permission.[53]

Lucia was invested with the jurisdictions of Melzo and Gorgonzola, and she was granted houses, tax exemptions and lucrative rights over mills and waterways (including the Naviglio della Martesana). Not surprisingly, Lucia's gifts and economic concessions increased once she became pregnant with Galeazzo's child. They were augmented further after the birth in April 1476 of this son named Galeazzo who came to be known as the 'contino di Melzo'.[54] By this time, Lucia maintained a small court in Milan, attended by thirty servants. The countess of Melzo and Gorgonzola was granted permission to incorporate the Sforza viper (*biscione*) into her own insignia of two doves on an azure background (illus. 71). Bonifacio Bembo and Giacomo Vismara painted ducal arms on the facade of her Milanese palace, destroyed in the 1870s but conveniently located quite close to the Castello Sforzesco.[55]

Galeazzo's expansion of Milan's hunting *barco* north of the castle provided a shortcut to Lucia's residence – through the garden of a small estate donated to his wife Bona of Savoy, no less. At first, Galeazzo tried to hide Lucia from Bona by visiting his mistress under the pretence of 'going to the stalls to see horses'. He likewise threatened death to anyone who told Bona about Lucia. When Bona became suspicious, however, Galeazzo endeavoured to convince her that Lucia was his brother's mistress and not his own.[56] While Bona may not have been persuaded by Galeazzo's lie, this misdirection was only plausible because of the ubiquitous, homosocial culture of mistresses shared among noble men.

Eventually Lucia became so prominent at court that Bona had little choice but abide her presence. Notes from Cicco Simonetta's diary suggest that the two women and Galeazzo all resided at least for a night at the Sforza villa at Gambolò, near Vigevano. Bona seems to have taken a lover too, a chamberlain from Ferrara, Antonio Tassino.[57] Galeazzo's affairs also brought about enmity with his sister Ippolita, married to Alfonso II, duke of Calabria, and heir to the Neapolitan throne. Ippolita and Galeazzo quarrelled following her less than subtle attempts, on Bona's behalf, to ascertain whether Galeazzo had lovers. He responded in the affirmative and angrily taunted his sister by adding that he nevertheless treated his wife better than her husband did. Early in their marriage, Ippolita had a servant follow Alfonso to track his philandering (with both women and young men). Ippolita eventually buddied up to some of Alfonso's mistresses after he and her father-in-law responded to her complaints and machinations by sending some of her attendants back to Milan.[58]

Galeazzo Maria's assassination on 26 December 1476 precipitated a sudden reversal of fortune for Lucia. She may have been present at the fatal mass in Santo Stefano in Brolo, on that saint's feast day. Bernardino Corio asserted that some of the lord's lovers were there, though he did not identify any by name. Lucia seems to have attended Galeazzo's hastily arranged funeral pregnant with their second child Ottaviano, who would become bishop of Lodi and then Arezzo.[59] Following the assassination, Lucia's emblems were removed throughout Sforza territory, including those painted by Bembo and Vismara on her Milanese *palazzo*. Many of her goods were confiscated. In 1479, Bona of Savoy showed the visiting duke of Ferrara Ercole d'Este her own gems, but when Ercole asked to view those previously belonging to the '*contessa* . . . that woman whom the duke of Milan kept', Bona granted his request but 'didn't want to see them' herself. Bona left the room while Ercole inspected these jewels and pearls that the Ferrarese ambassador estimated to be worth more than 40,000 ducats.[60]

Lands, titles and privileges, however, were returned to Lucia under Ludovico Sforza's rule. This included property at Cusago, a few kilometres west of Milan. The Sforza acknowledged and provided for Lucia's two children with Galeazzo: Galeazzo, Count of Melzo, and the bishop Ottaviano. Both served their Sforza siblings and cousins into the sixteenth century. Bolstered by the financial and political support of the Marliani, Raverti and Sforza dynasties, Lucia successfully navigated ecclesiastical networks in and around Milan for another four and a half decades and managed to wield substantial power. As a widow, in 1510, she even battled the bishop of Piacenza over costly tapestries that had been in the possession of a prior bishop, her relative Fabrizio Marliani. Lucia Marliani died on 15 December 1522, age seventy, outliving Galeazzo Maria Sforza by nearly 46 years.[61]

The Sforza–Marliani love affair had bound and been contracted by both men and women, not only the two lovers but additionally her husband and mother-in-law. Galeazzo furnished two of Lucia's sisters with sizeable dowries (of 2,000 ducats) for marriage into noble families from Lodi.[62] The involvement of Lucia's mother-in-law, together with the financial advantage enjoyed by Lucia and her sisters, attests to the ways that women operated and profited at the Renaissance court. Women were both agents and objects. Lucia, moreover, understood that a woman of her means could take matters into her own hands when necessary, particularly if supported by wider familial networks. In her first will, composed almost four decades after Galeazzo's death, Lucia pleaded with her daughter Orsina to abandon her violent husband, and she exhorted Orsina's siblings to take in their sister.[63]

Given the fame of Leonardo da Vinci's portrait of the Sforza mistress Cecilia Gallerani, the subject of the chapter that follows, scholars have long sought to identify portraits of Lucia Marliani, with little success. Recently, however, Edoardo Rossetti introduced a donor portrait of Lucia not as mistress but as exemplary wife and mother (illus. 72). Lucia dutifully folds her hands in prayer, kneeling with her husband, Ambrogio Raverti, and three of her children (each with their mother's reddish-blond tresses): two boys in black and one girl dressed in crimson like her mother. The husband's and wife's name saints Lucy and Ambrose advocate to Christ and Mary, backed by gilded pastiglia, on behalf of the family. This fresco in Santa Maria delle Grazie – the Dominican monastery vigorously patronized by Ludovico Sforza – can be connected with the tomb of Fra Giacomo da Sesto, whose cult Ludovico promoted following the friar's death in 1493. As part of the case for beatification, Lucia testified that Giacomo had intervened during the precarious birth of her first legitimate son, saving the life of mother and child. The friar is nowhere to be seen in this image, which has been transferred from its original location in the church. An early description suggests that Fra Giacomo was depicted in fresco on the tomb itself, which was surmounted by this votive representation of Lucia and her family.[64] The devotional portrait clearly reveals a pious and dignified identity for the former ducal mistress. The splendid golden surfaces and prime ecclesiastical location testify to the wealth of Lucia and Ambrogio and to the elite circles in which they continued to move.

72 Unknown Lombard painter, *Madonna and Child with Sts Ambrose and Lucia, with Donors Ambrogio Raverti, Lucia Marliani and Three Children*, c. 1493–4, fresco, Santa Maria delle Grazie, Milan (originally from the tomb of Fra Giacomo da Sesto).

To be sure, Galeazzo Maria Sforza enjoyed many lovers and begat many bastards. He ordered dozens of opulent, cloth-of-gold garments to be given to mistresses who remain anonymous to us: 'our secrets', as they were referred to in directives to the court official Gottardo Panigarola. These 'secreti' seem mainly to have been women, as some are identified as such and most of the garments were female attire. These seem not to be gifts for Lucia, however, because many others are explicitly intended for her ('the contessa', or 'the contessa di Melzo') in these same documents. Most 'secrets' were given one *gamurra* (or *camora*, the garment worn over the chemise) and a pair of sleeves. A few received stockings or shoes as well. In fact, a *gamurra* and a pair of sleeves seems to have been a regular sort of payment for the lord's passing lovers. Some sleeves were brocaded with exceedingly costly loops of golden thread (*riccio sopra riccio*). The *gamurre* were made of assorted silks: sendal; satin adorned with gold fringes; crimson figured velvet; and plush velvet of varying heights. In a few instances Galeazzo demanded that his tailor Emanuele Lanza produce the garment himself. Sforza sometimes commanded that it be sent immediately – 'make sure that it arrives here soon' or 'send these things straight away, so that we have them on time tomorrow' – signalling for us the fleeting nature of the trysts.[65]

Yet Galeazzo cherished Lucia Marliani above other lovers, presumably for her beauty but also because she hailed from an aristocratic family that had been closely involved with the Sforza state since its inception. Some gifts from Galeazzo, in fact, were extensions of earlier grants to the Marliani from Francesco Sforza and even Filippo Maria Visconti (who had conceded Melzo to the Marliani in 1412). Much of the countess of Melzo and Gorgonzola's territory was located in the vicinity of her natal dynasty's traditional holdings, which enabled the Marliani to consolidate regional power further. Even before Lucia came to Galeazzo's attention, a jealous courtier sarcastically complained that Melchione Marliani was so close to the Sforza that he pompously paraded around town as if he were 'another Cosimo de' Medici of Florence' – a biting quip that reveals courtly, Milanese disdain for the seigneurial posturing of republican Florence's leading dynasty.[66]

Galeazzo and Lucia's relationship emerged from their houses' decades-long alliance but also expanded Marliani networks of power. It afforded mutually beneficial, politically advantageous and multilineal bonds beyond those of marriage. When celebrated in art, adulterous relations among the nobility – like that between Pier Maria Rossi and Bianca Pellegrini – crucially underscored the lord's virility and patriarchal authority. This was the case too for Galeazzo's brother Ludovico Sforza and his mistress Cecilia Gallerani, best known as Leonardo da Vinci's *Lady with an Ermine*. It is to these two Renaissance men, and one Renaissance girl, then woman, to whom we now turn.

73 Leonardo da Vinci, *Girl with an Ermine* (Cecilia Gallerani), *c.* 1486–8, oil on walnut panel.

4

The Girl with an Ermine Between Men: Cecilia Gallerani, Leonardo da Vinci and Ludovico Sforza

Cecilia Gallerani is familiar today as the unassuming, yet attentive subject of Leonardo da Vinci's portrait known as *The Lady with an Ermine* (illus. 73).[1] In her own lifetime, Cecilia shifted from a precociously adept operator at the Sforza court, to a venerable and charismatic literary luminary. Leonardo's painting, now in Kraków, represents Cecilia when she was the adolescent mistress of Milan's de facto ruler, Ludovico il Moro Sforza. This chapter provides a new account of Cecilia's deft navigation of power – from a strikingly young age, through adulthood and well beyond Ludovico's reign. We centre Cecilia's experience and both her and Ludovico's investments in the portrait, to investigate the efficacy and resiliency of courtly art marshalled to seduce, persuade and dominate subjects.

In recent decades, *The Lady with an Ermine* has generally been dated to circa 1489–90, though in the last few years, a case has been made for 1486–8.[2] This chapter establishes that Cecilia and Ludovico's sexual relationship had begun by July 1485, when she was perhaps twelve. Better *The Girl*, then, rather than *The Lady with an Ermine*. Though this study makes no definitive claims about when precisely to date *The Girl with an Ermine*, it argues that limited evidence justifies the scholarly consensus of 1489–90. Art historians have tended towards the later date, in part, because they presume that Cecilia must have been a respectable seventeen or eighteen years old when she served as Ludovico's mistress. Crucially, the pages that follow will show that many of the assumptions made to support the later dating have often implicitly, and sometimes explicitly, obscured historical understandings of the relations of gender, sex and power that Leonardo's portrait puts on plain display.

I explore the social, political and sexual ramifications of Cecilia's youth. Virility, sexual violence and female agency are at the heart of this chapter. We need to keep in mind the immaturity of the objects of Renaissance men's desires, particularly those of the princes who patronized so much of the art and architecture that fill our survey classes. At the same time, it is vital to examine the other key actors within Renaissance networks of adultery – the girls and young women who were exchanged between men – and to do so attentive to the ways that they negotiated and capitalized on these experiences to their own advantage (yet might also suffer in the margins of these networks). Documentary, art-historical and sartorial evidence presented here affords a new look at Cecilia Gallerani's place and agency in Renaissance Milan and allows us to recognize that she operated on both her own and her family's behalf. Focusing on Leonardo's famous painting, moreover, enables us to appreciate and evaluate the potential efficacy of visual representation – the ways that Cecilia instrumentalized her portrait and the ways she and other women could benefit from this (artistic) visibility. Art did not merely flatter the beautiful mistress as a passive object to be gazed upon; rather, it provided the material through which Cecilia Gallerani could construct, in time, a virtuous persona as a noble poet. We extend our investigation well into the sixteenth century to explore the ways that Cecilia and her adherents cultivated her courtly identity beyond her prince's lifetime, manoeuvring within Milan's cultural milieu.

It is neither surprising nor scandalous that Leonardo painted Ludovico's mistress. Renaissance lords had for decades advertised such relationships within homosocial courtly environments and throughout their realms. Mistresses served as important instruments in political strategies and in economies of favours in fifteenth-century courts, and as a means to proclaim virility, political power and sexual prowess. Through actual and imaged women, princes communicated their status in relation to other men. Adultery was a masculine prerogative that advertised sexual pleasure and privilege, cemented bonds between aristocratic dynasties and amplified broader social networks. Extra-marital relationships were formative aspects of princely sexuality. They were normative, not exceptional.[3]

Critical analysis of Renaissance patriarchy requires close attention to multiple forms of authority's gendered configurations. Sexual violence and coercion encompassed essential components of lordly rule, and they were visualized through images of both noble men and women. Leonardo's familiar portrait may seem to be one of the most demurely charming and placid of Renaissance images of women, yet it speaks volumes about, at once revealing and blinding us to, dominant masculinities and their erotics of power. Cecilia, Leonardo and Ludovico seduce us still, just as they seduced Renaissance viewers enamoured by Gallerani's beauty and Sforza's patriarchal authority.

Signore Ludovico and Cecilia Fashionista

The prevailing dating of Leonardo's *Girl with an Ermine* to circa 1489–90 depends on a few key historical and art-historical assumptions. In this and the following section, they are dismantled, one by one. To start, that Cecilia Gallerani's relationship with Ludovico Sforza began only after her intended marriage to Giovanni Stefano Visconti was renounced (in June 1487) and about the time that her brothers petitioned for the return of confiscated lands (in May 1489); additionally, that Spanish or Neapolitan fashions and modes of adornment displayed by Cecilia in Leonardo's portrait only reached Milan in 1489 or '90; and, finally, that Leonardo would have painted Ludovico Sforza's mistress caressing an ermine only after 1488, the year in which, it is often claimed, he was inducted into the Neapolitan Order of the Ermine. We first examine the last of these assertions, which is the simplest to correct. Conventional wisdom regarding Spanish fashions is then reassessed, with evidence mobilized to reinterpret their arrival in Milan and to offer a more dynamic view of fashion's operations. Lastly, I shed new light on Ludovico's and Cecilia's sexual relationship, and on its start and duration, by considering a letter published in the nineteenth century but mainly ignored and, until recently, fundamentally misunderstood.[4] This missive confirms that the thirty-something prince's infatuation with Cecilia had begun long before she reached eighteen years of age.

The ermine was a remarkably multivalent creature for Renaissance Italians, and the painting's original viewers could ascribe an array of meanings to it. Among the most resonant meanings produced by the animal that Cecilia gracefully strokes are heraldic, in relation to the Neapolitan King Ferrante's conferral of the chivalric Order of the Ermine upon Ludovico Sforza.[5] When reading about *The Girl with an Ermine*, one often encounters the claim that Ludovico was invested with the chivalric honour in 1488, a date that stems from Carlo Pedretti's influential study of Cecilia's ermine as a 'political allegory'. It has been repeated countless times, by even the most diligent art historians, but is erroneous. It seems that 1488 derives from the title of Pedretti's source: Luigi Volpicella's *Regis Ferdinandi Primi Instructionum Liber (10 Maggio 1486–10 Maggio 1488)*, which, as its title indicates, published the diplomatic correspondence and instructions of King Ferrante (also known as Ferdinando) between May 1486 and May 1488.[6]

Yet, as Volpicella's book establishes, the investiture took place in 1486.[7] In October of that year, Ferrante provided his envoy exacting instructions for how the elaborate investiture ceremony would unfold in Vigevano the following month. The golden collar and ermine-lined crimson mantle of the order should be exhibited on the altar, while Giovanni Nauclero, a member of the order, holds aloft an additional white gown. Nauclero, Ludovico and assorted courtiers later move to the sacristy where Ludovico puts on the gown, assisted by these men. After a series of *Allelujas*, Sforza emerges from the sacristy and kneels piously before the altar, to be draped with the mantle and collar. We can appreciate the charged moment of the placement of the golden collar from an illuminated manuscript of an oration celebrating Ferrante's conferral of the order upon Federico da Montefeltro in 1474 (illus. 74). Three crimson, cloth-of-gold mantles converge in the image's centre. They bedeck Federico, Ferrante and the king's son Alfonso II, and they conspicuously reinforce the ritual's sumptuousness for the original audiences of the investiture and those of its painted representation.[8] Like Federico, Ludovico Sforza swore an oath to obey the order's chapters, with a notary present for certification. The brilliantly dressed lord sat upon a catafalque while alms were dispersed and more *Allelujas* were sung.

Correspondence confirms that Ferrante's instructions were followed and that Ludovico Sforza was invested with the Neapolitan Order of the Ermine in November 1486 (and not 1488). Next, we contend with the often-repeated claim that Cecilia's ostensibly Spanish clothing and hairstyle – in particular, the mantle (*sbernia*) draped over her left shoulder and the ribbons in her hair forming a long braid (*coazzone*) – could have only been worn in Milan following the wedding celebrations of the first cousins Gian Galeazzo Sforza

74 Unknown artist, 'King Ferrante of Naples investing Federico da Montefeltro with the Order of the Ermine', illuminated page from *Lucubrantiumcula in honorem Hermini Ordinis*, 1474.

and Isabella of Aragon. These extended festivities took place in January and February 1489 and in January 1490. Assessing Cecilia's fashion with fresh eyes will unsettle a few ostensibly settled matters about her clothing and hair.

The assertion that Spanish fashions – which on the Italian peninsula were most popular in Aragonese Naples – arrived in Milan in 1489 was made most influentially by Attilio Schiaparelli in 1921. It has been restated countless times since, though rarely critically examined.[9] Perhaps I should hesitate to dispute points of fashion with any member of the Schiaparelli clan, let alone Elsa's cousin (Attilio, son of the eminent astrologer Giovanni, helped the fourteen-year-old Elsa, well before she was the fabulous fashion designer, publish the scandalous poems for which she was sent, by her family, to a convent). Yet, as we shall see, a great deal of evidence ignored in scholarship on Cecilia's portrait demonstrates that Spanish styles were described and diffused throughout the peninsula in the last *few* decades of the fifteenth century.

Given the close diplomatic and marital connections between the Sforza and (Neapolitan) Aragonese courts, it should come as no surprise that fashions, garments and modes of adornment associated with Spain and Naples – alternatively identified as 'Spanish', 'Neapolitan', 'Castilian' or 'Catalan' – reached Milan time and again throughout the late 1460s and '70s. Ippolita Maria Sforza journeyed to Naples in 1465 to marry Alfonso II, duke of Calabria. When she returned to Milan for the first half of 1468 for her brother Galeazzo's wedding, the court was struck by her Neapolitan style of dress – 'sua vestita ala napolitana', in the Mantuan ambassador's words – which included a damask mantle worn over the shoulder, perhaps tailored not unlike Cecilia's *shernia*, to be discussed shortly. Spanish Neapolitan fashions spread quickly at the Sforza court, and a month later, in February 1468, Ippolita's sister Elisabetta arranged her hair 'al modo Napolitano'. In subsequent days Elisabetta donned a garment 'a la napoletana', while two fashionable Milanese ladies showed off their hair styled 'also *ala napoletana*'.[10]

The Sforza siblings Ippolita and Galeazzo identified and assessed Spanish clothing in the ensuing years. In May 1473, Ippolita effusively praised the work of the Milanese embroiderer Niccolò da Gerenzano, who had been sent to Naples to produce scintillating brocades.[11] Galeazzo was keen to keep pace with Neapolitan and Spanish fashions, and no doubt Gerenzano filled him in on his return to Milan. In May 1475, Galeazzo referred to Niccolò as 'our embroiderer', and over the course of the summer, the lord made no fewer than six orders for Spanish-style garments, including one tailored from tawny satin –

the colour of a lion's hide, which was presumably unavailable in Milan and had to be sent for in Venice. Some of this 'Spanish' attire was worn by Galeazzo, including a silver-brocaded crimson garment 'ala castigliana' lined with green sendal. Indeed, many of these garments were to be worn by Sforza or his male courtiers, though satin mantles 'a la castigliana' with silk buttons and sendal lining were feminine array.[12] While the sources do not always tell us expressly for whom this apparel was intended, nor specifically what distinguished these hair styles and these modes of adornment and tailoring from local ones, what is certain is that the lords and ladies of Milan did not need to wait until the 1489 spring season for the arrival of Spanish fashions.

Scholars are quick to label Cecilia's hairdo the *coazzone*, also known (from Spanish) as the *trenzale* or *trenzado*: a long braid parted in the centre and gathered and bound by ribbons in the back. The *coazzone* was made stylish by Milan's duchess Beatrice d'Este, who was called the 'inventrix of fashions' by a chronicler. Ludovico Sforza's young wife Beatrice sports the distinctive plait in the *Pala Sforzesca* (illus. 75 and 76).[13] A related form of the term, however, had long been in use in Milan. Sumptuary laws of 1396 forbade prostitutes from wearing silk braids, 'coazias pendentes'.[14] While the *coazzone* was associated with Neapolitan and Spanish fashion in 1490s Milan, moreover, noble Bolognese women had shown off the style prior to Isabella of Aragon's departure from Naples. Indeed, Sara van Dijk questions the Neapolitan origins of the *coazzone* and plausibly suggests that it may have been a North Italian fashion.[15] The multiplicity of terms to describe the style may also imply a multi-origin or coexistence within the peninsula.

Though Beatrice d'Este popularized the *coazzone* at the court of Milan, Neapolitan hairstyles were fashionable there before her arrival. Scholars routinely identify a *coazzone*, but it is not at all certain what sort of braid Cecilia Gallerani exhibits. Her hair is strictly parted in the centre, and it is held in place by an extraordinarily fine, translucent veil with woven, gilded border (seen above Cecilia's eyes), cinched by the black band running across her forehead. No strands noticeably cross the centre part, which runs quite high up Cecilia's head, with hair pulled down to either side. Yet the braid of gathered hair is difficult to make out, and its silk ribbons are barely visible, just obliquely glimpsed. Close inspection reveals strokes of paint evoking silk filaments in three or four areas, each one a different pattern of two or

75 Master of the Pala Sforzesca, *Virgin and Child Enthroned with the Doctors of the Church and the Family of Ludovico il Moro (Pala Sforzesca)*, *c.* 1496, tempera and oil on panel.

76 Beatrice d'Este, detail from the *Pala Sforzesca* (illus. 75).

three painted lines. *In toto*, they suggest silk's shimmer more than they represent the fabric itself. The viewer can hardly discern the material and form of the ribbons, let alone their precise arrangement. Leonardo may very well depict a particular hair fashion or adornment, but it is by no means certain that this is the distinctive braid that bedecked Beatrice's circle in the 1490s.

The *sbernia* or similar mantles worn over the shoulder were associated with Spanish attire by three Milanese sources in 1491–2: the Sforza chancellor Tristano Calco, who chronicled the double wedding festivities of Beatrice d'Este to Ludovico Sforza, and Anna Sforza to Alfonso d'Este; additionally, the compilers of two Sforza trousseaus, those of Anna just mentioned and of Ippolita, the daughter of Galeazzo's illegitimate son Carlo.[16] The *sbernia* was, for noble women at least, tailored from one sort or colour of iridescent silk and lined with another (and sometimes with fur). Its defining characteristic seems to be that it was draped over a shoulder. A Ferrarese chronicler asserted that the 'short mantles' known as 'bernie' were worn over 'the shoulder, as the Apostles had done'.[17] The *shernia* soon became *the* must-have garment for courtly women. Isabella d'Este made numerous orders for *shernie* in 1490–91, requesting black or crimson silks, but also seeking out mantles in what she termed 'strange' or unusual colours. In 1493, Isabella was informed that in Milan, during celebrations for the birth of her nephew Massimiliano Sforza, Beatrice d'Este (Isabella's sister and the newborn's mother) donned a *shernia* of blue silk; Isabella of Aragon, the baby's aunt (by marriage), wore one of crimson velvet; and his cousin Anna Sforza sported a sumptuously adorned *shernia* of crimson satin.[18] Significantly, the wedding trousseau of Elisabetta Gonzaga of Mantua included two luxurious *shernie* in 1488: one of crimson satin lined with ermine and another of murrey silk lined with blue sendal and adorned with pearls and jewels. This was more than a year before the garment was supposedly introduced to northern Italy by the Neapolitan princess Isabella of Aragon.[19] Indeed, as is the case with the *coazzone*, the *shernia* may not have been a Neapolitan import. They may not have been Spanish at all.

Cecilia's azure *shernia* worn over her left shoulder was not an original component of her ensemble. Recent analysis utilizing multi-spectral light technology by Pascal Cotte and his firm Lumière Technology suggests that Leonardo worked through multiple iterations of the portrait with significant overpainted additions.[20] According to Cotte's reconstruction, Leonardo added the blue *shernia* sometime after the painting's initial version had been completed. In Cotte's preliminary rendering (illus. 77), Cecilia wore only crimson array enhanced with the fashionable *gruppi* or knots motif intricately embroidered in threads of precious metal (and, indeed, eventually Cecilia had four garments adorned with 'groppi d'oro' in her trousseau).[21] This crimson attire, which is visible on the darker, left side of the painting and emerging beneath her *shernia*, featured ribbon-tied sleeves, but no mantle. Thus, even the painted Cecilia changed her clothes and updated her wardrobe.

While the chronology of the portrait's completion is far from settled, it is safe to say that we need a shifting date. Like many of Leonardo's paintings, *The Girl with an Ermine* was a work in progress encompassing an extended process of creation. This working method is what we should expect, of course, for it is generally how Leonardo painted. In sum, clothing confirms less about dating than art historians have assumed and does not provide a *terminus post quem*. The transmission of Neapolitan fashions and styles in Milan and throughout northern Italy was complex, dynamic and sustained – much more so than has been understood.

The Girl (with an Ermine)

Though the precise dating of Cecilia's portrait is not entirely clear, many facts about her life are coming into focus. The Gallerani were prominent bankers in Siena until their firm's collapse in the fourteenth century. In the early fifteenth, Cecilia's grandfather Sigerio was identified in notary documents as 'from Siena' and as a 'Milanese citizen' and merchant. Her father, Fazio, served the Sforza as a ducal tax official for decades and parlayed this position into noble status.[22] In the early sixteenth century, the poet Vincenzo Colli (known as il Calmeta) asserted that Cecilia had been raised and educated in a Milanese monastery after her father's death in December 1480. Calmeta may have exaggerated her penury for dramatic effect.[23]

The orphaned Cecilia was described as 'ten years of age' in December 1483, when she was betrothed to the 24-year-old Giovanni Stefano Visconti. The agreement stated that they could not marry until she was twelve, though the marriage was never consummated, or at least that was Cecilia's claim when it was annulled three and a half years later, in June 1487. The contract for the betrothal also affirmed, though the passage is visibly crossed out, that Cecilia is 'more than ten years of age, and less than eleven', a phrasing that nevertheless reckons her age the same – namely, ten.[24] This method of estimating children's ages was not unconventional. After their father Fazio's death, Cecilia's brothers were classified similarly: Sigerio as more than seventeen years of age, and less than nineteen; Federico as more than nine, and less than eleven; Galeazzo as more than five, but less than six. A document from May 1489 introduces additional ambiguity, moreover, and identifies Cecilia as 'fifteen, or thereabout'. It is not possible to pin down the year of Cecilia's birth with certainty, though the best guess points to 1473 or early 1474. The imprecision may have been based on legitimate ignorance; however, as Anthony Molho showed, families manipulated or obfuscated young brides' ages for any number of strategic reasons.[25] A traditional dating of Leonardo's portrait to 1489–90 would thus put Cecilia at fifteen or sixteen years old (and not seventeen or eighteen). Cecilia may have been even younger when Leonardo began to paint her.

Ludovico and Cecilia's sexual relationship began earlier, by July 1485, when he was 32 and she, according to the rough estimate, was between eleven and thirteen years of age. A letter that Ludovico composed but may not have sent in that month, to be discussed shortly, reveals that their affair was well underway. Twelve was old enough to marry legally, in Milan and elsewhere on the peninsula (in Venice, for example), and elite and noble wives tended to wed earlier than common ones.[26] Though historians locate the average arrival of menarche at around age fourteen or fifteen for early modern women, many wives younger than that conceived shortly after their marriages. Teenaged girls exercised increased power and agency and assumed new risks and responsibilities as they became women, physiologically and socially.[27] Children younger than twelve were legally protected but were often sexually abused; more than one-third of the documented victims of convicted rapists in Florence circa 1500 were girls not yet that age.[28]

Cecilia was not the only girl Ludovico desired. In early 1489, when his betrothed, Beatrice, was thirteen, the 36-year-old Ludovico charged an Este ambassador with seeking information: how big was Beatrice and how soon could she come to Milan?[29] Sforza was increasingly impatient to consummate the marriage because his nephew Gian Galeazzo could now produce a legitimate heir with Isabella of Aragon. Of course, Ludovico was hardly the only Renaissance prince lusting after much younger girls. Battista Sforza wed Federico da Montefeltro at age fourteen, and he 24 years older (illus. 13). Niccolò d'Este's second wife Parisina Malatesta was also fourteen and more than two decades younger than he when they married. Isotta degli Atti (illus. 62) caught the eye of Rimini's lord Sigismondo Malatesta when she was twelve (and he in his mid-twenties), and before long Isotta was pregnant. Just as scholars have too often ignored the ways that violence against women served as a constituent aspect of masculinity (as I argued in the previous chapter), many have overlooked, if not wilfully ignored, the very young ages of the objects of their desires. This, we must remind ourselves, is the world that Renaissance princes – and princesses – made.

In correspondence addressed in July 1485 to his brother, the cardinal Ascanio then in Rome, Ludovico Sforza gushed about 'the

77 Leonardo da Vinci, *Cecilia Gallerani* – 'Simulation of phase one', from Pascal Cotte, *Lumière on The Lady with an Ermine* (2014).

pleasure he had taken' with an unnamed Milanese girl, who was 'of noble blood' and was 'as beautiful as anyone could have possibly desired'. This letter was published by Léon Pélissier in 1893 with various mistranscriptions and misunderstandings, including the identification of the missive's recipient as an unknown (and non-existent) Este cardinal rather than Ascanio Sforza.[30] It was only recently connected with Cecilia, by Alessandro Ballarin. Ludovico continues: he had wanted to tell his brother about this girl immediately after the relationship began, but had decided to wait until she became pregnant. This had not yet happened, but Ludovico was now declaring his love because he realized that Ascanio could possibly help with a favour for her. If a gravely ill abbot near Casteggio (south of Pavia) were to die, could Ascanio do anything in Rome, perhaps with the pope's help, to see that this lucrative benefice, which Ludovico estimated to be worth close to 600 *lire* annually, pass to Galeazzo Gallerani, the brother of 'my young girl [*questa mia giovane*]'?

Cecilia is not explicitly named. Her brother Galeazzo is. What Ludovico called 'this first favour that she requested of me' never came to pass, though Galeazzo received benefices five years later. (He eventually renounced his vows, married and fathered at least one child.) The historian Maria Nadia Covini suggested that the letter may not actually have been sent to Ascanio but rather was merely written to impress or placate Cecilia.[31] These suspicions are certainly plausible. The Sforza were sophisticated manipulators of various sorts of dummy letters intended to deceive, misdirect or confuse.[32] Regardless of whether the note ever reached Ascanio in Rome, it proves two crucial points. First, it confirms that a sexual relationship began much earlier than many scholars have allowed. Second, it provides critical evidence of Cecilia's precocious wheeling and dealing on behalf of her clan, which will be taken up in further detail below.

In conversations with Florence's ambassador in Milan, the infatuated Ludovico Sforza again professed his love – presumably for Cecilia, though the object of his desire is not identified by name. In March 1487, the envoy informed Lorenzo de' Medici that Ludovico had already twice requested that he write to Lorenzo to tell him that he has 'fallen in love … and is caught up in your sonnets and similar sorts of things'. 'I could not hear a single thing that would make me happier' than this news of Ludovico's love, Lorenzo replied in a charming letter quoting Petrarch and musing on love's pains and pleasures.[33]

That Leonardo is not invoked may suggest that he had not begun the portrait, or perhaps that Ludovico has fallen for another girl (and, indeed, the love is characterized as a new one). Circumstantial evidence that she was Gallerani includes the fact that within three months of Ludovico and Lorenzo's exchange, Giovanni Stefano Visconti appointed a priest to respond to a suit brought by Cecilia to dissolve the matrimonial vows. Scholars have asserted that the Gallerani's difficulties raising money for the dowry led to the marriage's dissolution – they paid only one instalment, in March 1484, for 700 *lire* of the 4,800–6,400 stipulated in the original contract.[34] Crucially, no additional funds were transferred around the time of or after Ludovico's delirious letter to Ascanio about the girl. No doubt Cecilia's status as Ludovico's mistress precipitated the change of plans; she, not Visconti, initiated the litigation. Cecilia was backed by her family, and over the next two years, as we shall see, the Gallerani benefited mightily from the protection of Milan's de facto lord.

To recap the chronology: Cecilia and Giovanni Stefano Visconti are betrothed in December 1483; the only dowry payment is made to Visconti in March 1484; in July 1485, Ludovico Sforza tells his brother Ascanio about Galeazzo Gallerani's sister, who may or may not be the girl Lorenzo de' Medici hears about in March 1487; that June, the priest Giulio Mcrosi appears in an ecclesiastical court on Visconti's behalf, responding to Cecilia's suit to annul their vows. At some point in these years Leonardo set his brush to panel, bringing the Milanese girl to life.

It is unclear how Ludovico and Cecilia first met, though Covini offers a plausible explanation beyond the poet Vincenzo Calmeta's rather vague claim that fame of Gallerani's 'beauty and manners reached Ludovico's ears'.[35] Ludovico's chancellor, Aloisio da Terzago – who in 1489 would be executed for betraying his lord, in a salacious and scandalous case that rocked the Milanese court – had been the lover of Cecilia's elder sister Zanetta Gallerani since the early 1480s. Perhaps through Aloisio (one of the witnesses to Cecilia's marriage agreement with Giovanni Stefano Visconti), Ludovico heard about or met Zanetta and her sister.[36] Of course, Ludovico must have also known their father Fazio, the ducal tax official.

Aloisio da Terzago was not the only man in Milan interested in the beautiful Zanetta Gallerani. Nor was she the sole object of his desire. Two nuns fled the Milanese convent of Sant'Anna after being seduced by Aloisio (at least according to accusations levied against the disgraced ducal functionary), and the armourer Damiano Missaglia seems to have been forced to care for his illegitimate daughter Ippolita. The enamoured Aloisio conspired to beat up rivals for Zanetta's affections. One foe was the physician Francesco Taverna, who was murdered in 1489 by Sigerio Gallerani, the eldest brother of Cecilia and Zanetta. Sigerio, who lived across the street from Galeazzo Maria Sforza's former mistress Lucia Marliani and her husband Ambrogio Raverti(!), was pardoned thanks to Ludovico's intervention. By this time, Sforza's relationship with Cecilia was increasingly well known in Milan, and he was willing and able to assist her family, even if the case was murder (a crime that, it is worth reiterating, was bound up in Milanese networks of adultery). Cecilia's kin enjoyed other favours granted by Ludovico in 1489 and the early 1490s, including the return of confiscated land and clerical offices for her brothers Stefano and Galeazzo (the latter the subject of the letter to Ascanio Sforza).[37]

By 1490, Cecilia resided close to Ludovico in the Castello Sforzesco's *Rocchetta*, an internal wing of the castle with a well-defended entrance of its own. In November, Ludovico's *inamorata* was 'pregnant, and pretty as a flower', according to the Ferrarese ambassador Giacomo Trotti. Cecilia and Ludovico's son Cesare was born the following May, and two weeks later Sforza rewarded Cecilia with jurisdictional and economic rights to the town and territory of Saronno, gifts that indicate the significance of mistresses as providers of heirs.[38] Galeazzo Maria Sforza had granted these privileges to his brother Sforza Maria in 1471, and in 1480, following Sforza Maria's demise, their transfer to Ludovico was confirmed by Galeazzo's widow Bona of Savoy. The concession of 18 May 1491 decreed that Saronno and attendant economic rights would pass to Cesare after Cecilia's death, though this would be complicated during the French occupation of Milan following Ludovico's expulsion in 1499. King Louis XII granted Saronno to Giovanni Stefano Castiglione, though Cecilia and Cesare contested Castiglione possession of the territory with some measure of success for another decade.[39]

Ludovico asserted increased control over the Castello Sforzesco (and over his nephew Gian Galeazzo, who ostensibly ruled Milan) following Cesare's birth by displaying Cecilia and his new son in a room adjacent to the *Rocchetta*'s treasury.[40] When the poet Bernardo Bellincioni paid a visit to mother and child, he happily reported back to Ludovico, who was then travelling, that he had made the nine-month-old laugh, and that the child was 'fat, fat I say [*grasso, dico grasso*]'. Bernardo also proudly reminded Ludovico that he had predicted the child would be a boy.[41]

In one of Bellincioni's sonnets, Cecilia's 'beautiful eyes make the sun seem but a dark shadow', and Nature envies Leonardo's powers. Leonardo makes Cecilia 'appear to listen and not to speak'.[42] Bellincioni astutely captures what has struck so many of the painting's viewers: its immediacy, and the gentle but unmistakable movement of the complaisant Cecilia. The illumination from the right calls attention to her subtle torsion. Cecilia's body turns towards us as her head pivots away, balanced against the plane of her shoulders. She twists into the light source, glancing graciously towards an unseen figure who has captured her attention. Cecilia's pupils are directed right as well, echoing the head's movement. This shift can be perceived in the face's strong foreshortening, most noticeably in her far cheek. Cecilia's gaze is echoed by that of the watchful ermine; their eyes are almost precisely parallel. For both, the eye to the right is slightly higher than the other, suggesting a lifting or looking up in the turn. This is, at once, an arresting and arrested portrait.

Mistresses and bastards were celebrated in Renaissance painting and poetry, yet visibility at court also presented complications. Wives needed to be clearly distinguished from lovers. Following their wedding in January 1491, Ludovico Sforza employed no small amount of misdirection to convince his young wife Beatrice d'Este, and her father Ercole, that he would soon give up his mistress. The Este, in fact, had protested the pregnant Cecilia's residence in the Castello Sforzesco, which was seen to encroach upon, if not directly compete with, Beatrice's status.[43] A month later, the Ferrarese ambassador reported that while Ludovico and Beatrice seemed most affectionate with one another, Sforza confided that they had not consummated the marriage, though this was of little concern to Ludovico because Beatrice had not yet menstruated and, as he understood it, such women either would not get pregnant or would give birth to unhealthy or nonviable children.[44] Beatrice was fifteen, Ludovico 38. She had been promised to him at the age of five or six, and when she was ten, Cosmè Tura painted a portrait of her – specifically of her face and chest: 'dal naturale la faza et peto' – that was sent to the 33-year-old Ludovico. Tellingly, the art historian Adolfo Venturi, who first published the payment to Tura, claimed that she was fifteen, though his many studies of the Este and Sforza would suggest that he must have known better.[45] When Beatrice eventually joined Ludovico in Milan, their age difference caused the young wife significant anxiety (as correspondence between the Este ambassador Giacomo Trotti and the girl's father details). Months passed before the marriage was consummated. There was substantial fear in Ferrara that it would be repudiated.[46]

Ludovico continued to visit Cecilia Gallerani during the first months of marriage, in spring of 1491, though he repeatedly pledged to Beatrice both that he was no longer having sex with his pregnant mistress, 'being as fat as she is', and additionally that he would not do so after the birth of Cecilia's child. Beatrice believed her husband's comforting words and publicly feigned ignorance of Cecilia, or at least this is what Trotti informed Beatrice's father in Ferrara. When Cesare was born on 3 May 1491, Beatrice – with Ludovico away at Vigevano – seemed quite pleased and satisfied with his reassurances. Once again, the ambassador Trotti is our source: Ludovico explained that he considered the boy merely a 'servant'; reiterated that he would not touch Cecilia again; and would not hurry back to Milan to see the newborn. These claims assuaged Beatrice's concerns for the moment, yet they were clearly disingenuous and disguised Ludovico's affection for the new mother and child. When Sforza returned to Milan a few days later, he stopped at the church of Sant'Eustorgio, visiting the miracle-working tomb of St Peter Martyr to offer thanks for the birth of his new heir.[47]

Nine months later, in February 1492, with boy and mother still residents of the *Rocchetta*, the sixteen-year-old Beatrice received a garment brocaded with drawn gold wire indistinguishable from one given to the nineteen-year-old Cecilia. Beatrice refused to wear it, and Ludovico had more explaining to do. Il Moro swore to the Este ambassador that Cecilia would either marry soon or would become a nun, and in July, no doubt at Ludovico's direction, she wed Count Ludovico Carminati di Brembilla, a Sforza courtier, soldier and knight known as Bergamino, son of the *condottiere* Giovanni Pietro Carminati di Brembilla.[48]

Cecilia's marriage trousseau contained dozens of iridescent garments. Significantly, a black silk *camorra* was decorated with the Sforza emblem of the pair of Genoese lighthouses, embodying and advertising her enduring affiliation with Ludovico's court even after her marriage. Cecilia's sixteen *sbernie* came in a variety of colours: white, black, murrey, blue, green and crimson; in an array of silk types and weaves: sendal, tabby or taffeta, damask, satin, velvet and shot silk; and embellished with various sorts of embroidery: gold- and silver-sheathed silk threads, drawn gold wire and more hefty golden cords, some arranged in patterns and knots (*groppi*). A blue satin *sbernia* lined with black sendal and embroidered with gold and silver wire in circular patterns recalls Cecilia's mantle worn in Leonardo's portrait, yet this is a distinct garment with a different silk lining and additional adornment. Leonardo's use of precious lapis lazuli for the painted blue *sbernia*, however, underscores the mantle's importance for Cecilia and for the portrait's original viewers.[49] Indeed, though Cecilia's clothing is often described as austere, simple or modest, Milanese audiences would have been dazzled by her garments' precious metals and radiant silks, including exceedingly costly crimsons.[50]

At the time of Cecilia's marriage to Ludovico Bergamino, Ludovico Sforza granted his mistress and their son Cesare the Palazzo Carmagnola, a short walk from the Castello Sforzesco (and today, much restored, the site of the Piccolo Teatro Grassi on Via Rovello). Ludovico confiscated the palace from the dal Verme dynasty in the mid-1480s. In the following decade, he paid for it to be restructured for Cecilia and Ludovico Bergamino by architects and artisans simultaneously employed at Santa Maria delle Grazie.[51] Vincenzo Calmeta declared that Cecilia's dowry was 'recompense' for her 'lost virginity'. To stress Cecilia's virtue, Calmeta emphasized that relatives had arranged the 'poor and simple' girl's relations with Ludovico, and this certainly may have been the case.[52] Indeed, offering sexual favours was a concrete means for mistresses and their families to amplify prestige and wealth.

Ludovico Sforza continued to promote Cesare. In August 1497, with the archbishop of Milan near death, Ludovico considered a bid to advance the candidacy of his six-year-old 'natural son born of Madonna Cecilia', as Cesare is identified by the Este ambassador Antonio Costabili, our source. Sforza, however, was dissuaded from doing so by the prior of Santa Maria delle Grazie, where Leonardo's *Last Supper* was then being painted.[53] Ludovico Sforza had also pressed, in negotiations with Maximilian, king of the Romans and later Holy Roman emperor, to amend his ducal investiture to make illegitimate sons eligible to succeed him as duke. The gambit was ultimately doomed to failure, however. When the marquis of Caravaggio Gian Paolo

Sforza – Ludovico's son with his mistress Lucrezia Crivelli – sought the title in 1535, the Milanese castellan conspired with Spanish officials of Emperor Charles v to destroy evidence of this privilege. Gian Paolo perished not long afterward, perhaps having been poisoned.

Though they never ruled the duchy, Cesare and Gian Paolo remained intermittently close to power. In July 1513, the pair attended the triumphal entry of their (legitimate) half-brother Massimiliano. They were dressed splendidly in white satin and velvet, traditional Sforza attire for rituals marking the assumption of lordship in Milan. Cesare died in his early twenties, in 1514, and was buried in Santa Maria delle Grazie near a pair of Sforza half-siblings.[54] He was survived by his stepfather Ludovico Bergamino, though only by a matter of months. His mother Cecilia, as we will see below, flourished in Milan and Cremona for another two decades.

Cecilia's Ermine

Cecilia Gallerani cradles and caresses an ermine. An ermine, more or less. While the beast has been classified as a ferret, weasel, polecat, stoat and marten, these animals all have heads and paws shaped differently than Leonardo's critter.[55] Perhaps a step back is necessary, to point out that, strictly speaking, the ermine is not a distinct species, but rather is any weasel-like mustelid in its white, winter coat. When we think of ermines, we generally have in mind dead animals or their carcasses, most frequently the white pelts of stoats. Renaissance lords did as well.

Leonardo's ermine (γαλέη/*galée* in Greek) puns on Gallerani's familial name, thus highlighting her patrilineal identity in addition to her status as Ludovico's mistress. Painted puns commonly played on the names of women, and certainly mistresses, in court culture, as with imagery related to Bianca Pellegrini explored in the previous chapter, or a picture representing Cupid within a little forest (*boschetto*) devised by Paride da Ceresara as an allusion to Isabella Boschetto, the noble mistress of Federico Gonzaga of Mantua (and the niece of Baldassare Castiglione).[56] Of course, Leonardo's earlier, Florentine portrait of Ginevra de' Benci backed by a juniper bush participated in just this sort of word play (illus. 86).

Leonardo showcases artifice and elegant design through Cecilia's elongated hand stroking the animal. Her hand curves subtly, parallel to the ermine's body. Fair, beautiful hands of both men and women were appreciated and celebrated in fifteenth-century courts. Ludovico's brother Galeazzo Maria, for instance, expected that praise of his hands would surpass that of his wife Bona of Savoy's hands. Though Leonardo emphasizes Cecilia's hand, the artist barely evokes her breasts, modelled through a bit of shadow. This may, of course, indicate the girl's immaturity. Just above, Cecilia's gleaming skin sets off her possibly perfumed agate beads. The black jet beads equally set off her flesh.

Cecilia's wiry, sinewy hand demands the beholder's attention. Leonardo juxtaposes the hand's fair skin with white fur and shimmering silk. He accentuates, even revels in, their sensual surfaces and tactility. Cecilia's delicate fingers gently caressing the creature arouse a sumptuous and gratifying sense of touch for both male and female viewers (illus. 78).[57] These intensely physical phenomena would have been familiar to the portrait's original audiences, the aristocratic men and women who wore ermine not just for warmth, but, crucially, to display status and wealth, along with an ideally pure and noble whiteness.[58] Through ermine fur, these men and women experienced privilege

78 Cecilia stroking the ermine, detail from Leonardo da Vinci, *Girl with an Ermine* (illus. 73).

tactilely; they no doubt recognized these pleasures and sensations in Leonardo's painting.

In 1486, live sables arrived from Muscovy at the Milanese court, brought by an ambassador of Grand Prince Ivan III (the Great) Vasily-evich. The envoy, Giorgio Percamota, also imported eighty sable hides and various falcons. He affirmed that his precious cargo had travelled over 4,800 kilometres (3,000 mi.). Viewers of Cecilia's portrait may have recalled these exotic creatures from faraway Russia, and perhaps Leonardo utilized one of these beasts as a model. Russian ermines were renowned for the candid whiteness of their winter pelts. In April 1474, the Sforza chancellor Cicco Simonetta made a list in his diary headed: 'These are the excellent things found in Russia.' The 'cose . . . excellenti' included peregrines and other falcons, fox and lynx furs, 'sable furs, ermines' and martens. Two years later, the Bolognese architect-engineer Aristotele Fioravanti wrote to Galeazzo Maria Sforza from Russia offering sables and 'ermines', both live animals and their pelts.[59] Of course, related mustelids were endemic much closer to home. In notes made at the Sforza court, Leonardo observed that in the mountains of Bormio northeast of Milan, 'ermines hide here [*qui nascono ermellini*]'.[60]

Ermine was a noble fur – the 'gentili ermellin' according to a fifteenth-century Florentine poet.[61] The fur was reserved for the aristocracy in sumptuary laws decreed throughout Italy. This included Milan and also Venice, which had a well-developed trade in ermine pelts imported from Russia. The doge of Venice was obligated to display his ermine-lined *bavaro* (a short cape worn around the shoulders) in no fewer than ten public ceremonies every year.[62] Generally, ermine fur lined clothing, both keeping the wearer warm and furnishing a soft insulation. Yet the men and women who wore costly furs, and their tailors, never missed the opportunity to turn the lining out at hems and edges, the better to flaunt the interior's sumptuous materiality.

Renaissance audiences looked for the ermine's easily discernible tails in life and in art (and in the latter, tails were sometimes schematically represented as black dots). Tails communicated the number of animals slaughtered to tailor and line the garment, and by extension its expense and the wearer's status. Isabella d'Este identified ermine tails when inspecting a velvet cap given to her brother Alfonso by Pope Alexander VI, whose daughter Lucrezia Borgia was marrying Alfonso. Isabella marvelled at the hat adorned 'with a tassel at the top made of tiny pearls, a braided ruffle with wrought gold around it, and hanging down from this a kind of stole lined with ermine with their tails hanging'.[63] Conventions for enumerating quantities of furs in terms of 'beasts', 'bellies' and 'backs' similarly underscored their animal-ness.

This leads, in my mind, to the most puzzling detail about *The Girl with an Ermine*. Where is the ermine's tail? Why does Leonardo not represent it? The black tail set against white fur is what viewers looked for when they discerned ermine pelts, sensitive as they were to clothing's materiality.[64] Leonardo's contemporaries at the court of Milan were obsessed with lavish textiles and furs. While they some-times conflated animals and furs, they were certainly mindful of hierarchies among them. As Bernardo Bellincioni voiced in a sonnet: 'I am not so thick or simple/ that I take weasel for ermine.'[65]

The ermine's missing tail introduces for us the paradoxes and poetics that characterize Leonardo's naturalism, in particular the ways that it generates meaning through occlusion, even omission – with Cecilia's braid and her ermine, art historians tend to perceive more than is actually presented. Pascal Cotte's recent technical study of Leonardo's painting may provide a more prosaic solution here. He detects, in a preliminary conception, traces of the fingers of Cecilia's right hand placed over her left wrist, suggesting to Cotte that she was not originally depicted holding something in her arms (illus. 77).[66] Indeed, the rear of the animal is decidedly illegible, almost shoved in, with no sense of its back legs. The elongated, tubular body bends around Cecilia, slinky-like; there is very little sense of her fingers here, presumably working to cradle and control the ermine. This unsuccess-ful passage may indicate a changing composition and conception, rather than a clear initial design.

If Leonardo began the painting without the ermine, its start could be located before Ludovico's investiture of the Order of the Ermine in November 1486. As multivalent and resonant as the animal is, however, potential meanings need not be limited to Sforza's chiv-alric honour, even if there is certainly something heraldic about the attentive ermine's raised left paw held almost like it is rampant. Per-haps the fact that the order's *impresa* and collar were first displayed at the Neapolitan wedding of Ippolita Sforza, Ludovico's sister, imbued the imagery with added resonance for some viewers in Milan.[67] Cotte argues that Leonardo subsequently, in a second conception,

79 Leonardo da Vinci, *Cecilia Gallerani* – 'Simulation of phase two', from
Pascal Cotte, *Lumière on The Lady with an Ermine* (2014).

depicted Cecilia stroking an ermine with her right hand, though this mustelid was smaller and slenderer than the one seen today; it was more akin to a stoat (what an ermine typically is) (illus. 79).[68] Leonardo then made the ermine bulkier and more muscular, with powerful legs and a more robust head. As the ermine became more substantial, the possibility of representing the tail diminished. Of course, the animal's large size, and its outsized proportions for a stoat, emphasize Cecilia's petite self and young age.

The ears of this disarming ermine are delicate and exceedingly thin; its eyes are penetrating and beady. Though the visible leg is powerful and muscular, its paw is awkwardly set and seems about to slide off the smooth silk. The ermine also appears, almost, to fold back the *sbernia* with its other paw, displaying for us the golden silk lining (illus. 78). While it is not certain that the claw actually hooks or pulls the fabric, viewers may have noticed Leonardo's visual witticism here. Once again, the artist offers plays between sumptuous, tactile surfaces and layers. The creature's triangular head and tapering muzzle, moreover, have suggested to scholars that Leonardo was looking at or thinking through his studies of bears: a silverpoint drawing of an ambling beast now at the Metropolitan Museum of Art (illus. 80) and a small, exquisite study of a bear's head that in 2021 sold for nearly £9 million (illus. 81).[69] As we saw in Chapter Two, Sforza lords eagerly hunted bears and displayed them as trophies.

The ermine was a symbolically suggestive creature, known both for its purity and for its lust and fecundity. The ermine's lascivious connotations led an eminent Milanese historian to dismiss the portrait's identification with Cecilia, presuming that Ludovico would not associate a noblewoman with an emblem of lust.[70] The ermine's fertility and sensuality may have been read encouragingly, however.[71] As we have seen, Ludovico anticipated that Cecilia would become pregnant as early as 1485, some six years before she gave birth to Cesare. It may be that either the second or third iteration of the painting – with the introduction or subsequent transformation of the mustelid – came late and related to Cecilia's pregnancy, accentuating the animal's apotropaic qualities alongside the many other meanings that viewers could have supplied.[72] Gallerani and other mistresses were indispensable because they provided potential heirs, generally faithful yet often relatively disposable illegitimate children who strengthened political networks and ensured a dynasty's survival in the face of high rates of

80 Leonardo da Vinci, *A Bear Walking*, c. 1482–5, silverpoint on paper.

81 Leonardo da Vinci, *Head of a Bear*, c. 1480s, silverpoint on paper.

infant mortality and the risks of childbirth for mothers. Indeed, Ludovico's wife Beatrice d'Este and niece Anna Sforza (who had celebrated a jubilant double wedding together in 1491) both died in childbirth in 1497. Scores of illegitimate and often legitimated children populated Renaissance courts, manifesting the prince's virility and potency while consolidating political authority and securing inheritance. These children, Cecilia's son Cesare among them, were tangible political benefits of the prerogatives of sexual pleasure and mastery enjoyed by the Sforza and their seigneurial peers.[73] In Ludovico's case, heirs legitimate and otherwise were essential as he laid the groundwork to usurp the rule of his nephew Gian Galeazzo.

Ludovico Sforza was also identified with the pure, white ermine, which one fifteenth-century Florentine bestiary possessed by Leonardo – the *Fior di virtù* – characterized as the 'most courtly and noble animal in the world'.[74] Bernardo Bellincioni dubbed Ludovico 'tutto ermellin' and the 'bianco Ermellino', playing the ermine's white purity off the darkness of il Moro.[75] We can imagine *The Girl with an Ermine* as something of a double portrait, one exceedingly rich with meaning, openly invoking Ludovico and his princely, virile identity, while depicting his mistress. The portrait, however, is not disguised or intended to hide the adulterous relationship, as some scholars still insist.

In animal lore, the ermine signalled chastity, moderation and purity, because it would rather surrender to a hunter than soil its pure, white fur in an attempted escape. Thus the beast adorns all manner of Renaissance material and visual culture in printed, painted and sculpted form: from pennants in Triumphs of Chastity performed at court and represented on *cassone* panels (illus. 82), to the intarsia of Federico da Montefeltro's *studioli* (illus. 83); from a brooch set with diamonds, rubies and a pendant pearl worn by Ludovico's mother Bianca Maria, to the walnut plinth of Marguerite de Navarre's mirror.[76]

A poignant passage in Leonardo's notebooks connects an ermine in the mud to Ludovico's ill-fated nephew Gian Galeazzo Sforza. And in a small drawing (9 cm (3½ in.) in diameter), Leonardo illustrated the ermine giving itself up to a hunter menacingly armed with a pick, shovel and branch or switch (illus. 84).[77] As the art historian Leah Clark pointed out, Leonardo's ermine here approximates the appearance of the enamelled ermine of the order's late fifteenth-century collar, though the drawn creature's head swivels towards the hunter.[78] Leonardo's *cartellino* subtly and elegantly parallels the ermine's body, with its left edge whipped back, echoing the animal's turned head. It is often thought that this drawing is Leonardo's design for a medal commemorating Ludovico's induction into the Order of the Ermine. If so, the scroll ultimately may have contained the order's motto *decorum*, or perhaps *malo mori quam foedari* (Better to die than be dishonoured) or an abbreviated version such as *non mai* seen in Federico da Montefeltro's *studioli* (illus. 83).

Like Ludovico's ermine, Cecilia and other mistresses at court were rewards of virile political authority. The noble ermine, moreover, was both sensuous and chaste, and thus very much akin to Renaissance mistresses defined by both their 'sexualized body and feminine chastity'.[79] The ermine embodies a fundamental contradiction inherent in cultural constructions of normative Renaissance femininity, expressed, for instance, in an essential tenet of courtly love as enacted in fifteenth-century Italian courts: the demand that the woman remain virtuous, yet surrender to her lover. Sexualized and chaste, political and

82 Triumph of Chastity, with ermine banner and bound Cupid, detail from Francesco Pesellino, *The Triumphs of Love, Chastity and Death*, c. 1450, *cassone* panel, tempera and gold on panel.

83 Giuliano da Maiano, *Ermine*, late 1470s, intarsia, *Studiolo*, Palazzo Ducale, Urbino.

84 Leonardo da Vinci, *Allegory of the Ermine*, c. 1494, pen and brown ink on paper.

chivalric, Gallerani's ermine encompasses the complex character of Cecilia and other mistresses: carnal, yet respectable; pure, yet seduced.

Cecilia Gallerani Between Men (and Without Them)

Renaissance men conceptualized the exchange of their daughters, wives, sisters and mistresses in terms of commerce. For instance, Tristano Sforza described his brother Galeazzo Maria's soon-to-be wife Bona of Savoy as 'merchandise' when in France enacting wedding rituals in Galeazzo's stead. The Gonzaga ambassador in Milan, moreover, reported that Galeazzo had 'bought' his mistress Lucia Marliani 'from her husband', and in the same letter asserted that she 'was sold' by her husband and mother-in-law.[80] The homosocial sharing and exchange of women between men at court afforded opportunities for considerable financial gain for the patrilineal and marital families of these mistresses, and for the women themselves. For mistresses such as Lucia Marliani and Cecilia Gallerani, these relationships were so potentially lucrative that we might suppose that they and their families endeavoured to attract the prince's attention. Some mistresses created significant room to manoeuvre within courts, realizing financial and political prominence. Lucrezia d'Alagno aspired to become queen of Naples; Isotta degli Atti temporarily controlled Rimini after the death of Sigismondo Malatesta; and Lucia Marliani amassed territories and jurisdictions as the countess of Melzo and Gorgonzola.[81]

The act of honouring a mistress accentuated the man's agency. Toril Moi influentially interpreted the desire of the female object of devotion as 'non-existent or entirely cultural', essentially serving to authorize masculine judgement, to ennoble and civilize the lover through chivalric discourse, and to provide lords with a legitimizing ideology.[82] That said, scholars should take care not to construct actual women, especially privileged aristocratic women, as passive victims with little room to act. Mistresses, princes, consorts, bastards, courtiers, ambassadors and everyone else we have encountered in these pages operated to position themselves for the greatest advantage within their particular sets of social relations and within the discourses and institutions that constrained and empowered them. Chief among these spaces at court were the homosocial, patriarchal continua within which mistresses were celebrated.

While men bonded over female bodies, aristocratic women were not merely objectified or inevitably rendered powerless by their artistic visibility. Of course, neither were they necessarily liberated by it. Female viewers, like all who had internalized Renaissance patriarchal discourse, could interpret and subvert such representations. Women and men could take these stories imaginatively as models. As we saw in the previous chapter, for instance, adulterous iconography relating to Bianca Pellegrini was spread throughout Pier Maria Rossi's territory around Parma, on castle facades and within churches, where it would have been creatively evaluated by women of all social ranks.

Women at court could fashion their identity around these models, raise their standing through reference to these ideals, and derive pleasure both from viewing their own representation in painting and from the recognition and material benefits that came with this visibility. The extent to which patronage of *The Girl with an Ermine* can be assigned to Cecilia Gallerani or Ludovico Sforza remains uncertain. The art historian Jacqueline Musacchio intriguingly proposed that Cecilia may have commissioned the painting.[83] Leonardo, for his part, may have taken the initiative to suggest Cecilia as a potential portrait subject to either she or Ludovico. Artistic patronage was a matter of negotiation, and in this case perhaps one with unrecoverable dynamics. What is certain is that the process of painting the duke's mistress – of rendering a woman of even the minor nobility visible at court in this way – must have involved the consideration or input of both lovers. Because of Cecilia's age, members of her family may have also played a role, perhaps her mother Margherita Busti or her formidable siblings Zanetta and Sigerio.

Cecilia moved within artistic circles at Ludovico's court, as Bellincioni's visit in February 1492 proves. Even as a girl Cecilia operated successfully, and to her own benefit (though, of course, it is difficult for us to disentangle Cecilia's own motivations and choices from those of her wider family). In the earliest evidence of Cecilia and Ludovico's relationship – il Moro's letter to his brother Ascanio – Gallerani manoeuvred on her family's behalf, no doubt also supported or guided by them. If Cecilia could initiate annulment proceedings and see to it that her brother got away with murder, could she not commission a portrait? Alternatively, the painting may have been a gift from Ludovico, or less likely, Leonardo, when Cecilia resided within the Sforza castle. It may have been a wedding gift from Ludovico given to Gallerani well after it was painted.

If Cecilia did not commission Leonardo's portrait, she nevertheless took possession of it at some point during Ludovico's reign. She utilized the painting to shape and control her self-representation. In April 1498, Isabella d'Este asked Cecilia if she could borrow the picture, so that she could compare the image with 'certain beautiful portraits' painted by Giovanni Bellini. Isabella must have been familiar with *The Girl with an Ermine* because her younger sister Beatrice (though by then deceased) had been Ludovico's wife and Cecilia's rival. Isabella clearly understood the portrait to be in Cecilia's possession. Gallerani, now the Countess Bergamina, sent the painting to Mantua straight away, via the courier whom Isabella had specifically charged with the task. Cecilia demurely protested that she, now in her mid-twenties, no longer resembled herself represented as a girl by Leonardo:

> I would send it more willingly if it better resembled me. Do not, your lordship, believe that this defect is the fault of the master [Leonardo], for in truth I believe that there is no one to be found who equals him, but only because the portrait was made at such an immature age and I have since changed so much from that likeness, that seeing it and me together, there is no one who would judge that it had been made for me.[84]

Cecilia's invocation of her 'immature age [*età … imperfecta*]' and the corresponding remove from her appearance in Leonardo's painting lends additional credence to an earlier date. Isabella must have sympathized with Cecilia looking back wistfully at her youthful portrait – the two were about the same age.

Through Leonardo's painting, and ownership of it, Cecilia stood out within courtly networks, beyond her life at Ludovico's court. The ready favour to Isabella d'Este soon paid dividends for Cecilia, who was housed by the *marchesa* in Mantua after Milan fell to the French and some properties were confiscated (though most would be returned). Cecilia's brothers Sigerio and Federico, moreover, were at this time protected by the Gonzaga, to the displeasure of the French government occupying Milan.[85] No doubt the alliance between the Gonzaga and these Milanese rebels was consolidated by their sister having willingly lent the portrait that Isabella so coveted. Cecilia's loan of her prized Leonardo was a politically shrewd manoeuvre, indeed.

Attention centred around Cecilia Gallerani well into the sixteenth century. She cultivated a salon and composed Latin and Italian poetry. The literati sought Cecilia out in person and in epistolary correspondence.[86] Cecilia lived well into her fifties, if not her sixties. By the time of her death – not in 1536, as is often reported, but prior to 22 February 1533 – Cecilia had spent nearly two decades as a widow, without her son Cesare or husband Ludovico Bergamino, who died in 1514 and 1515, respectively.[87] Ludovico Sforza had long since wasted away in a French dungeon, at Loches in 1508. Leonardo da Vinci also died in France, at Clos Lucé in May 1519.

Numerous sources extol Cecilia's poetry alongside her creativity and clever wit, but her verses do not seem to survive, at least to my knowledge. Vernacular poetry flourished in Sforza Milan in the late fifteenth century, and in the first decades of the sixteenth, a number of noble women poets orbited Isabella d'Este's courtly ambit in Mantua and beyond. Cecilia Gallerani was thus well positioned to craft an identity as one of a new sort of virtuous learned women with increased cultural authority and social prestige.[88] The literary historian Virginia Cox counts Gallerani among the learned, female vernacular lyricists emerging in these decades in the courts of Mantua, Milan, Naples and Ferrara. Cecilia is one of seven such modern women poets in something of a canon proposed by Matteo Bandello.[89]

In the first decade of the sixteenth century, Antonio Tebaldeo celebrated 'Cicilia Bergamena' in two sonnets lamenting the death of the poet Serafino Aquilano, and Vincenzo Calmeta praised her affable and ingenious speech (both Calmeta and Aquilano had enjoyed the patronage of Beatrice d'Este, Ludovico's wife, and Aquilano also that of Ascanio Sforza, to whom Ludovico's letter about the young Gallerani had been addressed).[90] Cecilia's letter to the humanist Gian Giorgio Trissino in 1512 reveals a friendly, even affectionate, personal and literary relationship between the two. The humanist and physician Giulio Cesare Scaligero also lauded 'Caecilia Bergamina' as a muse in his epigrams known as the *Heroinae*, which celebrated illustrious women ancient and modern.[91]

The soldier and bishop Matteo Bandello praises Cecilia's chastity and compares her to Sappho in a sonnet. Bandello extends these

85 Sappho, detail from Raphael, *Parnassus*, *c*. 1509, fresco, Stanza della Segnatura, Musei Vaticani.

themes throughout his *Novelle*. The dedication invokes the discussion of one of Gallerani's sonnets in Milan, in a conversation between Ippolita Sforza Bentivoglio (daughter of Galeazzo's illegitimate son Carlo) and the poets Niccolò Amanio and Girolamo Cittadino. Bandello later counts Cecilia and Camilla Scarampa of Asti 'our two Muses . . . in our time two great lights of the Italian tongue'. He again designates Cecilia 'the modern Sappho', who 'so elegantly . . . composed' verse in Latin and Italian.[92] Sappho emerged as a resonant, and decorous, antecedent and symbol for early sixteenth-century women poets, who themselves soon figured as 'emblem[s] of the revival of antiquity'. That Sappho was by no means an indecent or improper foremother, for the Renaissance learned elite, is also suggested by her appearance in Raphael's frescoed *Parnassus* from Pope Julius II's Stanza della Segnatura (illus. 85).[93] Bandello, moreover, refers to the 'molto magnifica e vertuosa . . . Contessa

Bergamina'.[94] Cecilia is not just magnificent, but virtuous, affirming that her time as a young mistress hardly tarnished her later years. Her noble status and chaste marriage trumped suspicions about an adulterous past.

In the cornice or frame of one of Bandello's *Novelle*, the reader dines with Cecilia, and in another story finds her at baths outside Milan, where she is called upon by soldiers, musicians, architects, painters, philosophers and poets. Elsewhere, the narrator visits Cecilia's estate at San Giovanni in Croce, west of Cremona, interrupting 'her usual, pleasurable study of Latin and Italian poetry'. The following day, a *novella* is offered to Cecilia's 'museo' – a reminder of the museum's origin as the house of the Muses – where it will reside with other poetry and prose written and collected by the Muse Cecilia. Soon enough, we return to the Milanese palace of the 'Contessa Bergamina', where a tale about her former lover, Ludovico Sforza, is recounted.[95] For decades, Cecilia continued to advertise and realize the courtly identity and reputation that she had fashioned at the Sforza court. Cecilia persisted, even flourished, in navigating Milan's networks of power.

The Girl with an Ermine visualizes patriarchal expectations. Through the painting, we recognize the ways that Italian seigneurial authority is grounded in portraits of women. On the one hand, images of mistresses seem to convey less about specific historical women than about aristocratic, patriarchal ideologies of representation and rule. These portraits are more like mirrors, or screens for projection, than they are windows. One can rightly argue, for instance, that Cecilia's beauty served to flatter Ludovico as much as Cecilia, and that Leonardo's painting united the audience as much with their prince as with the portrait's sitter.

These claims, however, threaten to disempower Cecilia, to lose her between the genius artist and the magnificent, cocksure lord. Indeed, art historians increasingly acknowledge the ways that Renaissance women deployed artistic patronage and representation to their advantage even or expressly when they, or images of them, were exchanged between men. Ginevra de' Benci may have commissioned her portrait from Leonardo da Vinci (illus. 86). Like Cecilia, Ginevra was a poet in her own right and was celebrated in verses penned by a powerful man (Bernardo Bembo, the Venetian ambassador in Florence and father of the famous poet and scholar Pietro Bembo). Through her visual

86 Leonardo da Vinci, *Ginevra de' Benci*, c. 1474–8, oil on panel.

and poetic representation within men's homosocial exchange, Ginevra acquired prestige.[96]

Privileged by her beauty, intellect and noble status, and trafficked between men, Cecilia Gallerani marshalled her representation to accrue esteem, distinction and authority. Artistic representations of mistresses reified courtly manhood. Yet these images could simultaneously bolster women. For Cecilia Gallerani, later Cecilia Bergamina, this unfolded over decades. The Contessa Bergamina capitalized on Leonardo's portrait of *The Girl with an Ermine*, and on her youthful access to power, deploying both to her advantage.

87 Various artists (attr.), including Baldassare d'Este and Bonifacio Bembo,
'Borso d'Este', illuminated page from *Genealogia dei Signori d'Este*, c. 1474–5.

5

Borso d'Este and the History of Lordly Sexuality

In love and war, fifteenth-century lords exercised power, fulfilled desires and flaunted privilege through aggression, force and intimidation. Yet constructions and ideals of masculinity, then as now, are conflicting, overlapping and multifaceted, and so this chapter moves beyond the prevalent, if often appropriate, associations between manhood, violence and the seduction of women, correlations that have become almost a default interpretative key within the study of Renaissance masculinity. Though courtliness and nobility were carefully displayed by the prince's body, modern assumptions about one's clearly legible, individual identity have (mis)led us to search, instead, for indications of sexual identity. This chapter critically investigates noble self-fashioning and representation, moving towards a history of fifteenth-century aristocratic male sexuality, by focusing on the image and reputation of Borso d'Este, the lord of Ferrara famous in his own time for his elegance and charisma and infamous now for his anomalous bachelorhood. The analysis here orbits around an illuminated portrait of Borso that has been seen as problematically effeminate but that I instead interpret as an efficacious exemplar of patriarchal, aristocratic authority (illus. 87). By examining Borso, we can recalibrate our accounts of Renaissance Italy's variegated panorama of masculinities.

A number of surviving portraits of Borso d'Este are posthumous, which demands that we explore the ways that his brother and successor Ercole shaped Borso's image to bolster his own authority. Accordingly, this chapter examines patterns of Este succession within the vicissitudes of Borso's and then Ercole's assumption of Ferrara's *signoria*. Neither his father Niccolò III nor his predecessor (and brother)

Leonello ever designated Borso as heir. He was not intended to rule the Este state, and his rise to power was an improbable one. Though his image is exceedingly familiar to students of Renaissance art history, particularly through the frescoes of the Palazzo Schifanoia, Borso – one among many of Niccolò's sons – was by comparison historically invisible, at least in terms of artistic representation, before he became Ferrara's *signore*.

In Leonello's final years, Borso collaborated ever more closely with his brother in the governance of the Este state, laying the groundwork for his eventual lordship. I would not, however, characterize Borso as having lucked into rule of Ferrara, as scholars sometimes do, echoing Pope Pius II's dismissive assessment of him.[1] Borso was a shrewd, ambitious operator who had endeavoured, albeit unsuccessfully, to succeed Filippo Maria Visconti as lord of Milan. Following Leonello d'Este's death in October 1450, Ferrara's populace (*popolo*) and the communal officials of the *Savi* ('wise-men') proclaimed Borso their lord. He was 37 years old. This fourteenth Este marquis soon became the dynasty's first duke, when Emperor Frederick III elevated Borso to the rank of duke of Modena and Reggio in 1452. Pope Paul II made Borso duke of Ferrara in 1471.

Contemporary apologists credit Borso for a peaceful and prosperous two-decades-long rule, and they inevitably praise his subjects' devotion. Supporters of the Este regime stressed that Borso's body augmented his dynasty's nobility through its pulchritude and radiance. By most accounts, Borso d'Este was an affable, jocund and elegant prince. His charisma was amplified by the gems and brocades on display in the Palazzo Schifanoia's frescoes, where the lavishly attired duke smiles and laughs, at the centre of attention (illus. 2, 32). Not only Borso, but his entire entourage visually constituted and reinforced lordship and courtliness. The homosocial, almost exclusively male court's aristocratic splendour is relentlessly reiterated in visual form at Schifanoia, where Borso is surrounded by beautiful, often blond, youths with slender bodies and shining faces.

Schifanoia's cortège presents an idealized version of Borso's court, to be sure. The lord's half-brother Baldassare d'Este – a painter and artisan – repainted, updated or somehow restyled 36 of the cycle's portraits not long after they were frescoed and just before Borso's death in 1471. Baldassare additionally produced a large canvas with portraits of Borso and his courtiers Alberto d'Este, Teofilo

Calcagnini and Lorenzo Strozzi on horseback – this painting may have served as a model or template for his adjustments to the frescoes.[2] Experienced and grey, though still cheerful, charismatic and conspicuously aristocratic, Borso commands the attention of his charming lads who, together with their prince, embody the Este courtly realm. Indeed, the Salone dei Mesi's walls display one of the most carefully fashioned and effective images of Italian Renaissance lordship.[3]

Towards a History of Lordly Sexuality

An illuminated portrait of Borso d'Este donning supposedly gay apparel, in a dynastic genealogical manuscript known as the *Genealogia dei Signori d'Este*, has led scholars to wonder if the image might expose Borso's (homo)sexual identity (illus. 87). Much on display in the striking, full-length portrait seems to undermine normative masculinity. Borso's 'indolence' and 'effeminate ease' are, for the historian Werner Gundersheimer, 'heightened by the … enormous jewel that festoons his breast and by the languid pose of his left hand … dangling limply'. This gesture and the seigneurial baton, held with the 'genteel attenuated docility of an Edwardian dandy holding a teacup', ostensibly effeminize Borso. Pejorative, gendered language seems inescapable: 'Admittedly, the word *embonpoint* is normally applied to women, and yet it came to me as an almost unavoidable way of characterizing Borso.'[4]

Further suspicions about Borso's sexuality have been raised: he never married; recognized no heirs; adorned himself in gems and brocades; and gave magnificent gifts, even palaces, to male courtiers.[5] Borso's homosexuality has not only been implied but has been declared as fact. For one art historian, Borso rode a 'gay wave' at court and 'chased trousers' (a rather imprecise sartorial metaphor for men clad in stockings). Supporting evidence for this conclusion included the jewels and sequins worn at the Este court, its lack of 'macho' courtiers and the peace enjoyed in Borso's realm, since, after all, 'gays are for non violence … [and] making love, not war!'[6] More recently, Luke Syson exposed the implicit homophobia of some scholars who seek to deny a homosexual orientation for Borso and argued instead that the lord's ostentation manifested a self-evident homosexuality and that his court style expressed his individual identity.[7] These claims, of course, are imbued with an ahistoricist sense of homosociability and presuppose a sexual identity known through essential, transhistorical somatic markers and manners. They rely, moreover, on the modern stereotype of the flamboyant, vain or merely well-groomed, gay urban man.

Queer or same-sex and -gender desires and affinities have always existed, yet their expressions cannot be assumed to be immediately visible or available based on our experiences. Reliance on hetero- or homosexual as categories places historical actors into a system of sexuality that conceptualizes one's choice of sexual object to be the principal, even singular, basis for classification, and that inevitably presents heterosexuality as the norm.[8] Like that of homosexuality, the category 'heterosexuality' is a nineteenth-century invention; it carries much ancillary baggage (including ideals of domesticity, procreation and parenting) that were hardly relevant for Renaissance aristocratic men. Heterosexuality continually denies its own construction through claims to be stable, natural and universal, and we must not confer upon this paradigm the historical privilege that it asserts but does not deserve.[9] Fifteenth-century men and women neither classified themselves nor their sexual acts and desires according to our hetero-/homosexual dichotomy, the one unavoidably calling the other into play and further consolidating heterosexuality as the norm.[10] We need, instead, to denaturalize heterosexuality through interrogations of its historical formation and subsequent, shifting modes, and by exploring the chronologies, discontinuities and genealogies of early modern sexualities.[11]

As we shall see, Borso rejected one culturally normative model of sexual self-fashioning that in certain ways aligns with our ideals of heterosexuality, yet such a manoeuvre does not make him homosexual by default. We should be cautious when identifying visual clues in physical appearance, mannerisms or deportment for a time when they were not legible in the same way as they could be today.[12] Pronouncing a homosexual orientation for Borso maps modern, Western bourgeois historical constructs onto the past, further reifying our (ostensibly self-evident) constructions of sexuality and sexual orientation as natural and inevitable rather than variable, ever-changing and historically contingent. Such a claim also dangerously marginalizes, even renders invisible, less familiar queer practices, affinities and constructions of both the Renaissance and today, reducing those of both the past and the present to normative configurations and prevailing stereotypes.

Queer is an essential theoretical concept here; it denaturalizes dominant constructions of both hetero- and homosexuality, and in so doing elucidates the indeterminacy, messiness and shifting nature of sexualities. For investigations of pre-modern societies, queer's value lies in multiplying historical sexual manifestations, desires, acts and fashionings and in revealing their lack of coherence or stability. 'Queer' is at times used as a relatively straightforward synonym for 'homosexual', and in other cases it deliberately destabilizes monolithic or hegemonic constructions of homosexuality and heterosexuality. Peril lies, to my mind, in always assuming that its use in the former mode necessarily accomplishes the work intended by the latter. The term can also reify our pervasive homo-/heterosexual binary (and, concomitantly, modern constructions of sexuality), by suggesting that erotic acts and desires that do not fit our paradigms must have been subversive or non-normative in the past. Identifying, or even idealizing, Borso d'Este as suspiciously masculine, for instance, threatens to overlook the dominance and brutal rule that he and his peers inflicted on subjects – and elides the pleasures and privileges afforded by their aristocratic status.

This chapter rejects both heteronormativity and the binary opposition of homo- and heterosexual (and I deliberately avoid utilizing the latter terms elsewhere in the book as anachronistic), in order to explore if or how we can replace our conception of heterosexuality before its formation as a category and for a class of people for whom it is illegible as an identity.[13] Moving towards a history of noble, male sexuality in fifteenth-century Italy, I can only begin to consider what constituted 'normative' sexuality for *signori*, and then suggest that we extend this investigation. Though they do not easily fit our categories, the actual and ideal behaviours, appearances and desires of and for lords were essential, constituent elements of the resilient operations of aristocratic power in Renaissance Italy.

Bodily splendour, adornment and elegance bolstered patriarchal authority, as much as the exercise of virility through sexual domination did. Being perceived to have broken down the 'traditional confines between male and female' does not prove that Borso is homosexual, as Syson would have it, but neither should the duke be considered respectably heterosexual or chaste, as those the scholar is justly reacting against would.[14] Attempts to 'out' historical figures often neglect or leave aside the more radical or interesting implications of sexual desires, experiences and conventions different from ours by restricting them to specific individuals rather than interpreting their wider social and cultural ramifications and meanings.[15] We cannot understand Borso or princely power if we label as gay any sign of masculinity that seems suspiciously non-normative, no matter how much pleasure it might bring to discover prominent homosexual men and women hidden in the past.[16] Modern identity categories obscure as much as clarify, exclude as much as reveal.

Of course, Borso was not homosexual in our sense, as a member of an identity group whose sexual orientation is based on one's object choice and manifests an intrinsic truth about the self. But Quattrocento courts were homosocial arenas in which it neither was nor is easy to distinguish between the sexual, political, erotic and intimate. We might instead think in terms of queer inclinations, affinities, tendencies and sensibilities rather than identities or essential orientations.[17] Galeazzo Maria Sforza instructed an ambassador to single out young Neapolitan men of 'noble and beautiful appearance' to serve as chamberlains, and we can well imagine Borso doing the same.[18] Their courts were organized around hierarchies of power and the promotion of younger, often specifically beautiful male favourites, much like the structures of desire based on class and age that, as the historian Michael Rocke showed, flourished in Florence and served as foundational elements of Italian Renaissance masculinity.[19] Homosocial age and power differentials are displayed on the walls of the Palazzo Schifanoia's Salone dei Mesi, where the wizened and grey Borso is surrounded by splendidly dressed, bright young things with beaming faces, blond hair, narrow waists and lithe legs. Whether one hopes to find an essential homosexual orientation or respectable and reassuring heterosexuality, these identities belong not to Borso's time but to ours – or, increasingly, to our recent past (for, when looking back at the essentialism vs social construction debates, the identities held up by partisans of the former now seem, ever more glaringly, to be historically specific manifestations of the late twentieth century). Indeed, the transformation and proliferation of embodiments, genders and sexualities in this century should discourage us from attempts to pin down essentialized (sexual) identities.[20]

It would be unwise, however, to deny, definitively, sexual activity with either women or young men for Borso. Not all sex, nor all desire, is necessarily publicly acknowledged or available to historians, for an array of reasons. Indeed, correspondence between Borso's brother Leonello d'Este and the humanist Pier Candido Decembrio confirms how knowledge about lordly sexuality might be managed or suppressed. Leonello had twice read Decembrio's biography of Filippo Maria Visconti and advised Decembrio to eliminate, or at least make 'more subtle and allusive', his discussion of Visconti's 'secret and never to be mentioned vice'. The recently deceased duke of Milan – according to the edited text that has come down to us (and that Leonello subsequently approved of) – 'shared . . . his pleasures' and his bed with beautiful boys and young men, who as adults became Visconti's most trusted and best rewarded courtiers. We can only guess what details the biography originally reported.[21] Crucially, Leonello's admonition and Decembrio's revisions make clear that one lord's sex with boys was an open secret among elite Renaissance men, and equally that they believed it should be hidden from certain audiences. Desires and acts revealed, concealed and enacted were circumscribed by factors including rank, gender, privilege and age. The degree to which they are legible to contemporaries, or to historians, depends on complex dynamics of political expediency, historical visibility and cultural intelligibility.

Tutti Figli di Niccolò: Este Bastards and Succession

Borso d'Este's image evolved after his death, under the direction of his brother Ercole. A closer look at the *Genealogia dei Signori d'Este* and the manuscript's sole full-length portrait within the context of the dynasty's traditions of succession thus affords a more sophisticated understanding of Borso's putatively dubious masculinity. From 1352 until 1471, a series of illegitimate, though typically legitimated, Este rulers continuously led Ferrara. Borso was the last in a line of ten. As the historian Jane Fair Bestor has masterfully shown, the Este maintained continuity through the employment of practical, creative and ductile strategies of succession and legitimation based on paternal recognition rather than legality, primogeniture or straightforward legitimacy. An excess of potential rivals, however, could escalate the threat of internecine conflict. Successions were contested, and disputes turned violent. Following Azzo VIII's death in 1308, for instance, strife between his illegitimate son Fresco and two of Azzo's brothers drew Venetian and papal armies into Ferrarese territory and led to the Este's decade-long banishment from the city.[22]

Competing heirs imperilled rule in the fifteenth century as well. Niccolò III d'Este (illus. 88) fathered dozens of children: legitimate, illegitimate and legitimated. A chronicler claimed that Niccolò had eight hundred lovers and nearly a thousand sons and daughters living in Ferrara, plus many others buried in the ground. His sons Leonello, Borso and Ercole ruled Ferrara for 64 years. Niccolò, a veritable *pater patriae*, was nicknamed the 'cock [*gallo*] of Ferrara' by Matteo Bandello, who likewise declared that Niccolò fathered enough bastards to form an army.[23] Niccolò was immortalized in jokes and *facezie* as well, most famously the rhyme 'Di quà, di là, sul Pò/ Tutti figli di Niccolò' ('Here and there along the Po/ All are children of Niccolò').[24] Following the beheading of his son Ugo for adulterous, incestuous relations with Parisina Malatesta, Niccolò's second wife and thus Ugo's stepmother – a remarkable episode discussed in Chapter Three, and one that Pope Pius II believed to have been 'just vengeance' for the amorous conquests of this 'devotee of pleasure' – Niccolò advanced Leonello, born of his Sienese mistress Stella de' Tolomei. Niccolò secured papal legitimation for Leonello and protected his line by stipulating that succession would fall to Leonello's eldest legitimate son, passing over Niccolò's other sons, even the legitimate Ercole.[25]

Following his death in 1450, however, Leonello was succeeded by his brother Borso (who was not considered for the *signoria* in their father's will) rather than by his son Niccolò, who had been named after his grandfather to safeguard his position. Ignoring his brother's designs, Borso hastened his own investiture before the twelve-year-old Niccolò di Leonello could return from Mantua, where he had been with his maternal relatives (his mother was Leonello's first wife, Margherita Gonzaga). Borso further strengthened his position against his nephew by having Pope Nicholas V annul Niccolò di Leonello's claim.[26] Nevertheless, Niccolò served Borso dutifully. As a teen, he received in magnificent fashion the eleven-year-old Galeazzo Maria Sforza at the Este villa of Fossadalbero, on Borso's behalf. Borso rewarded his nephew with lavish clothes, armour and other paraphernalia for jousts. Niccolò di Leonello held key positions in the Este state, competed in jousts, dressed radiantly in brocades and

88 Various artists (attr.), including Baldassare d'Este and Bonifacio Bembo,
'Niccolò III d'Este with his three wives and some of his sons, including Leonello
and Borso', illuminated page from *Genealogia dei Signori d'Este*, c. 1474–5.

commissioned manuscripts, including a book of hours illuminated by Taddeo Crivelli. A poet lauded Niccolò as 'a polished knight . . . graceful, beautiful . . . [and] so much beloved' by Borso.[27]

Yet soon after Borso breathed his last in August 1471, his brother Ercole seized Ferrara. Niccolò di Leonello was passed over for the second time. With his window of opportunity slamming shut, Niccolò orchestrated a coup. It failed, and he was banished from Ferrara. Tellingly, one of Ercole's very first artistic commissions as lord was to have Gherardo di Andrea da Vicenza paint the new duke's emblems in a room previously occupied by Niccolò, mere weeks after Borso's death. Ercole also sent Niccolò mourning attire, which was both an expression of familial piety and a demonstration of uncle Ercole's dominance.[28]

The new duke of Ferrara had a more dastardly gift in mind – one that would have made Marcel Mauss proud. In December 1471, Ercole dispatched the courtier Niccolò Ariosto to Mantua to arrange for Niccolò d'Este to be poisoned.[29] If we believe Niccolò di Leonello's account – narrated to Lorenzo de' Medici in a letter soliciting sympathy and military support – it would be difficult to imagine a more bumbling and inept assassination attempt. Ercole, in Niccolò's own words, was not content with merely maintaining Borso's 'fraud' of 'occupying my state', but additionally tried to 'take my life'. Ercole sent Ariosto to Mantua under cover of delivering a civet cat, though he bore more sinister cargo to be supplied to Cesare Prondo, one of Niccolò's attendants who was inveigled by Ariosto's promise of castles to be bestowed by Ercole in return for this loyal service fraught with danger.[30] Cesare was given a knife with a toxic blade plus an ampule of poison to sprinkle into his victim's drink in case he lacked the will or courage (the *animo*) to stab Niccolò. Cesare evidently lacked such mettle, and because of nervousness – or, in Niccolò's account, because God and the Virgin Mary were displeased and sent him 'una vertigine' – he became dizzy and collapsed. Believing that he had poisoned himself while handling the toxins, and convinced that his demise was imminent, Cesare spilled the (ricin) beans, as it were. He spontaneously confessed the plot and admitted that he 'deserved a thousand deaths' for his crime. Cesare only died once, however, though quite painfully and ignominiously so. Dragged through Mantua by a donkey, he was hanged and then beheaded and quartered. His remains were exhibited, scattered among the city gates, with his head set on a pike.[31] The noble Niccolò Ariosto, protected by Ercole, returned alive to Ferrara. His son, the poet Ludovico Ariosto, author of *Orlando Furioso*, was born three years later.

The birth of Ercole's heir Alfonso four and a half years after the botched assassination attempt spurred the now 38-year-old Niccolò di Leonello to invade Ferrara. On 1 September 1476, Niccolò's men, hidden under straw, arrived in five boats from Mantua while Ercole was away at the villa of Belriguardo, recovering from an illness. Niccolò hoped to turn the populace against their *signore*, but the coup was swiftly put down by troops rallied by Ercole's brothers Sigismondo and Rinaldo.[32] Niccolò and his cousin Azzo d'Este were beheaded in the castle courtyard – thus executed in a manner befitting their aristocratic rank. Niccolò's men, including his chancellor and a Greek falconer, were hanged and more publicly exposed. More than twenty corpses were suspended from the windows of the Palazzo della Ragione and from the merlons of Ferrara's castle. Niccolò's foot soldiers killed in the fighting were left to rot outside the city, and one of Ercole's officers sought to punish all survivors with the loss of an eye and a hand, though most were spared this fate in a show of mercy. It was essential, however, that the noble body receive altogether different treatment than those who were ingloriously and spectacularly maimed or hanged. Niccolò's neck and head were seamlessly sewn together, as a chronicler put it, 'so it did not seem that his head had been cut off'.[33]

Ercole decreed that 'every gentleman, doctor, citizen and official' must 'go to honour the body of messer Niccolò da Este', who was dressed in crimson cloth of gold 'as a prince [*a modo di principe*]'. The magnificent funeral procession wound its way through Ferrara to San Francesco, where Niccolò was buried within the dynasty's porphyry tomb, alongside kin including his uncle Ugo, who had been beheaded fifty years prior for adultery with his stepmother Parisina Malatesta. Among Niccolò's mourners was the duchess Eleonora of Aragon, who 'was not able to contain her very strong tears', even though she had been terrorized, hiding in the Castelvecchio with her young children – the infant heir Alfonso, and toddlers Beatrice and Isabella d'Este – as Niccolò and his men rode through town rousing the *popolo*.[34]

The singular circumstances of Niccolò di Leonello's execution and burial make clear the extent to which Ercole d'Este at once forcefully asserted his domination and simultaneously endeavoured to preserve an image of dynastic integrity and of a smooth and peaceful transition. The Este understood the consequences of internal dynastic conflict and had exhorted its avoidance at all costs. They likewise sought to minimize the dissatisfaction or hostility of noble families connected through marital alliances.[35] The Gonzaga were furious that Margherita's son Niccolò was denied his rightful lordship. The marriage pact forged by Leonello and Margherita's father Gianfrancesco Gonzaga had promised eventual succession from Leonello to the first-born son of the union. Thus on the day Niccolò was beheaded, Ercole wrote to Ludovico Gonzaga, personally letting him know that he had wanted to jail or banish Niccolò for life, but that he had no choice but to execute him. Ercole assured Ludovico, however, that Niccolò was 'buried most honourably as is appropriate for one of our dynasty'. This was a key part of Ercole's wider campaign to control the narrative. According to Ugo Caleffini, Ercole dispatched letters to 'all the lords, governments, and communes in Italy'. Caleffini himself wrote many of the missives in Ercole's name.[36]

Borso d'Este's image and relations were calculated to manage threats to his rule, both during his life and posthumously, to the extent that he and then Ercole could contrive to do so. Aristocratic marriages were arranged affairs, and arguing that Borso never married on account of his sexual identity overlooks the fact that most princes had wives chosen for them at an early age. Borso was not intended to rule by his father or brother. He assumed Ferrara's *signoria* in his mid-thirties, well past the age that most noble men married in fifteenth-century courts. Borso's exact contemporary Pier Maria Rossi – both were born in 1413 – married at age fifteen, no doubt because Pier Maria was his father's only legitimate son and thus heir apparent.[37] Niccolò III d'Este first married when thirteen, and the mortal enemies Sigismondo Malatesta and Federico da Montefeltro took their first wives at sixteen or seventeen. Exceptions prove the rule. Borso's younger brother Ercole married in his early forties, and only subsequent to Borso's death, while Ludovico Sforza wed Borso's niece Beatrice in his late thirties. Like Borso, as youths Ludovico and Ercole were not intended for rule, and so their fathers and other elders had not arranged wives for them.

No doubt Borso's bachelorhood was initially not a personal decision but rather his father's strategy, one that Borso extended by never marrying and by not legitimating or recognizing his children (and more soon about Borso's children). These manoeuvres strategically evaded dynastic complications. The judicious management of progeny – deciding who was to be married to whom, and who was to be directed towards an ecclesiastical career, for example – was one of the most critical challenges that Renaissance lords faced. Indeed, that neither his brother Ercole nor his nephew Niccolò di Leonello (who was reported to have fathered four illegitimate children) married during Borso's lifetime further attests to his regulation of the dynasty's marital relations as a means to curtail discord and dissent with and among potential successors.[38] For generations, the Este had handled these complicated operations with relative success and with the utmost concern, as Borso's contemporaries appreciated. One of Ludovico Carbone's *facezie* (humorous stories) plays on just this knowledge. Carbone narrates that Pope Eugenius IV – visiting Ferrara for the ecclesiastical council of 1438 – asked Niccolò III about his plans for his sons. Niccolò replied that Meliaduse was destined for priesthood, Leonello would succeed his father as lord and Borso was training to become a *condottiere*. The pope laughed and told Niccolò that he had it all wrong: Meliaduse is the soldier and Leonello the priest, and Borso is the ideal 'bel signore'.[39]

Numerous princes – Sigismondo Malatesta, Pier Maria Rossi and Ludovico Sforza, among others – advertised lordly virility and patriarchal privilege through artistic representations of their mistresses. Borso, for his part, also carefully managed the image or impression of sexual behaviour. Chastity, continence and temperance were crucial

89 Pisanello, *Chastity and Unicorn in a Moonlit Landscape* (reverse of Cecilia Gonzaga medal), 1447, lead alloy.

aspects of Borso's lordly self-fashioning, and these ideals were made more poignant or resonant for subjects because of the degree to which his peers flaunted their sexual prowess. Among Borso's most widely publicized emblems was the unicorn, a creature often associated with chastity and virginity in the fifteenth century. On the reverse of one of Pisanello's medals (illus. 89), for example, a decidedly goat-like unicorn cozies up to the *virgo* Cecilia Gonzaga, who rejected her arranged marriage to Oddantonio da Montefeltro even though her father Gianfrancesco Gonzaga had promised her would-be father-in-law that he would convey Cecilia to them to marry, even 'if they had to send her all tied up'. Only after Gianfrancesco's death and Oddantonio's assassination (both in 1444) was Cecilia able to enter the Clarissan convent of Santa Lucia in Mantua. In 1447, with Cecilia's chaste and pious reputation quickly spreading, and the Gonzaga looking to profit from it, Pisanello struck Cecilia's medals, presumably at her brother Ludovico's direction.[40]

Though other members of the Este dynasty utilized the unicorn emblem, its association with Borso is indicated by a goldsmith's enamel work on a chest transforming Leonello's *impresa* of the blindfolded lynx into a unicorn, following Leonello's death.[41] In 1473,

90 Ambrogio di Giacomo da Milano and Antonio di Gregorio (attr.), *Unicorn under a Date Palm*, 1460s, marble, entry portal, Palazzo Schifanoia, Ferrara.

91 Unknown Ferrarese painter, *The Muse Urania*, c. 1455–60, tempera on panel.

92 Unicorns pulling Minevra's triumphal chariot, from Francesco del Cossa, *March*, late 1460s, fresco, east wall, Salone dei Mesi, Palazzo Schifanoia, Ferrara.

Eleonora of Aragon was served aspic or gelatin dishes covered with what were described as the 'date tree and unicorn of duke Borso's device' at a Roman feast, as she travelled north from Naples to meet her new husband Ercole in Ferrara. The unicorn must have been interpreted for Eleonora by a member of the Este entourage accompanying her – perhaps by Ercole's brother Sigismondo, who had resided in Naples as a child. That it was here identified with Borso two years after his death confirms the extent to which Ercole sought to connect their rules.[42] Unicorns are illuminated in Borso's manuscripts and struck on his medals. A unicorn under a date palm graces Schifanoia's marble portal (illus. 90) and the belltower of Ferrara Cathedral. The beasts adorn the throne of the Muse *Urania* from the *studiolo* at Belfiore (illus. 91), and they lead Minerva's triumphal chariot in *March* at Schifanoia, visibly straining and panting under its weight. The extraordinarily long, pointy horns painted *a secco* have deteriorated in the frescoes, however (illus. 92).[43]

The unicorn's horn magically detected or removed poison when dipped into water, and, accordingly, this emblem of purification advertised the duke's extensive land reclamation projects.[44] Yet seigneurial devices were multivalent and dynamic, and many subjects may have also understood the unicorn to figure Borso's mastery of sexual desire. The unicorn was a crucial component of Borso's lordly image, and additional evidence corroborates the fact that he recognized and recommended the versatile instrumentality and rhetoric of sexual restraint. In instructions provided to ambassadors to the court of the Hafsid Caliph Abu 'Amr 'Uthman, so that all perceive that the Ferrarese envoys serve a 'signore da honore', Borso directed his men to 'avoid women and all lascivious things', and thus avoid scandal.[45]

Ercole and the *Genealogia dei Signori d'Este*

Ercole d'Este cultivated images of dynastic unity and harmony. This second duke of Ferrara would have well understood why a chronicler connected the claim that Borso had no wife or children to the assertion that he reigned 'triumphantly and peacefully for twenty-one years'. To shore up his rule and emphasize continuity from Borso, Ercole deployed carefully edited genealogies, mythological epics such as Tito Vespasiano Strozzi's *Borsiad*, and chivalric poems, notably Matteo Maria Boiardo's *Orlando Innamorato*.[46] To memorialize fraternal piety,

Ercole even availed himself of Borso's corpse. The embalmed body was dressed in crimson cloth of gold, and Borso's heart and viscera were consigned to Ercole, who enshrined his brother's heart within a column in the church of San Paolo. This monumental reliquary seems to have been destroyed when San Paolo was damaged in Ferrara's cataclysmic earthquake of 1570.[47]

Ercole utilized the *Genealogia dei Signori d'Este* to shape Este history and make his usurpation of Ferrara's *signoria* seem legitimate, even inevitable. Now divided between Modena and Rome, the manuscript presents a simplified Este genealogy with nine medallion portraits per page (typically one lord in the top, centre medallion, surrounded by wives and children) (illus. 88). The medallions, each accompanied by a short text, economically set down a genealogy of radiant Este ancestors culminating in Ercole and his offspring – including a portrait of Isabella d'Este (illus. 93), here a toddler – for the manuscript's intended audience of present and future members of the dynasty. The *Genealogia* was begun after Borso's death in 1471 and was illuminated by 1475. This was not a static work of art, however, but one in which the ever-developing story of the dynasty unfolded. Brief texts were added to blank medallions throughout the 1470s, as Ercole fathered additional progeny (illus. 93): Beatrice (Ludovico Sforza's eventual wife) born in June 1475; Alfonso (Ercole's successor) born in July 1476; and their brothers Ferrante and Ippolito, born in September 1477 and March 1479, respectively. Other updates were also appended. The passage above Niccolò di Leonello's portrait matter-of-factly informs the reader that he 'died in 1476 on September the 4th in Ferrara' (illus. 94). There is no mention of Niccolò's coup attempt, execution or reattached head.

The usual format of three rows of three medallions encircling bust portraits is disrupted by the full-length depiction of Borso and a substantial text. One explanation for Borso's magnification is that he fathered no recognized heirs, and so the image and description of his most noteworthy deeds could be given the full page. Indeed, the text indicates precisely this, though it additionally, and significantly, informs the reader that Borso occupies so much space because he was the first of 'his most illustrious' dynasty to achieve the rank of duke.[48] The visual emphasis on Borso alone served Ercole by underscoring fraternal succession and bolstering his position against Niccolò di Leonello's challenges. Though Niccolò is depicted in the manuscript as Leonello's

93 Various artists (attr.), including Baldassare d'Este and Bonifacio Bembo, 'Ercole d'Este with his wife Eleonora of Aragon and his children Lorenzo, Lucrezia and Isabella', illuminated page from *Genealogia dei Signori d'Este*, c. 1474–5.

son and flanks his father with a parallel profile, he is not shown as a *signore*; he lacks the gold background and sceptre that distinguish lords from other Este kinfolk (illus. 88, 94). Above all else, this manuscript constructs an efficient, streamlined image of succession from Niccolò III to Leonello, then to Borso, and finally to Ercole.

94 Various artists (attr.), including Baldassare d'Este and Bonifacio Bembo, 'Niccolò di Leonello and Leonello d'Este', illuminations from *Genealogia dei Signori d'Este*, *c.* 1474–5.

A previous portrait in the *Genealogia dei Signori d'Este* visually connects Borso to his father, as did Ludovico Carbone's tale in which Pope Eugenius IV comments to Niccolò III that Borso 'with his noble aspect . . . resembles you'.[49] Of Niccolò's 25 children represented over three folios, it is Borso's roundel portrait, significantly, that is located immediately below the dynasty's patriarch (illus. 95). The gazes and jowly profiles of father and son are conspicuously aligned, emphasizing the alliance and physical resemblance between the two, though Borso is here represented with youthful blond tresses. Their similar double chins and nearly identical noses propose a semblance suggesting continuity. These telling similarities and subtle distinctions – and the fact that Borso is depicted twice, with varying somatic markers that differentiate his age and attendant status (blond as Niccolò's son, grey-haired when alone as lord in his own right) – confirm that the manuscript's illuminators and patron were attuned to the specifics of dynastic, brotherly succession, essential as they were for Ercole's authority.

Encomiastic texts composed during Borso's life insist upon his continence and chastity and suggest that these values reflect the lord's

95 'Niccolò III and Borso d'Este', detail from illuminated page in *Genealogia dei Signori d'Este* (illus. 88).

laudable self-control. In the mid-1460s, Ludovico Carbone affirmed Borso's chastity within the context of his moderation and temperance. Carbone commented that Borso avoided sexual relations that would dilute the purity of his lineage.[50] Later in the decade, Carlo da Sangiorgio explained that continence is a lord's most worthy virtue, and invoking 'Plato, Aristotle and all the other philosophers', reminded readers that whoever conquers their own desires, conquers all things. Thus, he asserted, the admirably chaste Borso turned his mind to hunting, to drive away lust by chasing deer.[51]

Borso's reputation for chastity was proclaimed with greater immediacy, urgency and precision following his death. Only now did sources insist not just that Borso never married or that he hunted to fend off sexual desire, but additionally, and in no uncertain terms, that he never fathered children.[52] The text accompanying Borso's full-length portrait in the *Genealogia dei Signori d'Este*, for instance, maintains that he 'never had a wife' and 'never had children' (and it records the dates that he assumed Ferrara's *signoria* and was invested by Emperor Frederick III and Pope Paul II, respectively, with the titles of duke of Modena and Reggio and then of Ferrara).[53] Both word and image bolstered Ercole's claim to Ferrara's *signoria* by offering an uncontested succession from the dynasty's first duke to the second.

Bachelors father children, of course. Aristocratic bastards were not always formally recognized or legitimated. Their acknowledgement and historical visibility were tied, above all else, to dynastic needs. Some were promoted, others ignored.[54] Borso d'Este may have fathered at least two children. A certain Maddalena Anzeleri nursed and reared Borso's daughter Bartolomea (and may have been her mother). In 1453, the duke paid for clothing for the girl. Additionally, in June 1470, an (unnamed) young petitioner declared himself to be Borso's son.[55] Significantly, Borso's offspring emerge from historical invisibility after he became lord of Ferrara in 1450, even though Bartolomea was born beforehand. They were not legitimated or otherwise designated as potential heirs, though Borso knew of their existence. If Ercole did as well, it would have been all the more imperative for him to insist upon Borso's lack of children. Ercole had a vested interest in representing Borso's dedication to chastity and fraternal unity, putting dynastic above personal interests. The disavowal or erasure of his brother's progeny, of course, benefited Ercole regardless of Borso's sexual desires or acts.

While Borso may have sacrificed the well-being of his illegitimate children, encomiastic texts composed after his death declared that he unfailingly treated brothers and nephews with love and devotion, enhancing Ercole's picture of dynastic concord. Never was there a 'bad word' or deed between Borso and any brothers or nephews, according to a chronicler, at least not until Borso's health deteriorated and enmity arose between Ercole and Niccolò di Leonello. Other writers avowed that Borso 'was benevolent with all of his brothers, nephews, and with all those of the Este dynasty', and that he 'unified, principally with love, his brothers and nephews'.[56] Ercole, for his part, informed Borso about a conspiracy orchestrated by the Pio of Carpi. Though the Pio intended to advance Ercole once Borso was ambushed and killed while hawking, he calculated that the risks from a failed plot outweighed the rewards of informing on the Pio, two of whom were beheaded.[57]

Borso's political enemies had conspired against him many times, seizing upon his spurious birth both when he assumed the *signoria* and throughout his reign. One chronicler even reported the rumour that Borso was done in by a poisoned melon.[58] Pope Pius II prefaced harsh criticisms of Borso with an indictment of his dynasty: 'Here is an extraordinary fact about the family: within recent memory no legitimate son has ever inherited the title; fortune has smiled so much more on the children of the mistresses than on those of the wives. It is a circumstance contrary not only to Christian teaching but to the law of almost every nation.' Borso and Pius were once allies, in part because Borso's mother hailed from a Sienese family connected to the pope's. As a key member of Emperor Frederick III's entourage, Enea Piccolomini – the future pope – supported Borso's elevation to duke of Modena and Reggio and delivered an oration lauding his virtues. In a biography of Leonello d'Este, moreover, Piccolomini sounded the right tone for praise of a lord by commenting that Borso 'was extremely beautiful … more beautiful than one could describe'. To celebrate Piccolomini's election to the papacy, Borso declared a holiday in Ferrara, complete with a horse race with a green damask *palio* as first prize. Nine months later, Borso housed the pope and several cardinals in magnificent fashion on their journey to the Council of Mantua.[59]

The friendship soured, however, after Pius declined a number of Borso's requests, most notably to be raised to the rank of duke of Ferrara. In response, Borso refused to travel to Mantua, and he withheld promised financial support for the pope's crusade. As Pius tells it, Borso offered lame excuses: warnings from his astrologer, a fever and his love of hunting. Motivated to attack Borso's character, Pius II turned customary praise of *signori* into scathing criticism (and, indeed, the pope slandered other princes who insufficiently supported his calls for crusade). Thus, while Borso possessed seigneurial virtues, he did so either immoderately or superficially, according to Pius: Borso was loved by his subjects, but spoke only to hear the sound of his own voice; he was a skilled hunter, but this obsession kept him from more pressing matters, and 'he would rather spend his time with beasts than human beings'; perhaps most damning, Borso 'wanted to appear magnificent and generous – rather than genuinely to be so'.[60]

Borso's illegitimate origins aggravated even Ercole, who bitterly complained that his brother, a mere 'bastardo', had enjoyed lucrative rights over the production and trade of woad flowers – from which were extracted a valuable blue dye – while he was denied these privileges. A Milanese ambassador rudely but perceptively reminded Ercole that he should not disparage his brother, or else Borso's 'defect' might put his own position in doubt.[61] Aware that his predecessor's illegitimacy could be used against him at every turn, Ercole would not have implied through the *Genealogia* that Borso was suspiciously unlordly. The manuscript presents Borso as a paragon of noble, elegant and courtly masculinity embodying patriarchal authority for future Este rulers to emulate.

This is precisely how images of Borso were viewed following his death in August 1471. In September, Galeazzo Maria Sforza requested that Ercole send him a portrait of Borso recently painted by their half-brother Baldassare d'Este. When the painting arrived, Galeazzo profusely thanked Ercole 'because we have always desired to have a representation of this lord, whom we still love as a father'. Galeazzo additionally asserted that he would mirror the 'legacy and behaviours' of Borso, which he considered to be 'most commendable and truly worthy of a prince'. Galeazzo affirmed that the image painted by Baldassare – whom he lauded with unreserved praise – was all the more dear because Borso seemed alive, lacking only a soul.[62] Sforza's promise that he would forever keep the portrait near underscores the crucial importance of art within diplomatic networks in Renaissance Italy. That Galeazzo asserted that he would do so both to memorialize Borso and to be always reminded of Ercole's generosity, moreover, prompts us to be attentive to the ways that the object itself *and* the identities of the giver and recipient shape the affective experiences of gift-giving.

The Gestures of Courtly Masculinity

Borso's 'left hand . . . dangling limply' in the *Genealogia*'s full-length portrait troubled Werner Gundersheimer. The duke's slender rod (*bacchetta* or *bastone*) struck him as particularly unmanly.[63] In the context of the manuscript's many portraits, moreover, Borso's *bacchetta* unites him with earlier rulers (illus. 94 and 95). Each of the splendidly attired Este *signori* brandishes a slender rod, visually linking one another from page to page. Both the object that Borso holds and the manner with which he presents himself would have persuaded viewers that this was a lord to admire.

Bacchette signified seigneurial authority throughout the Italian peninsula. The painter Costantino da Vaprio gilded two *bastoni* for Galeazzo Maria Sforza's use in the spectacular cavalcade celebrating the feast of St George, and Galeazzo gifted Ercole d'Este a *bastone* decorated with an image of his namesake Hercules slaying the Hydra. In republican Florence, the epithet 'signore a bacchetta' slandered Lorenzo de' Medici. The baton's conferral was frequently fixed at an astrologically propitious time, which further indicates its symbolic power in fifteenth-century Italy.[64] The *bacchetta* manifested patriarchal authority as an indispensable component of the rituals marking the assumption of rule. Francesco Sforza was presented the sceptre when crowned duke of Milan, as were his sons Galeazzo (at Francesco's funeral) and Ludovico. When Ercole d'Este informed Lorenzo de' Medici of the death of Borso, 'who for his excellent virtues deserved to live forever', he added that 'our most faithful community ... unanimously elected me to be their prince and lord and presented me the *bacheta de la Signoria*'.[65] Three decades prior, Leonello d'Este was

96 Unknown artist, 'Borso d'Este proclaimed lord of Ferrara and invested with a *bacchetta*', illumination from Michele Savonarola, *De felici progressu illustrissimi Borsii Estensis*, late 1450s.

offered two *bacchette* when invested as *signore*: the first from the civic officials of the *Savi* ('wise-men'), symbolizing the *popolo*'s consent, and the second from the bishops of Ferrara and Ravenna. An illumination in Michele Savonarola's *De felici progresso illustrissimi Borsii Estensis* depicts this ritual (illus. 96). A kneeling member of the *Savi* grants Borso a book of laws and a thin *bacchetta*. The lord – arrayed in crimson brocades – gracefully takes the rod with two fingers. Savonarola's text asserts that Borso wielded the '*bacchetta* of justice' to eradicate three impediments to his citizens' peace: dissension, discord and extortion.[66]

Similar scenes were represented elsewhere in Ferrara. In *May*'s first decan from the Salone dei Mesi's astrological register, an elegantly dressed, blond youth lifts his left hand over the head of a kneeling subject, while his right gracefully supports in his fingertips a slender rod (*virga* in related astrological sources) (illus. 97). The later insertion of a door destroyed the scene immediately below, in which a seated Borso holding a *bacchetta* joyfully received a basket of fruit from a kneeling peasant.[67] These parallel seigneurial objects and gestures linked the frescoes' registers for the room's visitors. While Renaissance princes' batons were commonly more substantial than Borso's in the *Genealogia*, visual evidence suggests that lost monuments celebrating Alberto and Niccolò III d'Este depicted these lords grasping slender *bacchette*.[68] In the presentation manuscript of Andrea Pannonio's *De origine clarissime illustrissimeque domus Estensis* (On the Origin of the Most Famous and Illustrious House of Este), moreover, the enthroned Ercole d'Este is portrayed in a flowing, crimson cloth-of-gold mantle, holding between his fingers an even more narrow sceptre (illus. 98).[69]

A text describing his triumphal entry into Reggio Emilia celebrating the first ducal investiture affirmed that Borso received a sceptre because virtue shone through him. In Reggio's cathedral, the new duke was exhorted to avoid 'wicked, vicious, rebellious and factious men' and to punish insolent malefactors with his *bacchetta*. Indeed, as we saw in Chapter One, *The Flower of Battle* (illus. 21) owned by Borso's father instructs how to wield the baton both to attack and to defend.[70] Hardly the dandy's accessory, Borso's *bacchetta* symbolized communal and imperial investiture and rule, and might even be cast as a weapon. These batons, moreover, were guarded in dynastic treasuries, where they perpetuated lordly authority and continuity. In Old St Peter's Basilica in 1471, Pope Paul II presented Borso a golden staff. Borso died soon after his return to Ferrara and was exhibited to subjects clutching a golden *bacchetta* and clad in crimson brocades. Two decades later, an inventory recorded this *bacchetta* 'covered in gold that Pope Paul gave to Duke Borso when he made him duke'.[71]

In art, Quattrocento princes displayed willowy *bacchette* with exceedingly elegant gestures. Piero della Francesca depicted Sigismondo Malatesta, dressed in a cloth-of-gold mantle and crimson *calze*, devoutly kneeling before a virile, bearded St Sigismund, who delicately holds a narrow rod with his fingers (illus. 99). Some viewers would have associated the saint with Emperor Sigismund and thus imperial authority. Malatesta, moreover, possessed a 'small golden rod' according

97 Decan with a *bacchetta*, from Francesco del Cossa, *May*, late 1460s, fresco, east wall, Salone dei Mesi, Palazzo Schifanoia, Ferrara.

to a posthumous inventory.[72] The ironclad, adulterous prince Pier Maria Rossi daintily grips a similar *bacchetta* in two scenes from Torrechiara's Camera d'Oro (illus. 8, 61). That the *bacchetta* signified Rossi lordship is confirmed by the sixteenth-century testimony of a nonagenarian from Roccabianca (near Parma) who had heard that Pietro Rossi, on his deathbed, passed down 'la bacchetta della signoria' to his son Pier Maria.[73]

One of European literature's most tyrannical lords holds a remarkably slender *bacchetta* and exercises an excess of domination in frescoes from Roccabianca Castle. The most extensive surviving visual narrative of the cruel trials that Gualtieri of Saluzzo inflicted upon patient

98 'Ercole d'Este', illumination from Andrea Pannonio, *De origine clarissime illustrissimeque domus Estensis*, 1470s.

99 Piero della Francesca, *St Sigismund*, *c.* 1451, fresco, San Francesco, Rimini.

Griselda was painted in the 1460s–70s in a room that served (at times) as the *podestà*'s audience chamber. Gualtieri elegantly supports a thin *bacchetta* surrounded by hounds, young courtiers and a trusted advisor whispering into his ear, in a heavily damaged fresco compositionally similar to Mantegna's scene of Ludovico Gonzaga holding court (illus. 30, 100). Elsewhere, Gualtieri delicately clasps his *bacchetta* upright between his left thumb and index finger as he orders his newborn daughter to be sent away and (ostensibly) left for dead (illus. 101). He also maliciously banishes the defrocked Griselda from the

100 Unknown Emilian or Lombard Artist, *Advisor Whispers in Gualtieri's Ear*, c. 1470, fresco, Camera di Griselda, Castello Sforzesco, Milan, originally from Roccabianca Castle.

palace (illus. 102). As she steps away, Gualtieri holds a long, narrow *bacchetta* with these same two fingers conspicuously posed even more nimbly. He presses the rod against Griselda, mercilessly expelling her. Borso d'Este's gesture was not unmanly to fifteenth-century eyes; rather, it visualized imperious, patriarchal authority.

Manifestations of masculinity that may seem to modern viewers to lack virility were not necessarily met with suspicion or condemnation in Renaissance Italy, and neither were they typically associated with what we would understand as homosexuality.[74] Benvenuto Cellini extolled a soldier as 'the most courteous warrior I ever came across, with the exquisite manners of a young girl, and yet, when necessary, showing himself incredibly bold and ruthless'.[75] Matteo Bandello described Niccolò III d'Este, Ferrara's supreme bastard-begetter who fathered scores of illegitimate children, as the 'most womanly man [*il più feminil uomo*]' of his time, because 'as many women as he saw, that many he desired'. Bandello here echoed a millennia-long perception of effeminacy as a manner generally constituted and performed through extreme desire for women, or excessive time spent loving them or seeking their attention. Bandello's criticism of Niccolò's boundless heteroeroticism, in fact, demonstrates that what effeminized a man was the very loss of masculine self-control that Borso's apologists lauded.[76]

The fact that Borso fathered children does not mean that he abstained from sex with men or boys. Evidence that he did not – or that contemporaries believed that he did not abstain – may be Giovanni Pontano's insinuation, two decades after the duke's death, about Borso's motives for building palaces for courtiers. Pontano alleged that he had heard the Ferrarese say that these men enjoyed Borso's favour because they were in the flower of their youth. This posthumous condemnation, however, can also be put within the context of Pontano's censure of profligate lords, and it came as beliefs about normative masculinity and rule were undergoing marked transformations propelled by the dynamics of Italy's invasion.[77] Some decades

101 Unknown Emilian or Lombard Artist, *Gualtieri Sends Daughter Off* (ostensibly to be left for dead), *c.* 1470, fresco, Camera di Griselda, Castello Sforzesco, Milan, originally from Roccabianca Castle.

102 Unknown Emilian or Lombard Artist, *Griselda Evicted from the Palace*, c. 1470, fresco, Camera di Griselda, Castello Sforzesco, Milan, originally from Roccabianca Castle.

later, Pietro Aretino called Borso's courtiers 'real men at arms' in the prologue of his mock courtly and homoerotic comedy *Il Marescalco*. Though the title character's sexual attraction to boys looms over the play, Aretino seems not so much to defame Borso as to parody an old-timer constantly invoking 'the good old days'. If Borso is here ridiculed or maligned, it is as a representative of the splendidly attired fifteenth-century lords that Aretino's contemporaries, among them Baldassare Castiglione and Francesco Guicciardini, by the 1530s regarded as suspiciously unmasculine and the cause of Italy's ruin (though for reasons other than sexual desire for men).[78]

Among Borso's courtiers, one who is sometimes proposed to have been his lover is Teofilo Calcagnini, who was knighted by the lord on Christmas Day in 1464. Teofilo received similar honours from Emperor Frederick III in 1469 and from Pope Paul II two years later, when Borso was made duke of Ferrara in Rome. Teofilo, the patron of an illuminated *Decameron* now at Oxford, was the recipient of a manuscript on horses and their care commissioned by Borso. He also serves, along with Battista Guarino, as interlocutor in a treatise on dogs and horses (*Sermone del cane e del cavallo*).[79] In many ways, then, Teofilo Calcagnini is the ideal courtly Renaissance man. He sponsored a magnificent joust the day following his first knighthood, and his *barberi* horses ran in Ferrara's *palio* races. At important spectacles in Ferrara and beyond, Teofilo often accompanied Borso, who granted him castles and lands, including Bellombra, Benvignante, Cavriago and Maranello, in addition to a palace in the vicinity of the Palazzo Schifanoia.[80]

In the late seventeenth century, Alfonso Maresti claimed that Teofilo astounded audiences at Schifanoia by playing the lute and singing verses lauding Borso, while clad in flesh-coloured clothing so skin-tight that he 'decisively seemed nude'.[81] Maresti further asserted that Borso – so enamoured with this courtier, whom Maresti called a 'heartthrob' (literally, a 'heart magnet', *calamita de Cuori*) – directed that the spectacle be commemorated by a painted portrait of Teofilo in this attire. A sculpture was also ordered, which Maresti identified as the nude, music-making *putto* standing atop a candelabra with his back to us on Schifanoia's marble portal (illus. 103). The tale is an improbable one almost certainly invented by Maresti; or, perhaps it came down to him from some tradition, a fantasy based on the marble relief. Maresti fumbles many chronological specifics – about Calcagnini's age and his grants from Borso, and regarding the construction history of the palace. More importantly, the sculpted lutenist is clearly naked (for the most part). The chubby rolls of fat in his legs are not held by hose or any other garment, though he seems to have a tie or ribbon around his calf, on the right. This is not a depiction of flesh-coloured clothing. Nor is this an ideally beautiful youth – lithe and slender – according to fifteenth-century standards of courtly male beauty that we see throughout Schifanoia's frescoes. This is instead a plump *amorino* or sprite, much like those making music in the margins of other courtly images, including numerous Este manuscripts or the lunettes of Torre-chiara's Camera d'Oro, dating within a decade of Schifanoia's marble *putto* (see illus. 8, to the left, or illus. 27, to the right). The sculpture undoubtedly inspired the (almost certainly apocryphal) performance, rather than the other way around.

Perhaps the most compelling visual evidence at Schifanoia for homosocial if not queer erotic intimacy or companionship is found in the pair of courtiers standing at far left in the *March* scene of Borso's

103 Ambrogio di Giacomo da Milano and Antonio di Gregorio (attr.), *Putto Playing the Lute*, 1460s, marble, entry portal, Palazzo Schifanoia, Ferrara.

court (illus. 104). Their arms are clearly intertwined, with their bodies pulled together tight and legs quite close together too, with feet almost interlocking. The two figures in the same location in *April* (illus. 32) may also be arm in arm, though not, for us, visibly so. Could this be the long-sought proof of queer love at Borso's court? In *March*, the nearby monkey hugging, perhaps humping, a young page's leg assuredly hints at sexual desires and acts. A scholar who elsewhere declares that Borso's 'homosexuality' was 'well known', convincingly identifies the couple as Borso's brothers Ercole and Alberto and interprets them as figures of fraternal accord.[82] One of these two men was long considered to be Teofilo Calcagnini, in a tradition echoed by Ferrarese scholars for centuries. Calcagnini has recently been more plausibly associated with the confidently smiling or laughing courtier on horseback next to and turned to face Borso and the viewer in a number of scenes (see

104 Borso d'Este among courtiers, including two with intertwined arms (perhaps Alberto and Ercole d'Este), and a page whose leg is humped by a tethered monkey, detail from Francesco del Cossa, *March* (illus. 2).

him just below the sprinting hares, for instance, in illus. 34). This face might be recognized as well in the extravagantly dressed man with his back to us in *April*, with large wing-like sleeves covered in pearls and gilded metal adornments (at far right in illus. 32).[83] These identifications are by necessity tentative, of course. What we can say with certainty about the men with locked arms among the crowd of courtiers surrounding their lord is that, once again, evidence confirms the fundamental importance of male homosociality, which may have been erotic, affective, intimate and sexual, but was by no means confined to that.[84]

It should not be at all surprising if evidence eventually emerges confirming that Borso had sex with men or boys; a substantial percentage of men did in contemporary Florence, for example, although most later married women.[85] The courtiers who have been proposed as Borso's lovers eventually married women as well, following their lord's death. For instance, Teofilo Calcagnini – father of at least six children, including one illegitimate son and a son named after Borso – wed Marietta Strozzi, granddaughter of the famous (and infamously exiled) Florentine humanist Palla Strozzi. According to Giorgio Vasari and other sixteenth-century sources, Marietta, who was raised in Florence, was among the town's great beauties and was represented in a marble bust by Desiderio da Settignano (well before she married Calcagnini).[86]

Gifts of palaces, clothing and jurisdictional rights to Teofilo Calcagnini and Borso's other courtiers seem akin to grants made to mistresses discussed in the previous two chapters. Gifts to Teofilo and others were both affective and political, as efforts to cement the loyalty of these men whose holdings and jurisdictional powers were strategically positioned on the confines of Este territory.[87] It had long been and would continue to be conventional in Ferrara to demonstrate magnificence by providing courtiers with palaces, thus situating, extending and fortifying the prince's authority. Of course, magnanimity and liberality were fundamental to Renaissance lordliness. This is how Ferrara was expanded under Ercole, through the *Addizione Erculea*. It would be difficult to underestimate the constitutive nature of such patterns of gift-giving to the town's urban, social and political history.[88]

Leonello d'Este's courtier Folco da Villafora, moreover, had been provided richly brocaded clothing and a palace at Savenuzzo (east of Ferrara) lavishly decorated at his lord's expense. Folco was portrayed by Andrea Mantegna in a double portrait with Leonello, though given this *signore*'s modest reputation and two wives, scholars' suspicions seem never to have been raised by the very dear friendship between the two.[89] Ercole d'Este also granted villas to his men. In 1481, he awarded Verginese, 20 kilometres (12 mi.) southeast of Ferrara, to the Neapolitan Sigismondo Cantelmo, and he promoted young, handsome courtiers, notably Giulio Cesare Tassoni.[90]

Ercole continued to support Borso's noblemen, a fact that underscores the importance of political continuity and homosocial networks, beyond individual desires. This included Teofilo Calcagnini. An anonymous chronicler referred to Calcagnini as Borso's 'compagno', which some scholars have taken as evidence that they were lovers. A close reading of this chronicle, however, confirms that 'compagno' was utilized for a wide variety of men in Ferrara – other courtiers of Borso, and those of Niccolò III, Niccolò di Leonello, Ercole and Alberto d'Este. The word is also used in this text for a courtier of Galeazzo Maria Sforza – Gaspare Vimercati, patron of the wedding oration we saw in Chapter One (illus. 15) – who visited Ferrara in the duke of Milan's stead. Perhaps most tellingly for our purposes, the chronicler explains that one of Ercole's first acts as lord was to make 'il magnifico messer Teophilo Calcagnino' his own 'compagno', and to confirm all the 'honors and emoluments' that Teofilo had enjoyed during Borso's reign.[91] In the end, what we know about Borso and his men, including Teofilo Calcagnini, tells us less about a sexual identity than about the resolutely masculine and homosocial, intimate and erotic nature of power in fifteenth-century Italy.

Power seduces. The chronicler and notary Ugo Caleffini characterized Niccolò III d'Este as 'more courtly than a beautiful lady'. French women who 'saw this noble lord' – as he travelled while on pilgrimage to Santiago de Compostela – 'fell in love with him more than with their husbands'. Whether or not this is true is beside the point. What is significant is Caleffini's claim that aristophiliac women fell in love with Niccolò on sight, because of his nobility. Courtliness and aristocratic rank were erotically charged, and beauty manifested both social status and sexual desirability. These categories were not distinct. According to Enea Piccolomini, the future Pope Pius II, Borso's subjects honoured him 'like a god'. Caleffini even asserted that he himself was 'so very in love with', or 'enchanted by', Borso's body.[92] The desire aroused by his lord's courtly body was at least in part sexual, and we must avoid erasing amorous and erotic sentiment from it. Though this claim might strike us as hyperbolic, it speaks volumes about the operations of power in Renaissance Italy, and it clearly indicates the crucial element of love and desire in the ways that subjects imagined and articulated their relationship to their rulers. Elegance, radiance and courtliness incited love and admiration for lords. These values, when embodied and visualized in life and art, amplified authority.

The *Genealogia dei Signori d'Este*'s full-length portrait of Borso d'Este offers an exemplary lord, much grander than the manuscript's other bejewelled ancestors, for Ercole and his successors to emulate. The image of this self-assured and charismatic prince reveals just how dynamic were Renaissance aristocratic masculinities – magnetic, elegant and seductive. The display of noble, courtly men emerges here as fundamental to Renaissance power, often visualized and embodied in erotic terms. At the courts of Borso and other lords, homosocial configurations and hierarchies may have facilitated, even animated, sexual relations between men and boys of contrasting status. Queer intimacies, desires and pleasures were not radically transgressive, nor marginal, but were embedded in the structures of Renaissance authority, at their very apex or centre.[93] These were the privileges of power.

REFERENCES

All translations are my own, unless otherwise stated.

Introduction: Making Renaissance Men

1 Antonio Cappelli, 'Notizie di Ugo Caleffini notaro ferrarese del secolo
  XV con la sua Cronaca in rima di Casa d'Este', *Atti e memorie delle Regie
  Deputazioni di storia patria per le provincie modenesi e parmensi*, II (1864),
  p. 292.
2 For aristophilia, see James A. Schultz, *Courtly Love, the Love of Courtliness,
  and the History of Sexuality* (Chicago, IL, 2006).
3 For swords, for instance, see Kristen B. Neuschel, *Living by the Sword:
  Weapons and Material Culture in France and Britain, 600–1600* (Ithaca, NY,
  2020), pp. 1–23.
4 Timothy McCall, *Brilliant Bodies: Fashioning Courtly Men in Early
  Renaissance Italy* (University Park, PA, 2022).
5 Ruth Mazo Karras, *From Boys to Men: Formations of Masculinity in Late
  Medieval Europe* (Philadelphia, PA, 2003); Alexandra Shepard, 'Manhood,
  Patriarchy, and Gender in Early Modern History', in *Masculinities,
  Childhood, Violence: Attending to Early Modern Women and Men*, ed. Amy
  E. Leonard and Karen L. Nelson (Newark, DE, 2010), pp. 77–95; Patricia
  Simons, *The Sex of Men in Premodern Europe: A Cultural History* (Cambridge,
  2011); Douglas Biow, *On the Importance of Being an Individual in Renaissance
  Italy: Men, Their Professions, and Their Beards* (Philadelphia, PA, 2015);
  Elizabeth Currie, *Fashion and Masculinity in Renaissance Florence* (London,
  2016); Jacqueline Murray, 'Reflections on the Male Body and Social
  Masculinity', in *The Male Body and Social Masculinity in Premodern Europe*,
  ed. Jacqueline Murray (Toronto, 2022), pp. 9–21.
6 The fundamental study remains R. W. Connell, *Masculinities*, 2nd edn
  (Berkeley, CA, 2005). See too Judith Butler, *Bodies That Matter: On the
  Discursive Limits of Sex* (London, 1996); Jack Halberstam, *Female Masculinity*
  (Durham, NC, 1998); R. W. Connell and James W. Messerschmidt,
  'Hegemonic Masculinity: Rethinking the Concept', *Gender and Society*,
  XIX/6 (2005), pp. 829–59; Ben Griffin, 'Hegemonic Masculinity as a
  Historical Problem', *Gender and History*, XXX/2 (2018), pp. 377–400.
7 Ulrich Pfisterer, 'Die Erotik der Macht: Visualisierte Herrscher-Potenz
  in der Renaissance', in *Menschennatur und politische Ordnung*, ed. Andreas
  Höfele and Beate Kellner (Paderborn, 2016), p. 179. See too Rebecca Zorach,

Blood, Milk, Ink, Gold: Abundance and Excess in the French Renaissance (Chicago, IL, 2005).

8 The classic account of homosociality is Eve Kosofsky Sedgwick, *Between Men: English Literature and Male Homosocial Desire* (New York, 1985). See too Michael Rocke, *Forbidden Friendships: Homosexuality and Male Culture in Renaissance Florence* (Oxford, 1996); Patricia Simons, 'Homosociality and Erotics in Italian Renaissance Portraiture', in *Portraiture: Facing the Subject*, ed. Joanna Woodall (Manchester, 1997), pp. 29–51.

9 Matteo Bandello, *Tutte le opere di Matteo Bandello*, ed. Francesco Flora, 4th edn (Milan, 1966), vol. I, p. 518.

10 Robert Mills, *Seeing Sodomy in the Middle Ages* (Chicago, IL, 2015); Roland Betancourt, *Byzantine Intersectionality: Sexuality, Gender, and Race in the Middle Ages* (Princeton, NJ, 2020); Leah DeVun, *The Shape of Sex: Nonbinary Gender from Genesis to the Renaissance* (New York, 2021).

11 Diane Watt, 'Why Men Still Aren't Enough', GLQ: *A Journal of Lesbian and Gay Studies*, XVI/3 (2010), p. 452.

12 Connell, *Masculinities*; Connell and Messerschmidt, 'Hegemonic Masculinity', pp. 837, 848; Shepard, 'Manhood, Patriarchy, and Gender', pp. 82–7; Simons, *The Sex of Men*, pp. 73–8.

13 Diego Zancani, 'Il *De Herculei filii ortu et de urbis Ferrariae periculo ac liberatione* di Antonio Cornazzano', *Bollettino storico piacentino*, LXXIV/1 (1979), pp. 63, 69.

14 Werner L. Gundersheimer, *Ferrara: The Style of a Renaissance Despotism* (Princeton, NJ, 1973).

15 For humanism's erotics, start with Leonard Barkan, *Transuming Passion: Ganymede and the Erotics of Humanism* (Palo Alto, CA, 1991); Stephen J. Campbell, *The Cabinet of Eros: Renaissance Mythological Painting and the Studiolo of Isabella d'Este* (New Haven, CT, 2006); James Grantham Turner, *Eros Visible: Art, Sexuality and Antiquity in Renaissance Italy* (New Haven, CT, 2017).

16 Ruggero Rugolo, 'Medaglie', in *Pisanello: Una poetica dell'inatteso*, ed. Lionello Puppi (Cinisello Balsamo, 1996), pp. 156–7; Luke Syson and Dillian Gordon, *Pisanello: Painter to the Renaissance Court* (London, 2001), pp. 90–93; Ulrich Pfisterer in *The Renaissance Nude*, ed. Thomas Kren with Jill Burke and Stephen J. Campbell (Los Angeles, CA, 2018), p. 256. For Leonello and the nude, see also Stephen J. Campbell, 'Naked Truth: Humanism, Poetry, and the Nude in Renaissance Art', in *The Renaissance Nude*, ed. Kren, Burke and Campbell, p. 143.

17 McCall, *Brilliant Bodies*, pp. 106–44.

18 Stephen K. Scher, ed., *The Currency of Fame: Portrait Medals of the Renaissance* (New York, 1994), pp. 47–50; Rugolo, 'Medaglie', pp. 157–8; Raymond B. Waddington, 'Pisanello's *Paragoni*', in *Perspectives on the Renaissance Medal*, ed. Stephen K. Scher (New York, 2000), pp. 28–9.

19 Gino Arrighi, 'Canzone per Leonello d'Este raccolta da Felino Sandei dello studio di Ferrara in un codice lucchese del '400', *Rinascimento*, II/2 (1962), p. 208; Tim Shephard, *Echoing Helicon: Music, Art and Identity in the Este Studioli, 1440–1530* (Oxford, 2014), pp. 50–54.

20 Ovid, *Ars Amatoria: Book 1*, ed. A. S. Hollis (Oxford, 1977), p. 1.

21 Stephen Campbell and Tim Shephard have highlighted *amore*'s centrality for Leonello: Stephen J. Campbell, *Cosmè Tura of Ferrara: Style, Politics, and the Renaissance City, 1450–1495* (New Haven, CT, 1997), pp. 46–51, 60–61; Shephard, *Echoing Helicon*, pp. 54–7. See too Giuseppe Pardi, *Leonello d'Este, marchese di Ferrara* (Bologna, 1904), pp. 151–2; Arrighi, 'Canzone per Leonello d'Este'; Syson and Gordon, *Pisanello*, pp. 87–100, 123.

22 Niccolò Machiavelli, *Il Principe*, ed. Luigi Firpo (Turin, 1961), p. 61: 'è molto più sicuro essere temuto che amato, quando si abbia a mancare dell'uno de' dua'.

23 Richard W. Kaeuper, *Chivalry and Violence in Medieval Europe* (Oxford, 1999), p. 2.

24 Matteo Provasi, *Il popolo ama il duca? Rivolta e consenso nella Ferrara estense* (Rome, 2011), p. 10.

25 John M. Najemy, 'Politics: Class and Patronage in Twentieth-Century Italian Renaissance Historiography', in *The Italian Renaissance in the Twentieth Century*, ed. Allen J. Grieco, Michael Rocke and Fiorella Superbi Gioffredi (Florence, 2002), p. 120.

26 Stefano De Carolis, 'Le ricognizioni dei resti mortali di Sigismondo Pandolfo Malatesta: Un'anamnesi retrospettiva', *Penelope: Arte storia archeologia*, 1 (2002), p. 36; McCall, *Brilliant Bodies*, pp. 27, 52.

27 Giuseppe Pardi, ed., *Diario ferrarese dall'anno 1409 sino al 1502* (Bologna, 1928–33), p. 60; Provasi, *Il popolo ama il duca?*, pp. 68–9, 78–9.

28 Gerry Milligan, 'The Politics of Effeminacy in "Il cortegiano"', *Italica*, LXXXIII/3–4 (2006), pp. 345–66. See too McCall, *Brilliant Bodies*, pp. 151–2.

29 For the sophistication and inventiveness of these courtly frescoes, see Anne Dunlop, *Painted Palaces: The Rise of Secular Art in Early Renaissance Italy* (University Park, PA, 2009).

30 C. Jean Campbell, 'Pier Maria Rossi's Treasure: Love, Knowledge and the Invention of the Source in the Camera d'Oro at Torrechiara', in *Emilia e Marche nel Rinascimento: L'identità visiva della 'periferia'*, ed. Giancarla Periti (Azzano San Paolo, 2005), pp. 63–88; Timothy McCall, '"Questo misto di profano e di sacro": The *Studiolo Oratorio* of Torrechiara', *Predella*, 47 (2020), pp. 165–83.

1 Chivalry and Courtly Masculinity

1 Chad Coerver, '*Donna/Dono*: Chivalry and Adulterous Exchange in the Quattrocento', in *Picturing Women in Renaissance and Baroque Italy*, ed. Geraldine A. Johnson and Sara F. Matthews Grieco (Cambridge, 1997), pp. 198–9; Andrea Rizzi, *Vernacular Translators in Quattrocento Italy: Scribal Culture, Authority, and Agency* (Turnhout, 2017), pp. 47–55.

2 Christopher Celenza, 'Creating Canons in Fifteenth-Century Ferrara: Angelo Decembrio's *De politia litteraria*, 1.10', *Renaissance Quarterly*, LVII/1 (2004), p. 61.

3 The bibliography on chivalric texts in the libraries of fifteenth-century Italian lords is immense; to begin, and for further references, see Giulio Bertoni and Emilio Paolo Vicini, *Il castello di Ferrara ai tempi di Niccolò III: Inventario della suppellettile del castello, 1436* (Bologna, 1907), pp. 94–109; Élisabeth Pellegrin, *La bibliothèque des Visconti et des Sforza, ducs de Milan,*

au xve siècle (Paris, 1955); Antonia Tissoni Benvenuti, 'Il mondo cavalleresco e la corte estense', in *I libri di Orlando innamorato*, ed. Riccardo Bruscagli (Modena, 1987), pp. 13–33; Joanna Woods-Marsden, *The Gonzaga of Mantua and Pisanello's Arthurian Frescoes* (Princeton, NJ, 1988), pp. 22–6; and Maria Grazia Albertini Ottolenghi, 'La biblioteca dei Visconti e degli Sforza: Gli inventari del 1488 e 1490', *Studi petrarcheschi*, VIII (1991), pp. 1–238.

4 Ernst Kantorowicz, 'The Este Portrait by Roger van der Weyden', *Journal of the Warburg and Courtauld Institutes*, III/3–4 (1940), p. 172. For Francesco, see Timothy McCall, *Brilliant Bodies: Fashioning Courtly Men in Early Renaissance Italy* (University Park, PA, 2022), p. 155.

5 Andrew Martindale, 'Painting for Pleasure: Some Lost Fifteenth Century Secular Decorations of Northern Italy', in *The Vanishing Past: Studies of Medieval Art, Liturgy and Metrology Presented to Christopher Hohler*, ed. Alan Borg and Andrew Martindale (Oxford, 1981), pp. 109–31; Anne Dunlop, *Painted Palaces: The Rise of Secular Art in Early Renaissance Italy* (University Park, PA, 2009). For specific examples, see Bertoni and Vicini, *Il castello di Ferrara*, p. 117; Woods-Marsden, *The Gonzaga of Mantua*; Thomas Tuohy, *Herculean Ferrara: Ercole d'Este, 1471–1505, and the Invention of a Ducal Capital* (Cambridge, 1996), p. 215; Enrico Castelnuovo, ed., *Le stanze di Artù. Gli affreschi di Frugarolo e l'immaginario cavalleresco nell'autunno del Medioevo* (Milan, 1999); Marco Folin, 'Le residenze di corte e il sistema delle delizie fra Medioevo ed età moderna', in *Delizie estensi: Architetture di villa nel Rinascimento italiano ed europeo*, ed. Francesco Ceccarelli and Marco Folin (Florence, 2009), p. 95; Maria Teresa Sambin De Norcen, *Le ville di Leonello d'Este: Ferrara e le sue compagne agli albori dell'età moderna* (Venice, 2012), pp. 63, 277.

6 Woods-Marsden, *The Gonzaga of Mantua*, pp. 13–15, 23–6, 30; Micaela Torboli, *Il duca Borso d'Este e la politica delle immagini nella Ferrara del Quattrocento* (Ferrara, 2007), p. 14.

7 Cesarina Casanova, 'Mogli e vedove di condottieri in area padana fra Quattro e Cinquecento', in *Donne di potere nel Rinascimento*, ed. Letizia Arcangeli and Susanna Peyronel (Rome, 2008), p. 518.

8 Enrico Celani, 'La venuta di Borso d'Este in Roma. L'anno 1471', *Archivio della Regia società romana di storia patria*, XIII/3–4 (1890), pp. 380–82; Giulio Bertoni, L'"Orlando furioso" e la Rinascenza a Ferrara* (Modena, 1919), p. 92.

9 Amanda Luyster, 'Playing with Animals: The Visual Context of an Arthurian Manuscript (Florence Palatino 556) and the Uses of Ambiguity', *Word and Image*, XX/1 (2004), pp. 1–21; Jonathan J. G. Alexander, *The Painted Book in Renaissance Italy, 1450–1600* (New Haven, CT, 2016), p. 115.

10 Adriano Cappelli, 'Guiniforte Barzizza, maestro di Galeazzo Maria Sforza', *Archivio storico lombardo*, 3rd series, I/2 (1894), p. 404.

11 Marcello Simonetta, 'Il duca alla dieta: Francesco Sforza e Pio II', in *Il sogno di Pio II e il viaggio da Roma a Mantova*, ed. Arturo Calzona, Francesco Paolo Fiore, Alberto Tenenti and Cesare Vasoli (Florence, 2003), pp. 280–81. For orations performed by the young siblings, see Cappelli, 'Guiniforte Barzizza', pp. 422, 437–8; Monica Ferrari, *'Per non manchare in tuto del debito mio.' L'educazione dei bambini Sforza nel Quattrocento* (Milan, 2000), pp. 180, 186; Pius II, *Commentaries*, ed. Margaret Meserve and Marcello Simonetta (Cambridge, MA, 2003–7), vol. I, pp. 310–11; Marcello Simonetta,

Rinascimento segreto: Il mondo del segretario da Petrarca a Machiavelli (Milan, 2004), p. 116; Ippolita Maria Sforza, *Duchess and Hostage in Renaissance Naples: Letters and Orations*, ed. and trans. Diana Robin and Lynn Lara Westwater (Toronto, 2017), pp. 9–14, 173–85.

12 Cappelli, 'Guiniforte Barzizza', pp. 405–6, 425; Evelyn Welch, 'Sight, Sound and Ceremony in the Chapel of Galeazzo Maria Sforza', *Early Music History*, XII (1993), p. 158.

13 Augusto Campana, 'Atti, Isotta degli', in *Dizionario biografico degli Italiani*, vol. IV (Rome, 1961), p. 552; Stephen J. Campbell, *Cosmè Tura of Ferrara: Style, Politics, and the Renaissance City, 1450–1495* (New Haven, CT, 1997), pp. 46–8; Anthony F. D'Elia, *Pagan Virtue in a Christian World: Sigismondo Malatesta and the Italian Renaissance* (Cambridge, MA, 2016), pp. 196–7. For examples from Ovid, see *The Erotic Poems*, trans. Peter Green (London, 1982): *Amores*, pp. 87, 122–3, 127.

14 Maria Grazia Albertini Ottolenghi, 'L'altro "centro": Alessandro Sforza e Pesaro', in *Emilia e Marche nel Rinascimento: L'identità visiva della 'periferia'*, ed. Giancarla Periti (Azzano San Paolo, 2005), pp. 256–8. See too François Avril and Yolanta Załuska, eds, *Dix siècles d'enluminure italienne: VIe–XVIe siècles* (Paris, 1984), pp. 146–7.

15 Federico Cavalieri, 'Echi fiamminghi in Italia: Una tavola del '400', *Osservatorio delle arti*, IV (1990), pp. 42–9.

16 Jane Bridgeman, ed., *A Renaissance Wedding: The Celebrations at Pesaro for the Marriage of Costanzo Sforza and Camilla Marzano d'Aragona, 26–30 May 1475* (London, 2013), pp. 127, 159.

17 Bertoni and Vicini, *Il castello di Ferrara*, p. 43; Tuohy, *Herculean Ferrara*, p. 222; Cristelle Baskins, *The Triumph of Marriage: Painted Cassoni of the Renaissance* (Pittsburgh, PA, 2008).

18 Andrea Bayer, ed., *Art and Love in Renaissance Italy* (New York, 2008), pp. 140–41.

19 Niccolò da Correggio, *Opere*, ed. Antonia Tissoni Benvenuti (Bari, 1969), pp. 78, 93–4; Adrian W. B. Randolph, *Engaging Symbols: Gender, Politics, and Public Art in Fifteenth-Century Florence* (New Haven, CT, 2002), pp. 231–2; C. Jean Campbell, 'Pier Maria Rossi's Treasure: Love, Knowledge and the Invention of the Source in the Camera d'Oro at Torrechiara', in *Emilia e Marche*, ed. Periti, p. 73; Stephen J. Campbell, *The Cabinet of Eros: Renaissance Mythological Painting and the Studiolo of Isabella d'Este* (New Haven, CT, 2006), pp. 104–6; Dunlop, *Painted Palaces*, pp. 132–3; Maya Corry, 'The Homoerotics of Power: Art and Desire in Leonardo's Milan', in *The Male Body and Social Masculinity in Premodern Europe*, ed. Jacqueline Murray (Toronto, 2022), pp. 204–7.

20 Michael Rocke, *Forbidden Friendships: Homosexuality and Male Culture in Renaissance Florence* (Oxford, 1996); Campbell, *The Cabinet of Eros*, p. 178.

21 Elizabeth L'Estrange, 'Gazing at Gawain: Reconsidering Tournaments, Courtly Love, and the Lady Who Looks', *Medieval Feminist Forum*, XLIV/2 (2008), pp. 74–96; McCall, *Brilliant Bodies*, pp. 84–9, 144–9.

22 Georgia Clarke, 'Giovanni II Bentivoglio and the Uses of Chivalry: Towards the Creation of a "Republican Court" in Fifteenth-Century Bologna', in *Artistic Exchange and Cultural Translation in the Italian Renaissance City*, ed. Stephen J. Campbell and Stephen J. Milner (Cambridge, 2004), pp. 162–86.

23 Luigi Fumi, 'Una farsa rappresentata in Parigi contro Bartolomeo Colleoni', in *Miscellanea di studi storici in onore di Antonio Manno* (Turin, 1912), pp. 589–94.

24 Elizabeth Tobey, 'The *Palio* Banner and the Visual Culture of Horse Racing in Renaissance Italy', *International Journal of the History of Sport*, XXVIII/8–9 (2011), pp. 1269–82. For jousts generally, see Fabian Brenker, *Turniere und Lanzenspiele in Bildern aus dem Mittelalter und der frühen Neuzeit: Orte, Auftraggeber und soziale Funktionen* (Petersberg, 2021).

25 Maria Nadia Covini, *L'esercito del duca: Organizzazione militare e istituzioni al tempo degli Sforza (1450–1480)* (Rome, 1998), p. 320n173.

26 Bridgeman, ed., *A Renaissance Wedding*, pp. 13–14.

27 Antonio Cappelli, 'Notizie di Ugo Caleffini notaro ferrarese del secolo XV con la sua Cronaca in rima di Casa d'Este', *Atti e memorie delle Regie Deputazioni di storia patria per le provincie modenesi e parmensi*, II (1864), p. 286; Giuseppe Pardi, ed., *Diario ferrarese dall'anno 1409 sino al 1502* (Bologna, 1928–33), pp. 17, 44–5; Charles M. Rosenberg, 'Art in Ferrara during the Reign of Borso d'Este (1450–1471): A Study in Court Patronage', PhD thesis, University of Michigan, 1974, pp. 202–5, 223–5; Adriano Franceschini, *Artisti a Ferrara in età umanistica e rinascimentale: Testimonianze archivistiche* (Ferrara, 1993), vol. 1, pp. 625, 641; Marcello Toffanello, *Le arti a Ferrara nel Quattrocento: Gli artisti e la corte* (Ferrara, 2010), p. 13.

28 Pardi, ed., *Diario ferrarese dall'anno 1409*, p. 89; Bernardino Zambotti, *Diario ferrarese dall'anno 1476 sino al 1504*, ed. Giuseppe Pardi (Bologna, 1934–7), p. 163; Werner L. Gundersheimer, *Art and Life at the Court of Ercole I d'Este: The 'De triumphis religionis' of Giovanni Sabadino degli Arienti* (Geneva, 1972), pp. 69–71; Charles M. Rosenberg, 'Notes on the Borsian Addition to the Palazzo Schifanoia', *Musei ferraresi*, III (1973), pp. 32–42; Ugo Caleffini, *Croniche, 1471–1494* (Ferrara, 2006), pp. 52–4.

29 Franceschini, *Artisti a Ferrara*, vol. 1, pp. 512–13, 580, 656, 711, 731, 733, 737–8, 763, 765; Joseph Manca, *Cosmè Tura: The Life and Art of a Painter in Estense Ferrara* (Oxford, 2000), pp. 192–5.

30 Pardi, ed., *Diario ferrarese dall'anno 1409*, pp. 70, 86, 90; Alfonso Lazzari, *Il primo duca di Ferrara, Borso d'Este* (Ferrara, 1945), pp. 76–80.

31 Claudio Paolini, Daniela Parenti and Ludovica Sebregondi, eds, *Virtù d'amore: Pittura nuziale nel Quattrocento fiorentino* (Florence, 2010), pp. 256–7; Patricia Lurati, '"In Firenze non si fe' mai simile festa": A proposito del cassone di Apollonio di Giovanni con scena di giostra alla Yale University Art Gallery', *Annali di Storia di Firenze*, VII (2012), pp. 35–71. See also Lucia Ricciardi, *'Col senno, col tesoro e colla lancia': Riti e giochi cavallereschi nella Firenze del Magnifico Lorenzo* (Florence, 1992), pp. 138–42; Randolph, *Engaging Symbols*, pp. 196–201.

32 Ricciardi, *'Col senno'*, p. 139. Nerida Newbigin, ed., *'Le onoranze fiorentine del 1459. Poema anonimo'*, *Letteratura italiana antica*, XII (2011), pp. 58, 91–3. I thank Nerida Newbigin for providing the English translation.

33 The bibliography on these jousts is considerable; see Charles Dempsey, *The Portrayal of Love: Botticelli's Primavera and Humanist Culture at the Time of Lorenzo the Magnificent* (Princeton, NJ, 1992); Ricciardi, *'Col senno'*, pp. 166–86; Randolph, *Engaging Symbols*, pp. 193–241.

34 Eugène Müntz, *Les collections des Médicis au xve siècle; Le musée-la bibliothèque-le mobilier* (Paris, 1888), pp. 29–32; Richard Stapleford, *Lorenzo de' Medici at Home: The Inventory of the Palazzo Medici in 1492* (University Park, PA, 2013), pp. 30, 66, 135, 143, 152–3, 189–91; Newbigin, ed., *'Le onoranze fiorentine'*, p. 58. For jousting armour and equipment in general, see Brenker, *Turniere und Lanzenspiele*, pp. 34–57.

35 Carlo Morbio, *Codice visconteo-sforzesco, ossia raccolta di leggi, decreti e lettere famigliari dei duchi di Milano* (Milan, 1846), pp. 462–3; Giulio Porro Lambertenghi, 'Lettere di Galeazzo Maria Sforza, duca di Milano', *Archivio storico lombardo*, V (1878), p. 656; Emilio Motta, 'Armaiuoli milanesi nel periodo visconteo-sforzesco', *Archivio storico lombardo*, 5th series, I/1–2 (1914), p. 217; Franceschini, *Artisti a Ferrara*, vol. II, pt 1, pp. 533, 557; Toffanello, *Le arti a Ferrara*, pp. 198, 204, 211–12, 279, 281–3.

36 Giulio Porro, 'Nozze di Beatrice d'Este e di Anna Sforza (documenti copiati dagli originali esistenti nell'Archivio di Stato di Milano)', *Archivio storico lombardo*, IX/3 (1882), p. 529.

37 McCall, *Brilliant Bodies*, p. 24.

38 Carlo Magenta, *I Visconti e gli Sforza nel castello di Pavia e loro attinenze con la Certosa e la storia cittadina* (Milan, 1883), vol. I, p. 522; Francesco Malaguzzi Valeri, *La corte di Lodovico il Moro* (Milan, 1913–23), vol. I, p. 553; McCall, *Brilliant Bodies*, p. 96.

39 Zambotti, *Diario ferrarese dall'anno 1476*, p. 215.

40 *Carteggio degli oratori mantovani alla corte sforzesca (1450–1500)*, vol. VI: *1464–1465*, ed. Maria Nadia Covini (Rome, 2001), pp. 259–60.

41 Morbio, *Codice visconteo-sforzesco*, pp. 338–9, 345; Bertoni and Vicini, *Il castello di Ferrara*, p. 80; Malaguzzi Valeri, *La corte di Lodovico*, vol. I, p. 554; Woods-Marsden, *The Gonzaga of Mantua*, pp. 136–7; Stapleford, *Lorenzo de' Medici at Home*, p. 192. For lance heads: Pierre Terjanian, ed., *The Last Knight: The Art, Armor, and Ambition of Maximilian I* (New York, 2019), pp. 98–101.

42 Patricia Simons, *The Sex of Men in Premodern Europe: A Cultural History* (Cambridge, 2011), pp. 38–40, 112–13.

43 Luigi Alberto Gandini, 'Viaggi, cavalli, bardature e stalle degli Estensi nel Quattrocento', *Atti e memorie della Regia Deputazione di storia patria per le provincie di Romagna*, X (1892), p. 74. For Federico's injury and Piero's portrayal, see McCall, *Brilliant Bodies*, pp. 139–42.

44 Rachele Magnani, *Relazioni private tra la corte sforzesca di Milano e casa Medici, 1450–1500* (Milan, 1910), p. xliii; Edoardo Fumagalli, 'Nuovi documenti su Lorenzo e Giuliano de' Medici', *Italia medioevale e umanistica*, XXIII (1980), p. 163; Gregory Lubkin, *A Renaissance Court: Milan under Galeazzo Maria Sforza* (Berkeley, CA, 1994), p. 178.

45 Malaguzzi Valeri, *La corte di Lodovico*, vol. I, p. 554; Joachim K. Rühl, 'Regulations for the Joust in Fifteenth-Century Europe: Francesco Sforza Visconti (1465) and John Tiptoft (1466)', *International Journal of the History of Sport*, XVIII/2 (2001), pp. 193–208; Maria Serena Mazzi, *Come rose d'inverno: Le signore della corte estense nel '400* (Ferrara, 2004), p. 89.

46 Anthony B. Cashman III, 'Performance Anxiety: Federico Gonzaga at the Court of Francis I and the Uncertainty of Ritual Action', *Sixteenth Century Journal*, XXXIII/2 (2002), pp. 343–7.

47 Ibid.

48 Ferrari, *'Per non manchare'*, p. 48.

49 Magenta, *I Visconti e gli Sforza*, vol. II, p. 252; *Carteggio degli oratori mantovani alla corte sforzesca (1450–1500)*, vol. I: *1450–1459*, ed. Isabella Lazzarini (Rome, 1999), pp. 371–3. For Dorotea: McCall, *Brilliant Bodies*, pp. 85–8.

50 James A. Schultz, *Courtly Love, the Love of Courtliness, and the History of Sexuality* (Chicago, IL, 2006), p. 136. See also Richard W. Kaeuper, *Chivalry and Violence in Medieval Europe* (Oxford, 1999); Ruth Mazo Karras, *From Boys to Men: Formations of Masculinity in Late Medieval Europe* (Philadelphia, PA, 2003), pp. 21, 38.

51 Giuseppe Campori, 'Una visita del marchese di Mantova al duca Borso in Sassuolo', *Atti e memorie delle Regie Deputazioni di storia patria per le provincie dell'Emilia*, VI/1 (1881), p. 123.

52 Ken Mondschein, *The Knightly Art of Battle* (Los Angeles, CA, 2011), pp. 24, 32.

53 Luigi Firpo, ed., *Francesco Filelfo educatore e il 'Codice Sforza' della Biblioteca Reale di Torino* (Turin, 1967); Ferrari, *'Per non manchare'*, pp. 125–32; Alison Manges Nogueira, 'An Illuminated Schoolbook for Ludovico Sforza: Portraiture in Educational Manuscripts at the Court of Milan', *Manuscripta*, LIX/2 (2015), pp. 187–222.

54 Peter Mack, *A History of Renaissance Rhetoric, 1380–1620* (Oxford, 2011), pp. 14–17.

55 Nogueira, 'An Illuminated Schoolbook', pp. 214–15.

56 Achille Dina, 'Ludovico il Moro prima della sua venuta al governo', *Archivio storico lombardo*, 2nd series, III/4 (1886), pp. 749–55; Avril and Załuska, eds, *Dix siècles d'enluminure italienne*, p. 157; Lubkin, *A Renaissance Court*, p. 41; Alexander, *The Painted Book*, p. 134.

57 Porro Lambertenghi, 'Lettere di Galeazzo Maria Sforza', p. 268; Adolfo Venturi, 'Relazioni artistiche tra le corti di Milano e Ferrara nel secolo XV', *Archivio storico lombardo*, 2nd series, II/2 (1885), pp. 235–6, 248; Franceschini, *Artisti a Ferrara*, vol. II, pt I, p. 323; McCall, *Brilliant Bodies*, pp. 44–5. See also Tobias Capwell, 'Cradle to Grave: Armour in the Life of the Renaissance Nobleman', in *Iron Men: Fashion in Steel*, ed. Stefan Krause (Vienna, 2022), pp. III–14.

58 Attilio Portioli, 'Giacomo Galopini, prete e miniatore mantovano del secolo XV', *Archivio storico lombardo*, 3rd series, XI/22 (1899), pp. 332–3.

59 Alexander, *The Painted Book*, pp. 123–4, 274–5. See too Ferrari, *'Per non manchare'*, pp. 138–42; Terjanian, ed., *The Last Knight*, pp. 138–40; McCall, *Brilliant Bodies*, pp. 145–7.

60 Coerver, *'Donna/Dono'*.

61 Evelyn Welch, 'Painting the 15th-Century Palace', in *Mantegna and 15th-Century Court Culture*, ed. Francis Ames-Lewis and Anka Bednarek (London, 1993), p. 90; Kristen B. Neuschel, *Living by the Sword: Weapons and Material Culture in France and Britain, 600–1600* (Ithaca, NY, 2020), pp. 67, 73–4.

62 Magnani, *Relazioni private*, p. 35; Trevor Dean, *Land and Power in Late Medieval Ferrara: The Rule of the Este, 1350–1450* (Cambridge, 1988), pp. 127–8.

63 Lubkin, *A Renaissance Court*, p. 178.

64 *Cronache malatestiane dei secoli* XIV *e* XV, ed. Aldo Francesco Massèra (Bologna, 1924), pp. 110, 124–5; Corrado Ricci, *Il tempio malatestiano* (Milan, 1924), p. 24; Annalena Brini, Carlo Lalli, Giancarlo Lanterna and Maria Rizzi, 'Analisi stratigrafiche, morfologiche e caratterizzazione dei materiali eseguite sul corredo funerario di Sigismondo Malatesta e le problematiche del suo restauro', OPD *Restauro*, XV (2003), pp. 110–11. For (knights of the) golden spurs: McCall, *Brilliant Bodies*, pp. 74–5.

65 Marcello Simonetta, *The Montefeltro Conspiracy: A Renaissance Mystery Decoded* (New York, 2008), p. 63.

66 Luigi Napoleone Cittadella, *Notizie amministrative, storiche, artistiche relative a Ferrara* (Ferrara, 1868), vol. I, p. 245; Pardi, ed., *Diario ferrarese dall'anno 1409*, pp. 36, 56; Baskins, *The Triumph of Marriage*, pp. 50–54, 154–7; Anthony F. D'Elia, *A Sudden Terror: The Plot to Murder the Pope in Renaissance Rome* (Cambridge, MA, 2009), p. 29; Keith Christiansen and Stefan Weppelmann, eds, *The Renaissance Portrait from Donatello to Bellini* (New York, 2011), pp. 268–70.

67 Vincenzo Carrari, *Historia de' Rossi parmigiani* (Ravenna, 1583), p. 134; Angelo Pezzana, *Storia della città di Parma* (Parma, 1837–59), vol. II, pp. 152–3; Luchino dal Conte, 'Viaggio a Gerusalemme di Nicolò da Este', ed. Giovanni Ghinassi, in *Miscellanea di opuscoli inediti o rari dei secoli* XIV *e* XV (Turin, 1861), pp. 99–160; Pardi, ed., *Diario ferrarese dall'anno 1409*, p. 13; Richard M. Tristano, 'Ferrara in the Fifteenth Century: Borso d'Este and the Development of a New Nobility', PhD thesis, New York University, 1983, pp. 100–116; Matteo Maria Boiardo, *Orlando innamorato*, trans. Charles Stanley Ross (Berkeley, CA, 1989), pp. xxxvi, 457.

68 Antonio Frizzi, *Memorie per la storia di Ferrara: Con giunte e note del Conte Avv. Camillo Laderchi*, 2nd edn (Ferrara, 1847–50), vol. III, p. 392; dal Conte, 'Viaggio a Gerusalemme', pp. 139–40. For models of knightly piety, see Kaeuper, *Chivalry and Violence*, pp. 45–62.

69 Letizia Arcangeli, 'Principi, *homines* e "*partesani*" nel ritorno dei Rossi', in *Le signorie dei Rossi di Parma tra* XIV *e* XVI *secolo*, ed. Letizia Arcangeli and Marco Gentile (Florence, 2007), p. 283.

70 Celani, 'La venuta di Borso', pp. 373–4, 418, 420–21, 428–30; Adolfo Venturi, 'L'arte a Ferrara nel periodo di Borso d'Este', *Rivista storica italiana*, II (1885), p. 695; Pardi, ed., *Diario ferrarese dall'anno 1409*, p. 67; Franceschini, *Artisti a Ferrara*, vol. I, p. 642; Tuohy, *Herculean Ferrara*, p. 37.

71 Toffanello, *Le arti a Ferrara*, pp. 376–7.

72 Pardi, ed., *Diario ferrarese dall'anno 1409*, pp. 81–2; Tristano, 'Ferrara in the Fifteenth Century', p. 226; Tuohy, *Herculean Ferrara*, pp. 249–50.

73 Paul Nieuwenhuizen, 'Worldly Ritual and Dynastic Iconography in the Bentivoglio Chapel in Bologna, 1483–1499', *Mededelingen van het Nederlands Instituut te Rome*, LV (1996), p. 202.

2 Aristocratic Animals and Men at Court

1 Erica Fudge, *Animal* (London, 2002); Erica Fudge, 'Renaissance Animal Things', *New Formations*, LXXVI/76 (2012), pp. 86–100; Sarah Cockram, 'History of Emotions', in *Handbook of Historical Animal Studies*, ed. Mieke Roscher, André Krebber and Brett Mizelle (Berlin, 2021), pp. 409–22.

2 Cesare Foucard, *Relazioni dei duchi di Ferrara e di Modena coi re di Tunisi* (Modena, 1881), pp. 14–17; Elizabeth Horodowich, 'The Wider World: Foreigners, Travels, and Geography', in *Italian Renaissance Diplomacy: A Sourcebook*, ed. Monica Azzolini and Isabella Lazzarini (Toronto, 2017), pp. 193–202.

3 Beatrice Saletti, 'Imitation Games. Some Notes on the Envoys Sent by Borso d'Este to Uthman, Ruler of Tunis', *Legatio: The Journal for Renaissance and Early Modern Diplomatic Studies*, IV (2020), p. 88.

4 Loren Partridge and Randolph Starn, 'Representing War in the Renaissance: The Shield of Paolo Uccello', *Representations*, V (1984), p. 57.

5 Evelyn Welch, *Art and Authority in Renaissance Milan* (New Haven, CT, 1995), pp. 250, 324n41; Monica Ferrari, 'Lettere di principi bambini del Quattrocento lombardo', *Mélanges de l'Ecole française de Rome*, CIX/1 (1997), p. 353.

6 Archivio di Stato di Milano, Carteggio Sforzesco 1474 – Potenze Sovrane (Massimiliano Sforza), 2 June 1498. I thank John Gagné for this reference.

7 Lorenzo de' Medici, *Lettere*, vol. I: *1460–1474*, ed. Riccardo Fubini (Florence, 1977), pp. 239, 243; Evelyn Welch, 'Secular Fresco Painting at the Court of Galeazzo Maria Sforza, 1466–1476', PhD thesis, University of London, Warburg Institute, 1987, pp. 62, 277; Giancarlo Malacarne, *Le cacce del principe: L'ars venandi nella terra dei Gonzaga* (Modena, 1998), p. 44 (and pp. 42–8 for greyhounds more generally); Francesca Borgo, 'Leonardo's Hunts: Metaphors for the Physiology of Perception', in *Hunting without Weapons: On the Pursuit of Images*, ed. Maurice Saß (Berlin, 2017), pp. 37–40.

8 Borgo, 'Leonardo's Hunts', pp. 23–37.

9 Giorgio Vasari, *Vite de' più eccellenti pittori, scultori et architettori*, ed. Gaetano Milanesi (Florence, 1906), vol. V, pp. 303–4; Molly Bourne, *Francesco II Gonzaga: The Soldier-Prince as Patron* (Rome, 2008), pp. 112–13, 308–9. For Pliny's tales echoed in Renaissance Italy, see Sarah Blake McHam, *Pliny and the Artistic Culture of the Italian Renaissance: The Legacy of the 'Natural History'* (New Haven, CT, 2013), pp. 48, 107, 139, 325, 336, 344–5.

10 Victoria Kirkham, 'Petrarch the Courtier: Five Public Speeches', in *Petrarch: A Critical Guide to the Complete Works*, ed. Victoria Kirkham and Armando Maggi (Chicago, IL, 2009), p. 143.

11 Thomas Tuohy, *Herculean Ferrara: Ercole d'Este, 1471–1505, and the Invention of a Ducal Capital* (Cambridge, 1996), p. 84; Richard Stapleford, *Lorenzo de' Medici at Home: The Inventory of the Palazzo Medici in 1492* (University Park, PA, 2013), p. 69.

12 Rodolfo Signorini, 'A Dog Named Rubino', *Journal of the Warburg and Courtauld Institutes*, XLI/1 (1978), pp. 317–20; Malacarne, *Le cacce del principe*, pp. 33–5, 42–4; Kathleen Walker-Meikle, *Medieval Pets* (Woodbridge, 2012), p. 33; Timothy McCall and Sean Roberts, 'Introduction: Revealing Early Modern Secrecy', in *Visual Cultures of Secrecy in Early Modern Europe*, ed. Timothy McCall, Sean Roberts and Giancarlo Fiorenza (Kirksville, MO, 2013), pp. 5–7; Cockram, 'History of Emotions', pp. 413–14.

13 Adriano Franceschini, *Artisti a Ferrara in età umanistica e rinascimentale: Testimonianze archivistiche* (Ferrara, 1993), vol. I, p. 221.

14 Battista Guarino, *Sermone del cane e del cavallo*, ed. Gianluca Valenti (Rome, 2016), p. 5.

15 Malacarne, *Le cacce del principe*, pp. 24–48; Walker-Meikle, *Medieval Pets*, pp. 28–30, 34–7, 105–7; Cristina Arrigoni Martelli, 'Ducks and Deer, Profit and Pleasure: Hunters, Game and the Natural Landscapes of Medieval Italy', PhD thesis, York University, 2015, p. 110; Sarah Cockram, 'Sleeve Cat and Lap Dog: Affection, Aesthetics and Proximity to Companion Animals in Renaissance Mantua', in *Interspecies Interactions: Animals and Humans between the Middle Ages and Modernity*, ed. Sarah Cockram and Andrew Wells (London, 2017), pp. 34–65.

16 Cockram, 'Sleeve Cat and Lap Dog', pp. 49–51; Timothy McCall, 'Male Dress', in *Early Modern Court Culture*, ed. Erin Griffey (London, 2021), pp. 384–8.

17 Alessandro Cutolo, 'Nuovi documenti sull'esilio pisano di Ludovico il Moro e gli avvenimenti contemporanei (1477–79)', *Archivio storico lombardo*, new series, 1–2 (1939), p. 153; Lorenzo de' Medici, *Lettere*, vol. 11: *1474–1478*, ed. Riccardo Fubini (Florence, 1977), p. 262.

18 Francesca M. Vaglienti, 'Cacce e parchi ducali sul Ticino (1450–1476)', in *Vigevano e i territori circostanti alla fine del Medioevo*, ed. Giorgio Chittolini (Milan, 1997), p. 189; Arrigoni Martelli, 'Ducks and Deer', pp. 101–2.

19 Francesca M. Vaglienti, 'La detenzione del Conte Pietro dal Verme e la confisca del suo feudo ad opera di Galeazzo Maria Sforza, duca di Milano', *Nuova rivista storica*, LXXIV/3–4 (1990), p. 414.

20 Marcy Norton, 'Going to the Birds: Animals as Things and Beings in Early Modernity', in *Early Modern Things*, ed. Paula Findlen (London, 2012), pp. 54–8. Key, too, is Fudge, 'Renaissance Animal Things'.

21 Antonio Medin, 'Frammento di un cantare in morte di Galeazzo Maria Sforza', *Archivio storico lombardo*, 2nd series, 11/4 (1885), p. 803.

22 Elfriede R. Knauer, 'Fishing with Cormorants: A Note on Vittore Carpaccio's *Hunting on the Lagoon*', *Apollo*, CLVIII/499 (2003), pp. 32–9; Susannah Rutherglen, 'Painting at the Threshold: Pictures for Doors in Renaissance Venice', *Art Bulletin*, XCVIII/4 (2016), pp. 445–55; Peter Humfrey, *Vittore Carpaccio: Master Storyteller of Renaissance Venice* (Washington, DC, 2022), pp. 138–9.

23 Bourne, *Francesco II Gonzaga*, pp. 109, 128–33, 137–8, 389–90; Ali Smith, *How to Be Both* (London, 2015), pp. 49–50, 53.

24 Elena Past, 'Una ricetta per *longo e iocundo* vivere: *Il Libreto de tutte le cosse che se magnano*', in *Michele Savonarola: Medicina e cultura di corte*, ed. Chiara Crisciani and Gabriella Zuccolin (Florence, 2011), p. 123; Sarah Cockram, 'Interspecies Understanding: Exotic Animals and Their Handlers at the Italian Renaissance Court', *Renaissance Studies*, XXXI/2 (2017), pp. 277–96.

25 Malacarne, *Le cacce del principe*, pp. 40–41; Robin S. Oggins, *The Kings and Their Hawks: Falconry in Medieval England* (New Haven, CT, 2004), pp. 24–32, 85, 110; Stapleford, *Lorenzo de' Medici at Home*, p. 155.

26 Gregory Lubkin, *A Renaissance Court: Milan under Galeazzo Maria Sforza* (Berkeley, CA, 1994), pp. 91, 268–70; Malacarne, *Le cacce del principe*, pp. 62–83, 228–9.

27 Francesco Malaguzzi Valeri, *La corte di Lodovico il Moro* (Milan, 1913–23), vol. I, p. 724; Mario Tabanelli, *Sigismondo Pandolfo Malatesta, signore del Medioevo e del Rinascimento* (Faenza, 1977), p. 400; Bernardino Corio, *Storia di Milano*, ed. Anna Morisi Guerra (Turin, 1978), vol. II, p. 1409;

Franceschini, *Artisti a Ferrara*, vol. I, pp. 452, 562, 849; Tuohy, *Herculean Ferrara*, pp. 34, 245.

28 Dominique Cordellier and Paola Marini, eds, *Pisanello: Le peintre aux sept vertus* (Paris, 1996), pp. 255–63; Luke Syson and Dillian Gordon, *Pisanello: Painter to the Renaissance Court* (London, 2001), pp. 75–9.

29 Tuohy, *Herculean Ferrara*, p. 245; Maria Paola Zanoboni, *Artigiani, imprenditori, mercanti: Organizzazione del lavoro e conflitti sociali nella Milano sforzesca, 1450–1476* (Florence, 1996), p. 121; Malacarne, *Le cacce del principe*, pp. 80–81.

30 Lubkin, *A Renaissance Court*, p. 90; Tuohy, *Herculean Ferrara*, pp. 362–5; Malacarne, *Le cacce del principe*, p. 228; Marco Albertario, 'Documenti per la decorazione del Castello di Milano nell'età di Galeazzo Maria Sforza (1466–1476)', *Solchi*, VII/1–2 (2003), pp. 36–7.

31 Chiara Buss, ed., *Silk Gold Crimson: Secrets and Technology at the Visconti and Sforza Courts* (Cinisello Balsamo, 2009), p. 161; Jonathan J. G. Alexander, *The Painted Book in Renaissance Italy, 1450–1600* (New Haven, CT, 2016), pp. 117–18; Borgo, 'Leonardo's Hunts', p. 32.

32 Evelyn Welch, 'Between Italy and Moscow: Cultural Crossroads and the Culture of Exchange', in *Cultural Exchange in Early Modern Europe*, vol. IV: *Forging European Identities, 1400–1700*, ed. Herman Roodenburg (Cambridge, 2007), pp. 67, 76–7.

33 Pietro Ghinzoni, 'Rettifiche alla Storia di Bernardino Corio a proposito di Cristierno I Re di Danimarca', *Archivio storico lombardo*, 2nd series, VIII/1 (1891), pp. 60–71. For the loan, see Timothy McCall and Sean Roberts, 'Art and the Material Culture of Diplomacy', in *Italian Renaissance Diplomacy*, ed. Azzolini and Lazzarini, p. 231.

34 Pier Candido Decembrio, *Lives of the Milanese Tyrants*, trans. Gary Ianziti and ed. Massimo Zaggia (Cambridge, MA, 2019), pp. 116–19; Lubkin, *A Renaissance Court*, p. 235; Nicholas Webb, 'Giuniano Maio', in *Cambridge Translations of Renaissance Philosophical Texts*, vol. II: *Political Philosophy*, ed. Jill Kraye (Cambridge, 1997), p. 112.

35 Mario Borsa, *La caccia nel milanese: Dalle origini ai giorni nostri* (Milan, 1924), p. 209; Francesca M. Vaglienti, 'Le cacce ducali. Politica ambientale e tutela del territorio in età sforzesca', *Natura*, LXXXVII/2 (1996), pp. 70n24, 71n25; Sergio Giuntini, 'Sports under Visconti and Sforza Rule: Ball Games and Hunting for the Milanese Nobility', in *Artigianato e lusso: Manifatture preziose alle origini del Made in Italy*, ed. Maria Pia Bortolotti (Milan, 2013), pp. 182–3; Arrigoni Martelli, 'Ducks and Deer', p. 105.

36 Luigi Alberto Gandini, 'Viaggi, cavalli, bardature e stalle degli Estensi nel Quattrocento', *Atti e memorie della Regia Deputazione di storia patria per le provincie di Romagna*, X (1892), pp. 75–8; Giuseppe Pardi, *Leonello d'Este, marchese di Ferrara* (Bologna, 1904), pp. 85–6; Elizabeth Tobey, 'The *Palio* Horse in Renaissance and Early Modern Italy', in *The Culture of the Horse: Status, Discipline, and Identity in the Early Modern World*, ed. Karen Raber and Treva J. Tucker (New York, 2005), p. 70; Evan A. MacCarthy, 'The English Voyage of Pietrobono Burzelli', *Journal of Musicology*, XXXV/4 (2018), pp. 443–8.

37 Oscar Scalvanti, 'Cronaca perugina inedita di Pietro Angelo di Giovanni (già detta del Graziani), Parte II – (Anni 1461–1494)', *Bollettino della Regia Deputazione di storia patria per l'Umbria*, IX (1903), p. 73; Silvia Bianchessi,

'Cavalli, armi e salnitro fra Milano e Napoli nel secondo Quattrocento (1466–1492)', *Nuova rivista storica*, LXXXII/3 (1998), pp. 543–60.

38 Corio, *Storia di Milano*, vol. II, pp. 1380–81; Lubkin, *A Renaissance Court*, pp. 98–100; Nerida Newbigin, ed., '*Le onoranze fiorentine del 1459*. Poema anonimo', *Letteratura italiana antica*, XII (2011), p. 64.

39 Stapleford, *Lorenzo de' Medici at Home*, p. 69.

40 Foucard, *Relazioni dei duchi*, pp. 4, 16–18; Gandini, 'Viaggi, cavalli, bardature e stalle', pp. 47–52; Scalvanti, 'Cronaca perugina', p. 73; Giuseppe Pardi, ed., *Diario ferrarese dall'anno 1409 sino al 1502* (Bologna, 1928–33), pp. 66–7; Franceschini, *Artisti a Ferrara*, vol. I, pp. 639–40, 791–2; Tuohy, *Herculean Ferrara*, p. 161.

41 Leon Battista Alberti, *De equo animante*, trans. Antonio Videtta (Naples, 1991); Anthony Grafton, *Leon Battista Alberti: Master Builder of the Italian Renaissance* (Cambridge, MA, 2002), pp. 189–91.

42 Guglielmo Cavallo, ed., *I luoghi della memoria scritta: Manoscritti, incunaboli, libri a stampa di biblioteche statali italiane* (Rome, 1994), p. 249; Alessandra Coco and Riccardo Gualdo, 'Cortesia e cavalleria. La tradizione ippiatrica in volgare nelle corti italiane tra Trecento e Quattrocento', *Micrologus*, XVI (2008), pp. 13–65; Guarino, *Sermone del cane*; MacCarthy, 'The English Voyage', p. 444n42.

43 Alison Brown, 'The Early Years of Piero di Lorenzo, 1472–1492: Between Florentine Citizen and Medici Prince', in *Communes and Despots in Medieval and Renaissance Italy*, ed. John E. Law and Bernadette Paton (Farnham, 2010), p. 215.

44 Adolfo Maspes, 'Prammatica pel ricevimento degli ambasciatori inviati alla corte di Galeazzo Maria Sforza, duca di Milano (1468–10 dicembre)', *Archivio storico lombardo*, 2nd series, VII/1 (1890), pp. 148–9; Gandini, 'Viaggi, cavalli, bardature e stalle', pp. 63–6, 80–81; Lubkin, *A Renaissance Court*, pp. 22, 36, 130.

45 Tobey, 'The *Palio* Horse'; Elizabeth Tobey, 'The *Palio* Banner and the Visual Culture of Horse Racing in Renaissance Italy', *International Journal of the History of Sport*, XXVIII/8–9 (2011), pp. 1269–82; Timothy McCall, *Brilliant Bodies: Fashioning Courtly Men in Early Renaissance Italy* (University Park, PA, 2022), pp. 44, 163.

46 Gandini, 'Viaggi, cavalli, bardature e stalle', pp. 69–73; Pardi, ed., *Diario ferrarese dall'anno 1409*, p. 52; Franceschini, *Artisti a Ferrara*, vol. I, pp. 559–60, 580, 630, 637, 640, 659 and vol. II, pt I, p. 322.

47 Gandini, 'Viaggi, cavalli, bardature e stalle', p. 82; Isabella d'Este, *Selected Letters*, ed. and trans. Deanna Shemek (Toronto, 2017), p. 92; Carolyn James, *A Renaissance Marriage: The Political and Personal Alliance of Isabella d'Este and Francesco Gonzaga, 1490–1519* (Oxford, 2020), p. 59.

48 Tobey, 'The *Palio* Horse', pp. 65–6; Claudio Paolini, Daniela Parenti and Ludovica Sebregondi, eds, *Virtù d'amore: Pittura nuziale nel Quattrocento fiorentino* (Florence, 2010), pp. 258–61.

49 Alfonso Lazzari, 'Il "Barco" di Lodovico Carbone', *Atti e memorie della Deputazione ferrarese di storia patria*, XXIV (1919), pp. 11, 37; Tuohy, *Herculean Ferrara*, pp. 241–4; Christian Jaser, 'Beyond Siena: The Palio Culture of Renaissance Italy', *Ludica*, XXIII (2017), p. 26; James, *A Renaissance Marriage*, p. 24.

50 Marcello Toffanello, *Le arti a Ferrara nel Quattrocento: Gli artisti e la corte* (Ferrara, 2010), pp. 47–8, 63, 192–6, 199, 204, 211–15, 228, 280–83, 287–8.

51 Gandini, 'Viaggi, cavalli, bardature e stalle', p. 74n1.

52 Deanna Shemek, 'Circular Definitions: Configuring Gender in Italian Renaissance Festival', *Renaissance Quarterly*, XLVIII/1 (1995), pp. 8–9, 20.

53 Jaser, 'Beyond Siena', p. 28; Saletti, 'Imitation Games', p. 79.

54 Pardi, ed., *Diario ferrarese dall'anno 1409*, p. 67; Bernardino Zambotti, *Diario ferrarese dall'anno 1476 sino al 1504*, ed. Giuseppe Pardi (Bologna, 1934–7), pp. 64–5.

55 Jaser, 'Beyond Siena', pp. 27–9.

56 Tuohy, *Herculean Ferrara*, p. 241n38; Andrea Tonni, 'The Renaissance Studs of the Gonzagas of Mantua', in *The Horse as Cultural Icon: The Real and the Symbolic Horse in the Early Modern World*, ed. Peter Edwards, Karl A. E. Enenkel and Elspeth Graham (Leiden, 2012), pp. 263–6.

57 Alessandro Luzio and Rodolfo Renier, *Mantova e Urbino: Isabella d'Este ed Elisabetta Gonzaga nelle relazioni famigliari e nelle vicende politiche* (Turin, 1893), pp. 30–31n2; Giancarlo Malacarne, *Il mito dei cavalli gonzagheschi: Alle origini del purosangue* (Verona, 1995); Tobey, 'The *Palio* Horse', pp. 73–80; Bourne, *Francesco II Gonzaga*, p. 52.

58 Bourne, *Francesco II Gonzaga*, pp. 112–14, 147, 336, 496, 529, 537–40; Armelle Fémelat, 'Rubino, El Serpentino, Viola, and the Others: Renaissance Portraits of Dogs and Horses at the Court of the Gonzagas', in *Animals and Courts: Europe, c. 1200–1800*, ed. Mark Hengerer and Nadir Weber (Berlin, 2020), pp. 195–203.

59 Malacarne, *Le cacce del principe*, pp. 42, 50–51; For outfitting Sforza *canateri*: Giulio Porro Lambertenghi, 'Lettere di Galeazzo Maria Sforza, duca di Milano', *Archivio storico lombardo*, V (1878), pp. 255, 259, 271, 642, 662.

60 Webb, 'Giuniano Maio', pp. 111–12.

61 Pius II, *Commentaries*, ed. Margaret Meserve and Marcello Simonetta (Cambridge, MA, 2003–7), vol. II, pp. 76–7; Ken Mondschein, *The Knightly Art of Battle* (Los Angeles, CA, 2011), p. 30; Anthony F. D'Elia, *Pagan Virtue in a Christian World: Sigismondo Malatesta and the Italian Renaissance* (Cambridge, MA, 2016), p. 65.

62 Carlo Magenta, *I Visconti e gli Sforza nel castello di Pavia e loro attinenze con la Certosa e la storia cittadina* (Milan, 1883), vol. II, p. 252.

63 Carlo Morbio, *Codice visconteo-sforzesco, ossia raccolta di leggi, decreti e lettere famigliari dei duchi di Milano* (Milan, 1846), p. 454; Malaguzzi Valeri, *La corte di Lodovico*, vol. I, pp. 720–23; Lubkin, *A Renaissance Court*, p. 90; Vaglienti, 'Le cacce ducali'; Arrigoni Martelli, 'Ducks and Deer', pp. 115–17.

64 Borsa, *La caccia nel milanese*, pp. 98–9, 112–14, 128–9; Lubkin, *A Renaissance Court*, p. 235; Vaglienti, 'Cacce e parchi ducali', pp. 187, 190–94, 203–7; Arrigoni Martelli, 'Ducks and Deer', pp. 87–102.

65 Giulio Porro Lambertenghi, 'Preventivo delle spese pel ducato di Milano del 1476', *Archivio storico lombardo*, V (1878), p. 134; Luca Beltrami, *Il castello di Milano (Castrum Portae Jovis), sotto il dominio dei Visconti e degli Sforza* (Milan, 1894), pp. 687–90.

66 Lazzari, 'Il "Barco" di Lodovico Carbone'; Pardi, ed., *Diario ferrarese dall'anno 1409*, pp. 75, 81; Guido Antonioli, 'La caccia nel pensiero degli

umanisti della corte estense (xv secolo)', *F. D. Bollettino della 'Ferrariae Decus'*, xx (2003), p. 42.

67 Franceschini, *Artisti a Ferrara*, vol. ii, pt i, pp. 109, 625; Keith Christiansen and Stefan Weppelmann, eds, *The Renaissance Portrait from Donatello to Bellini* (New York, 2011), pp. 221–3; Marco Scansani, 'L'attività scultorea di Sperandio Savelli: Marmi, terrecotte e committenze francescane', *Studi di Memofonte*, xxiii (2019), pp. 55–7.

68 Luchino dal Conte, 'Viaggio a Gerusalemme di Nicolò da Este', ed. Giovanni Ghinassi, in *Miscellanea di opuscoli inediti o rari dei secoli xiv e xv* (Turin, 1861), p. 141; Borsa, *La caccia nel milanese*, pp. 124–6; Caterina Santoro, *Milano d'altri tempi* (Milan, 1938), p. 79; Decembrio, *Lives of the Milanese Tyrants*, p. 111; Tuohy, *Herculean Ferrara*, pp. 245–6; Malacarne, *Le cacce del principe*, pp. 174–7; Marco Masseti, 'Pictorial Evidence from Medieval Italy of Cheetahs and Caracals, and Their Use in Hunting', *Archives of Natural History*, xxxvi/1 (2009), pp. 37–47; Cockram, 'Interspecies Understanding', p. 283; Thierry Buquet, 'Hunting with Cheetahs at European Courts: From the Origins to the End of a Fashion', in *Animals and Courts*, ed. Hengerer and Weber, p. 29.

69 Emilio Motta, 'Il primo elefante in Milano?', *Bollettino storico della Svizzera italiana*, x/5–6 (1888), p. 106; Joan Barclay Lloyd, *African Animals in Renaissance Literature and Art* (Oxford, 1971), pp. 46, 60–62, 119–20; Werner L. Gundersheimer, *Art and Life at the Court of Ercole i d'Este: The 'De triumphis religionis' of Giovanni Sabadino degli Arienti* (Geneva, 1972), p. 69; Welch, 'Secular Fresco Painting', pp. 24, 31, 33, 119, 249, 254, 267, 339; Tuohy, *Herculean Ferrara*, pp. 34, 162, 245; Vaglienti, 'Le cacce ducali', p. 71n30; Masseti, 'Pictorial Evidence', pp. 37–9; Arrigoni Martelli, 'Ducks and Deer', pp. 110–11.

70 Lloyd, *African Animals*, p. 62; Warren Tressider, 'The Cheetahs in Titian's "Bacchus and Ariadne"', *Burlington Magazine*, cxxiii/941 (1981), pp. 481–5; Tuohy, *Herculean Ferrara*, pp. 34, 246; Cockram, 'Interspecies Understanding', pp. 284, 289–91; Buquet, 'Hunting with Cheetahs', p. 33.

71 Alan Ryder, *Alfonso the Magnanimous: King of Aragon, Naples and Sicily, 1396–1458* (Oxford, 1990), p. 350; Borgo, 'Leonardo's Hunts', p. 38.

72 Lloyd, *African Animals*, pp. 40–41; Lucia Ricciardi, *'Col senno, col tesoro e colla lancia': Riti e giochi cavallereschi nella Firenze del Magnifico Lorenzo* (Florence, 1992), pp. 116–22; Adrian W. B. Randolph, 'Il Marzocco: Lionizing the Florentine State', in *Coming About . . . A Festschrift for John Shearman*, ed. Lars R. Jones and Louisa C. Matthew (Cambridge, ma, 2001), pp. 11–18.

73 Emilio Motta, 'Una leonessa domestica in Venezia nel 1474', *Bollettino storico della Svizzera italiana*, vi/5 (1884), pp. 78–9; Cockram, 'Interspecies Understanding', pp. 277–81.

74 Pardi, ed., *Diario ferrarese dall'anno 1409*, p. 39; Cockram, 'Interspecies Understanding', p. 287.

75 Marco Parenti, *Lettere*, ed. Maria Marrese (Florence, 1996), p. 84; Newbigin, ed., *'Le onoranze fiorentine'*, pp. 104–5.

76 Newbigin, ed., *'Le onoranze fiorentine'*, pp. 104–6. See too Ricciardi, *'Col senno'*, pp. 148–51.

77 Foucard, *Relazioni dei duchi*, p. 8; Motta, 'Il primo elefante', p. 105; Borsa, *La caccia nel milanese*, pp. 167–8.

78 For example, Baldassare Castiglione, *Il libro del Cortegiano*, ed. Giulio Preti (Turin, 1965), p. 39; Bartolomeo Platina, *Bartholomaei Platinae De principe*, ed. Giacomo Ferraù (Palermo, 1979), p. 156; Guarino, *Sermone del cane*, pp. 4–5.

79 Welch, 'Secular Fresco Painting', pp. 61, 277; Evelyn Welch, 'Galeazzo Maria Sforza and the Castello di Pavia, 1469', *Art Bulletin*, LXXI/3 (1989), pp. 353, 360–61, 373; Evelyn Welch, 'The Image of a Fifteenth-Century Court: Secular Frescoes for the Castello di Porta Giovia, Milan', *Journal of the Warburg and Courtauld Institutes*, LIII (1990), pp. 171–4, 181–3; Lubkin, *A Renaissance Court*, pp. 83–4, 106–7; Borgo, 'Leonardo's Hunts', pp. 34–6.

80 Rachele Magnani, *Relazioni private tra la corte sforzesca di Milano e casa Medici, 1450–1500* (Milan, 1910), pp. 8, iv; Michael Mallett, 'Horse-Racing and Politics in Lorenzo's Florence', in *Lorenzo the Magnificent: Culture and Politics*, ed. Michael Mallett and Nicholas Mann (London, 1996), p. 257.

81 Magnani, *Relazioni private*, pp. 62–3, xliii; Edoardo Fumagalli, 'Nuovi documenti su Lorenzo e Giuliano de' Medici', *Italia medioevale e umanistica*, XXIII (1980), pp. 147–53, 161–2.

82 Magnani, *Relazioni private*, pp. 67, xli; Borsa, *La caccia nel milanese*, p. 177; Cicco Simonetta, *I diari di Cicco Simonetta*, ed. Alfio Rosario Natale (Milan, 1962), pp. 146, 155, 211–12; Arrigoni Martelli, 'Ducks and Deer', pp. 81, IIIn129.

83 Giuseppe Campori, 'Una visita del marchese di Mantova al duca Borso in Sassuolo', *Atti e memorie delle Regie Deputazioni di storia patria per le provincie dell'Emilia*, VI/1 (1881), pp. 119–25; Maria Nadia Covini, *Donne, emozioni e potere alla corte degli Sforza: Da Bianca Maria a Cecilia Gallerani* (Milan, 2012), p. 85.

84 Malaguzzi Valeri, *La corte di Lodovico*, vol. I, p. 556.

85 Magnani, *Relazioni private*, p. 89; Borsa, *La caccia nel milanese*, pp. 205–6.

86 Guido Rebecchini, *'Un altro Lorenzo': Ippolito de' Medici tra Firenze e Roma (1511–1535)* (Venice, 2010), p. 36.

87 Vasari, *Vite de' più eccellenti*, vol. VI, p. 273; Carl Brandon Strehlke, *Pontormo, Bronzino, and the Medici: The Transformation of the Renaissance Portrait in Florence* (University Park, PA, 2004), pp. 80–81; Rebecchini, *'Un altro Lorenzo'*, p. 38.

88 Welch, 'Secular Fresco Painting', pp. 20, 260; Monica Ferrari, *'Per non manchare in tuto del debito mio.' L'educazione dei bambini Sforza nel Quattrocento* (Milan, 2000), pp. 115–16, 183; Monica Ferrari, 'Stralci di corrispondenza famigliare nella seconda metà del Quattrocento: Il caso dei Gonzaga e degli Sforza', in *I bambini di una volta: Problemi di metodo; Studi per Egle Becchi*, ed. Monica Ferrari (Milan, 2006), pp. 31–2.

89 Ferrari, *'Per non manchare'*, p. 92; Ippolita Maria Sforza, *Duchess and Hostage in Renaissance Naples: Letters and Orations*, ed. and trans. Diana Robin and Lynn Lara Westwater (Toronto, 2017), pp. 16, 63–6.

90 Alessandro Giulini, 'Polidoro Sforza', *Archivio storico lombardo*, 5th series, I/1–2 (1914), pp. 257–71; Malacarne, *Le cacce del principe*, p. 35; Ferrari, 'Stralci di corrispondenza', pp. 39–40.

91 Ulinka Rublack and Maria Hayward, eds, *The First Book of Fashion: The Book of Clothes of Matthäus and Veit Konrad Schwarz of Augsburg* (London, 2015), pp. 57, 230–31; Pierre Terjanian, ed., *The Last Knight: The Art, Armor, and Ambition of Maximilian I* (New York, 2019), pp. 156–7; Fabian Brenker,

Turniere und Lanzenspiele in Bildern aus dem Mittelalter und der frühen Neuzeit: Orte, Auftraggeber und soziale Funktionen (Petersberg, 2021).

92 d'Este, *Selected Letters*, p. 213; James, *A Renaissance Marriage*, pp. 121–5.

93 Adriano Cappelli, 'Guiniforte Barzizza, maestro di Galeazzo Maria Sforza', *Archivio storico lombardo*, 3rd series, i/2 (1894), p. 410; Evelyn Welch, 'Sight, Sound and Ceremony in the Chapel of Galeazzo Maria Sforza', *Early Music History*, xii (1993), pp. 158–9; Ferrari, 'Lettere di principi bambini', p. 348; Ferrari, *'Per non manchare'*, pp. 110–13; *Carteggio degli oratori mantovani alla corte sforzesca (1450–1500)*, vol. v: *1463*, ed. Marco Folin (Rome, 2003), p. 286.

94 Welch, 'Secular Fresco Painting', pp. 29, 271; Carolina Manfredini, '"Vederò de asuefarme ad questo mestere al meglio poterò et credo havere honore del impresa": La spedizione milanese in Francia attraverso gli occhi (e gli scritti) del comandante Galeazzo Maria Sforza (1465–1466)', *Annuario dell'Archivio di Stato di Milano* (2018), p. 20.

95 Corio, *Storia di Milano*, vol. ii, p. 1399.

96 Ferrari, *'Per non manchare'*, pp. 248–9.

97 Monica Ferrari, *Lo specchio, la pagina, le cose: Congegni pedagogici tra ieri e oggi* (Milan, 2011), p. 143n92.

3 Courtly Mistresses: Representation and Power

1 Rebecca Zorach, *Blood, Milk, Ink, Gold: Abundance and Excess in the French Renaissance* (Chicago, il, 2005); Ulrich Pfisterer, 'Die Erotik der Macht: Visualisierte Herrscher-Potenz in der Renaissance', in *Menschennatur und politische Ordnung*, ed. Andreas Höfele and Beate Kellner (Paderborn, 2016), pp. 177–201; John Gagné, 'Collecting Women: Three French Kings and Manuscripts of Empire in the Italian Wars', *I Tatti Studies in the Italian Renaissance*, xx/1 (2017), pp. 127–84.

2 Helen S. Ettlinger, 'Visibilis et Invisibilis: The Mistress in Italian Renaissance Court Society', *Renaissance Quarterly*, xlvii/4 (1994), pp. 770–92; Timothy McCall, 'Traffic in Mistresses: Sexualized Bodies and Systems of Exchange in the Early Modern Court', in *Sex Acts in Early Modern Italy: Practice, Performance, Perversion, Punishment*, ed. Allison Levy (Farnham, 2010), pp. 125–36.

3 Chad Coerver, '*Donna/Dono*: Chivalry and Adulterous Exchange in the Quattrocento', in *Picturing Women in Renaissance and Baroque Italy*, ed. Geraldine A. Johnson and Sara F. Matthews Grieco (Cambridge, 1997), p. 200.

4 Carlo de' Rosmini, *Dell'istoria di Milano* (Milan, 1820), vol. iv, pp. 108, 121–5; Gregory Lubkin, *A Renaissance Court: Milan under Galeazzo Maria Sforza* (Berkeley, ca, 1994), p. 199.

5 Maria Nadia Covini, 'Il palazzo milanese di Elisabetta da Robecco, ultima amante di Francesco Sforza', *Nuova rivista storica*, lxxxviii/3 (2004), pp. 802–3, 808–10.

6 Jane Black, *Absolutism in Renaissance Milan: Plenitude of Power under the Visconti and the Sforza, 1329–1535* (Oxford, 2009), pp. 145–6.

7 Ettlinger, 'Visibilis et Invisibilis', p. 786.

8 E. Jane Burns, 'Courtly Love: Who Needs It? Recent Feminist Work in the Medieval French Tradition', *Signs*, xxvii/1 (2001), pp. 25, 35; James A.

Schultz, *Courtly Love, the Love of Courtliness, and the History of Sexuality* (Chicago, IL, 2006), pp. 38–9, 167. See too McCall, 'Traffic in Mistresses'; Pfisterer, 'Die Erotik der Macht'.

9 Andreas Capellanus, *The Art of Courtly Love*, trans. John Jay Parry (New York, 1986), pp. 91–107, 150, 161.

10 Paolo Giovio, *Elogi degli uomini illustri*, ed. Franco Minonzio, trans. Andrea Guasparri and Franco Minonzio (Turin, 2006), p. 645.

11 Alexis-François Rio, *Leonardo da Vinci e la sua scuola* (Milan, 1856), p. 43; Luigi Napoleone Cittadella, *Notizie amministrative, storiche, artistiche relative a Ferrara* (Ferrara, 1868), vol. I, p. 290; Alessandro Luzio and Rodolfo Renier, *Delle relazioni di Isabella d'Este Gonzaga con Ludovico e Beatrice Sforza* (Milan, 1890), p. 129; James Beck, 'The Dream of Leonardo da Vinci', *Artibus et Historiae*, XIV/27 (1993), p. 191.

12 Adriano Franceschini, *Artisti a Ferrara in età umanistica e rinascimentale: Testimonianze archivistiche* (Ferrara, 1993), vol. II, pt I, pp. 20, 188, 198–9; Joseph Manca, *Cosmè Tura: The Life and Art of a Painter in Estense Ferrara* (Oxford, 2000), pp. 212, 223.

13 Coerver, '*Donna/Dono*'; Giuseppa Z. Zanichelli, 'La committenza dei Rossi: Immagini di potere fra sacro e profano', in *Le signorie dei Rossi di Parma tra XIV e XVI secolo*, ed. Letizia Arcangeli and Marco Gentile (Florence, 2007), pp. 187–212; Timothy McCall, 'Secrecy and the Production of Seignorial Space: The *Coretto* of Torrechiara', in *Visual Cultures of Secrecy in Early Modern Europe*, ed. Timothy McCall, Sean Roberts and Giancarlo Fiorenza (Kirksville, MO, 2013), pp. 76–104.

14 Timothy McCall, 'Visual Imagery and Historical Invisibility: Antonia Torelli, Her Husband, and His Mistress in Fifteenth-Century Parma', *Renaissance Studies*, XXIII/3 (2009), pp. 273, 278.

15 Gerardo Rustici, *Cantilena pro potenti D. Petro Maria Rubeo Berceti comite magnifico et Noceti domino*, Parma, Biblioteca Palatina, MS Parm. 1992, fol. 9v–10r: 'il bel signore/ A cui e familiare la damisela . . . le quatre pelegrine poste al tecto'; Jacopo Caviceo, *Maximo humanae imbecilitatis simulachro fortunae bifronti vita Petrimariae de Rubeis viri illustris* (Venice, *c.* 1490), fol. 4r–4v: 'Mulieri Metropolitanae quam summopere deperibat aliud condidit Castellum, quod mulieris nomine Rochamblancham appellavit'.

16 Zanichelli, 'La committenza dei Rossi', pp. 201–10.

17 George Hill, *A Corpus of Italian Medals of the Renaissance before Cellini* (London, 1930), nos 280, 282, 289, 297.

18 Ibid., nos 282, 297.

19 Bella Mirabella, 'Embellishing Herself with a Cloth: The Contradictory Life of the Handkerchief', in *Ornamentalism: The Art of Renaissance Accessories*, ed. Bella Mirabella (Ann Arbor, MI, 2011), pp. 59–82. For noble, radiant beauty, see Timothy McCall, *Brilliant Bodies: Fashioning Courtly Men in Early Renaissance Italy* (University Park, PA, 2022), pp. 119–49.

20 Rustici, *Cantilena*, fol. 10r.

21 In Francesco Sforza's investiture of 1449, the jurisdiction was 'Arzenoldo'; Galeazzo Maria Sforza's investiture of 1470 referred to 'Rochablancha': Archivio di Stato di Parma (hereafter, ASPr), Archivio delle Famiglie, Rossi, 8 October 1400–3 March 1469 and 20 March 1470–1499.

22 Caviceo, *Petrimariae de Rubeis*, fol. 4r–4v; ASPr, Feudi e Comunità, Roccabianca, 186, Processo de testimonii essaminate sopra l'edificatione di Roccabianca, fol. 52r; Angelo Pezzana, *Storia della città di Parma* (Parma, 1837–59), vol. II, p. 173 and vol. IV, pp. 218–19; Augusto Campana, 'Atti, Isotta degli', in *Dizionario biografico degli Italiani* (Rome, 1961), vol. IV, p. 548.

23 Michael Camille, *The Medieval Art of Love: Objects and Subjects of Desire* (New York, 1998), pp. 94–104; Diane Wolfthal, *In and Out of the Marital Bed: Seeing Sex in Renaissance Europe* (New Haven, CT, 2010), pp. 166–85. See, now, Oliver Grimm, ed., *Raptor on the Fist: Falconry, Its Imagery and Similar Motifs throughout the Millennia on a Global Scale*, II vols (Kiel, 2020).

24 Gasparo Visconti, *I canzonieri per Beatrice d'Este e per Bianca Maria Sforza*, ed. Paolo Bongrani (Milan, 1979), pp. 20–21; Giancarlo Malacarne, *Le cacce del principe: L'ars venandi nella terra dei Gonzaga* (Modena, 1998), pp. 73–4.

25 Luke Syson and Dora Thornton, *Objects of Virtue: Art in Renaissance Italy* (London, 2001), p. 22.

26 Gabriele D'Annunzio, *Francesca da Rimini* (Milan, 1904), pp. 199–200; Matteo Bandello, *Tutte le opere di Matteo Bandello*, ed. Francesco Flora, 4th edn (Milan, 1966), vol. I, pp. 34–6; Daniel Devoto, *Textos y contextos: Estudios sobre la tradición* (Madrid, 1974), pp. 138–49; *Il Novellino*, ed. Alberto Conte (Rome, 2001), p. 148.

27 Vincenzo Carrari, *Historia de' Rossi parmigiani* (Ravenna, 1583), p. 134; Pezzana, *Storia*, vol. II, pp. 152–3; Luchino dal Conte, 'Viaggio a Gerusalemme di Nicolò da Este', ed. Giovanni Ghinassi, in *Miscellanea di opuscoli inediti o rari dei secoli XIV e XV* (Turin, 1861), pp. 99–160; Giuseppe Pardi, ed., *Diario ferrarese dall'anno 1409 sino al 1502* (Bologna, 1928–33), p. 13.

28 Marco Gentile, 'Un itinerario devozionale e i suoi orizzonti politici: Pietro Rossi pellegrino a Compostella', *Compostella*, XXVI (1999), pp. 5–13. For lords' parcelled-out body parts: Giovanni Ricci, *Il principe e la morte: Corpo, cuore, effigie nel Rinascimento* (Bologna, 1998), pp. 87–108.

29 Archivio di Stato di Milano, Archivio Sforzesco Ducale, Carteggio (Sforzesco), 835, 25 May 1471; Bonaventura Angeli, *La historia della città di Parma et la descrittione del fiume Parma* (Parma, 1591), p. 342; Vigenio Soncini, *La chiesa di S. Sepolcro in Parma. I suoi canonici regolari e i suoi cavalieri* (Parma, 1932), p. 155.

30 Francesco Sansovino, *Della origine et de' fatti delle famiglie illustri d'Italia* (Venice, 1582), fol. 76r; Silvana Tassetto, 'Gli emblemi del *Messale-Libro d'Ore* Lat. 757 della Bibliothèque Nationale di Parigi', *Arte lombarda*, CXXIII (1998), pp. 10–18.

31 'Aurea quem vestis redimebat tempora vitae/ Nunc Rubeum Petrum aspera petra tegit'. See, further, Angeli, *La historia della città di Parma*, pp. 239–40; Carrari, *Historia de' Rossi*, p. 138; McCall, *Brilliant Bodies*, p. 79.

32 Pezzana, *Storia*, vol. III, p. 324 and vol. IV, pp. 15–18; Marco Gentile, *Fazioni al governo. Politica e società a Parma nel Quattrocento* (Rome, 2009), pp. 46–54, 266; Timothy McCall, 'Pier Maria's Legacy: (Il)legitimacy, Inheritance, and Rule of Parma's Rossi Dynasty', in *Wives, Widows, Mistresses, and Nuns in Early Modern Italy: Making the Invisible Visible through Art and Patronage*, ed. Katherine A. McIver (Farnham, 2012), p. 35.

33 Jacopo Caviceo, *Il Peregrino*, ed. Luigi Vignali (Rome, 1993), p. 283.

34 David Chambers, 'Francesco "Cardinalino" (*c.* 1477–1511): The Son of Cardinal Francesco Gonzaga', *Atti e memorie della Accademia Virgiliana di Mantova*, XLVIII (1980), pp. 16–24; Marco Pellegri, *Un feudatario sotto l'insegna del leone rampante: Pier Maria Rossi, 1413–1482* (Parma, 1996), p. 75.

35 Giuseppe Bruscalupi, *Monografia storica della contea di Pitigliano* (Florence, 1906), pp. 252–5; Giancarlo Malacarne, 'L'adulterio nei documenti d'archivio. Un canovaccio millenario denso di suggestioni', in *Il più soave et dolce et dilectevole et gratioso bochone: Amore e sesso al tempo dei Gonzaga*, ed. Costantino Cipolla and Giancarlo Malacarne (Milan, 2006), pp. 229–44; Maria Nadia Covini, *Donne, emozioni e potere alla corte degli Sforza: Da Bianca Maria a Cecilia Gallerani* (Milan, 2012), pp. 12, 90; Christine Shaw, *Barons and Castellans: The Military Nobility of Renaissance Italy* (Leiden, 2015), pp. 69–71; Gary Ianziti, 'The Life of the Last Visconti: A Study in Tyranny?', *Renaissance Quarterly*, LXXV/3 (2022), pp. 767–70.

36 Campana, 'Atti, Isotta degli', p. 550; Trevor Dean, *Crime and Justice in Late Medieval Italy* (Cambridge, 2007), pp. 68–9.

37 Winifred Terni de Gregory, *Bianca Maria Visconti, duchessa di Milano* (Bergamo, 1940), p. 166.

38 Luigi Fumi, 'L'atteggiamento di Francesco Sforza verso Sigismondo Malatesta in una sua istruzione del 1462, con particolari sulla morte violenta della figlia Polissena', *Archivio storico lombardo*, 4th series, XIX/37 (1913), pp. 158–69; Anthony F. D'Elia, *Pagan Virtue in a Christian World: Sigismondo Malatesta and the Italian Renaissance* (Cambridge, MA, 2016), pp. 18, 188–9.

39 Bernardino Corio, *Storia di Milano*, ed. Anna Morisi Guerra (Turin, 1978), vol. II, p. 1408; Franca Leverotti, *'Governare a modo e stillo de' Signori … Osservazioni in margine all'amministrazione della giustizia al tempo di Galeazzo Maria Sforza duca di Milano (1466–76)* (Florence, 1994), p. 132.

40 Adolfo Venturi, 'L'arte ferrarese nel periodo di Ercole I d'Este, II', *Atti e memorie della Regia Deputazione di storia patria per le provincie di Romagna*, VI/4–6 (1888), pp. 381–2; Stefania Buganza, 'Intorno a Baldassarre d'Este e al suo soggiorno lombardo', *Solchi*, IX/1–3 (2007), pp. 62–3.

41 Isabella d'Este, *Selected Letters*, ed. and trans. Deanna Shemek (Toronto, 2017), p. 132.

42 Terni de Gregory, *Bianca Maria Visconti*, p. 169. Elisabetta's and Bianca's great grandfathers, respectively Galeazzo II and Bernabò Visconti, were brothers.

43 Alfonso Lazzari, *Parisina* (Florence, 1949), pp. 5–19. See also Lord Byron, *The Siege of Corinth, a Poem; Parisina, a Poem* (New York, 1816); Gabriele D'Annunzio and Pietro Mascagni, *Parisina: Tragedia lirica* (Milan, 1913); Bandello, *Tutte le opere*, vol. I, pp. 516–24.

44 Jane Fair Bestor, 'Marriage and Succession in the House of Este: A Literary Perspective', in *Phaethon's Children: The Este Court and Its Culture in Early Modern Ferrara*, ed. Dennis Looney and Deanna Shemek (Tempe, AZ, 2005), pp. 55–63; Mirna Bonazza, 'Stella de' Tolomei celebrata in un manoscritto raro conservato alla Biblioteca Ariostea', *Anecdota*, VI/1 (1996), pp. 71–8.

45 Matteo Griffoni, *Memoriale historicum de rebus bononiensium*, ed. Lodovico Frati and Albano Sorbelli (Città di Castello, 1902), p. 109; Pardi, ed., *Diario ferrarese dall'anno 1409*, p. 17; Lazzari, *Parisina*, pp. 70, 73; Franceschini, *Artisti a Ferrara*, vol. I, p. 119.

46 Franca Leverotti, 'Lucia Marliani e la sua famiglia: Il potere di una donna amata', in *Donne di potere nel Rinascimento*, ed. Letizia Arcangeli and Susanna Peyronel (Rome, 2008), p. 282. See also Lubkin, *A Renaissance Court*, pp. 196–9, 221.

47 Vincent Ilardi, 'Towards the Tragedia d'Italia: Ferrante and Galeazzo Maria Sforza, Friendly Enemies and Hostile Allies', in *The French Descent into Renaissance Italy, 1494–95: Antecedents and Effects*, ed. David Abulafia (Aldershot, 1995), p. 112; Covini, 'Il palazzo milanese', pp. 805–6.

48 Bortolo Belotti, *Storia di una congiura* (Milan, 1950), pp. 63–4, 76; McCall, *Brilliant Bodies*, pp. 27, 52.

49 Luigi Rossi, 'Di un delitto di Sigismondo Malatesta, signore di Rimini', *Rivista di scienze storiche*, VII (1910), pp. 362–82; Lauro Martines, *April Blood: Florence and the Plot against the Medici* (Oxford, 2003), p. 12; D'Elia, *Pagan Virtue*, p. 188.

50 Covini, 'Il palazzo milanese', pp. 803–7; Marcello Simonetta, *Rinascimento segreto: Il mondo del segretario da Petrarca a Machiavelli* (Milan, 2004), p. 112. For Francesco's illegitimate children, see Monica Ferrari, *'Per non manchare in tuto del debito mio.' L'educazione dei bambini Sforza nel Quattrocento* (Milan, 2000), pp. 244–6.

51 Corio, *Storia di Milano*, vol. II, pp. 1408–9; Lubkin, *A Renaissance Court*, pp. 201–2; Ferrari, *'Per non manchare'*, pp. 248–9; Simonetta, *Rinascimento segreto*, p. 119; Monica Azzolini, *The Duke and the Stars: Astrology and Politics in Renaissance Milan* (Cambridge, MA, 2013), pp. 100–101; McCall, *Brilliant Bodies*, p. 1.

52 Leverotti, 'Lucia Marliani', pp. 282–4. Additionally, see Giulio Porro Lambertenghi, 'Lettere di Galeazzo Maria Sforza, duca di Milano', *Archivio storico lombardo*, V (1878), pp. 109, 123–4, 261, 263, 267–8, 639, 651–3, 660; Timothy McCall, 'Galeazzo's Gem and *Ghellero* in the Uffizi Portrait by Piero Pollaiuolo', *Source: Notes in the History of Art*, XXXIX/3 (2020), pp. 154–8; McCall, *Brilliant Bodies*, pp. 39, 51.

53 de' Rosmini, *Dell'istoria di Milano*, vol. IV, pp. 109, 112, 120; Lubkin, *A Renaissance Court*, pp. 198, 214–18; Leverotti, 'Lucia Marliani', pp. 282–5, 288; Fabrizio Alemani, 'Il terzo incomodo: Il marito Ambrogio Raverta con la discendenza legittima', *Storia in Martesana*, II (2009), pp. 1–11.

54 de' Rosmini, *Dell'istoria di Milano*, vol. IV, pp. 108–34; Lubkin, *A Renaissance Court*, p. 199; Roberta Martinis, 'Il palazzo del Banco Mediceo: Edilizia e arte della diplomazia a Milano nel XV secolo', *Annali di architettura*, XV (2003), p. 42; Leverotti, 'Lucia Marliani', pp. 284–6.

55 de' Rosmini, *Dell'istoria di Milano*, vol. IV, p. 117; Michele Caffi, 'Di altri antichi pittori milanesi poco noti', *Archivio storico lombardo*, VIII/1–2 (1881), p. 57; Francesco Malaguzzi Valeri, *La corte di Lodovico il Moro* (Milan, 1913–23), vol. I, p. 512; Edoardo Rossetti, 'Il volto di Lucia: Un ritratto ritrovato', *Storia in Martesana*, IV (2010), p. 7.

56 Francesca M. Vaglienti, 'Cacce e parchi ducali sul Ticino (1450–1476)', in *Vigevano e i territori circostanti alla fine del Medioevo*, ed. Giorgio Chittolini (Milan, 1997), pp. 203, 238; Leverotti, 'Lucia Marliani', p. 284.

57 Cicco Simonetta, *I diari di Cicco Simonetta*, ed. Alfio Rosario Natale (Milan, 1962), p. 211; Lubkin, *A Renaissance Court*, pp. 202, 227.

58 Evelyn Welch, 'Between Milan and Naples: Ippolita Maria Sforza, duchess of Calabria', in *The French Descent*, ed. Abulafia, pp. 128–31, 134; Ippolita

Maria Sforza, *Duchess and Hostage in Renaissance Naples: Letters and Orations*, ed. and trans. Diana Robin and Lynn Lara Westwater (Toronto, 2017), pp. 12, 19, 25, 91, 109.

59 Belotti, *Storia di una congiura*, p. 110; Corio, *Storia di Milano*, vol. II, p. 1400. For Lucia's children, both Galeazzo's two sons and those fathered by Ambrogio Raverti, see Leverotti, 'Lucia Marliani', pp. 288, 309–11; Rossetti, 'Il volto di Lucia'; Andrea Terreni, 'Testamenti di Lucia Marliani e Ambrogio Raverta', *Storia in Martesana*, IV (2010), pp. 1–17.

60 Malaguzzi Valeri, *La corte di Lodovico*, vol. I, p. 390; Belotti, *Storia di una congiura*, p. 176; Leverotti, 'Lucia Marliani', p. 287.

61 Emilio Motta, 'Morti in Milano dal 1452 al 1552', *Archivio storico lombardo*, 2nd series, VIII/2 (1891), p. 277; Emilio Motta, 'Arazzi in Milano', *Archivio storico lombardo*, 3rd series, XIX/38 (1903), p. 486; Leverotti, 'Lucia Marliani', pp. 288, 302–11; John Gagné, *Milan Undone: Contested Sovereignties in the Italian Wars* (Cambridge, MA, 2021), pp. 140, 159–60, 179–80.

62 Lubkin, *A Renaissance Court*, pp. 196–9, 221; Leverotti, 'Lucia Marliani', pp. 282–5, 302–4.

63 Terreni, 'Testamenti di Lucia Marliani', p. 3.

64 Porro Lambertenghi, 'Lettere di Galeazzo Maria Sforza', pp. 111–12; Rossetti, 'Il volto di Lucia'. For Lucia's red hair, see Leverotti, 'Lucia Marliani', p. 282.

65 Porro Lambertenghi, 'Lettere di Galeazzo Maria Sforza', pp. 120–21, 127, 269, 274, 638, 643, 647–9, 656, 659, 666.

66 Leverotti, '*Governare a modo e stillo de' Signori*', pp. 23n63, 69; Leverotti, 'Lucia Marliani', pp. 289–302.

4 The Girl with an Ermine Between Men: Cecilia Gallerani, Leonardo da Vinci and Ludovico Sforza

1 For the portrait, start with Józef Grabski and Janusz Wałek, eds, *Leonardo da Vinci (1452–1519): Lady with an Ermine* (Vienna, 1991); Janice Shell and Grazioso Sironi, 'Cecilia Gallerani: Leonardo's Lady with an Ermine', *Artibus et Historiae*, XIII/25 (1992), pp. 47–66; Barbara Fabjan and Pietro C. Marani, eds, *Leonardo: La dama con l'ermellino* (Cinisello Balsamo, 1998); Luke Syson, *Leonardo da Vinci: Painter at the Court of Milan* (London, 2011), pp. 110–22.

2 Alessandro Ballarin, 'Nota sul *Ritratto di Cecilia Gallerani*', in *Leonardo a Milano: Problemi di leonardismo milanese fra '400 e '500: Giovanni Antonio Boltraffio prima della Pala Casio*, vol. I (Verona, 2010), pp. 256–7; Carmen C. Bambach, *Leonardo da Vinci Rediscovered* (New Haven, CT, 2019), vol. I, pp. 357–8.

3 Helen S. Ettlinger, 'Visibilis et Invisibilis: The Mistress in Italian Renaissance Court Society', *Renaissance Quarterly*, XLVII/4 (1994), pp. 770–92; Jane Fair Bestor, 'Bastardy and Legitimacy in the Formation of a Regional State in Italy: The Estense Succession', *Comparative Studies in Society and History*, XXXVIII/3 (1996), pp. 549–85.

4 Ballarin, 'Nota sul *Ritratto*', pp. 246–8.

5 For the Order of the Ermine generally: Leah R. Clark, *Collecting Art in the Italian Renaissance Court: Objects and Exchanges* (Cambridge, 2018), pp. 158–207.

6 Luigi Volpicella, ed., *Regis Ferdinandi primi instructionum liber (10 Maggio 1486–10 Maggio 1488)* (Naples, 1916), pp. 46–51; Carlo Pedretti, 'La dama dell'ermellino come allegoria politica', in *Studi politici in onore di Luigi Firpo*, ed. Silvia Rota Ghibaudi and Franco Barcia, vol. 1 (Milan, 1990), pp. 172, 176.

7 Agata Rona, 'L'investitura di Lodovico il Moro dell'ordine dell'Armellino', *Archivio storico lombardo*, 10th series, III (1979), pp. 346–58; Ballarin, 'Nota sul *Ritratto*', pp. 233–9; Clark, *Collecting Art*, p. 190; Marco Versiero, 'Leonardo da Vinci, Cecilia Gallerani e Ludovico il Moro: Arte, amore e politica nella Milano nel Rinascimento', in *La donna nel Rinascimento: Amore, famiglia, cultura, potere*, ed. Luisa Secchi Tarugi (Florence, 2019), p. 100.

8 Clark, *Collecting Art*, pp. 194–5. For crimson brocades: Timothy McCall, *Brilliant Bodies: Fashioning Courtly Men in Early Renaissance Italy* (University Park, PA, 2022), p. 40.

9 Attilio Schiaparelli, *Leonardo ritrattista* (Milan, 1921), pp. 120–44. The notable exception is Sara van Dijk, '"Beauty adorns virtue": Dress in Portraits of Women by Leonardo da Vinci', PhD thesis, University of Leiden, 2015, pp. 89–97.

10 *Carteggio degli oratori mantovani alla corte sforzesca (1450–1500)*, vol. VIII: *1468–1471*, ed. Maria Nadia Covini (Rome, 2000), pp. 69, 78, 80–81. See too Gregory Lubkin, *A Renaissance Court: Milan under Galeazzo Maria Sforza* (Berkeley, CA, 1994), p. 45; Serena Ferente, 'Women and Men', in *Italian Renaissance Diplomacy: A Sourcebook*, ed. Monica Azzolini and Isabella Lazzarini (Toronto, 2017), pp. 148–9.

11 Francesco Malaguzzi Valeri, 'Ricamatori e arazzieri a Milano nel Quattrocento', *Archivio storico lombardo*, 3rd series, XIX/37 (1903), pp. 43–4; Maria Paola Zanoboni, *Rinascimento sforzesco: Innovazioni tecniche, arte e società nella Milano del secondo Quattrocento* (Milan, 2005), p. 38.

12 Giulio Porro Lambertenghi, 'Lettere di Galeazzo Maria Sforza, duca di Milano', *Archivio storico lombardo*, V (1878), pp. 274, 637, 643–6, 652, 663.

13 Paola Venturelli, '"Novarum Vestium Inventrix". Beatrice d'Este e l'apparire: Tra invenzioni e propaganda', in *Beatrice d'Este, 1475–1497*, ed. Luisa Giordano (Pisa, 2008), pp. 147–59; Evelyn Welch, 'Art on the Edge: Hair and Hands in Renaissance Italy', *Renaissance Studies*, XXIII/3 (2009), pp. 247–9; McCall, *Brilliant Bodies*, p. 82.

14 Ettore Verga, 'Le leggi suntuarie milanesi: Gli statuti del 1396 e del 1498', *Archivio storico lombardo*, 3rd series, IX/17 (1898), p. 40.

15 Tristano Calco, *Mediolanensis historiographi, Residua e bibliotheca patricij nobilissimi* (Milan, 1644), p. 92; Ballarin, 'Nota sul *Ritratto*', pp. 243–6; van Dijk, '"Beauty adorns virtue"', pp. 81, 93–7; Paola Venturelli, *La moda alla corte degli Sforza: Leonardo da Vinci tra creatività e tecnica* (Cinisello Balsamo, 2019), pp. 24–5.

16 Calco, *Mediolanensis historiographi*, p. 92; Venturelli, *La moda alla corte*, pp. 20–24.

17 Giuseppe Pardi, ed., *Diario ferrarese dall'anno 1409 sino al 1502* (Bologna, 1928–33), p. 144.

18 Evelyn Welch, *Shopping in the Renaissance: Consumer Cultures in Italy, 1400–1600* (New Haven, CT, 2005), p. 263; Giancarlo Malacarne, *Fruscianti vestimenti e scintillanti gioie: La moda a corte nell'età gonzaghesca* (Verona, 2012), vol. I, pp. 35, 39, 86, 132 and vol. II, p. 17.

19 Alessandro Luzio and Rodolfo Renier, *Il lusso di Isabella d'Este, marchesa di Mantova* (Rome, 1896), p. 20; van Dijk, '"Beauty adorns virtue"', pp. 91–4.

20 Pascal Cotte, *Lumière on The Lady with an Ermine by Leonardo da Vinci: Unprecedented Discoveries* (Saint-Fargeau-Ponthierry, 2014), pp. 164, 170–82, 200–205.

21 Margherita Bellezza Rosina, 'Tre corredi inediti della seconda metà del Quattrocento', in *Tessuti serici italiani, 1450–1530*, ed. Chiara Buss, Marina Molinelli and Grazietta Butazzi (Milan, 1983), p. 68. For Cecilia's embroidery, see Venturelli, *La moda alla corte*, pp. 119–20.

22 Vittorio Pini, 'Presenza della "magnifica et generosa Cecilia" Gallerani, nonché delle famiglie paterna, materna e maritale in imbreviature notarili dal 1407 al 1573, all'Archivio di Stato di Milano', *Raccolta vinciana*, XXXI (2005), pp. 7–8, 24–7.

23 Vincenzo Colli, 'Cecilia Gallerani e Giulia Farnese', in *Prose e lettere edite e inedite*, ed. Cecil Grayson (Bologna, 1959), pp. 26, 30; Ballarin, 'Nota sul *Ritratto*', pp. 250–53; Maria Nadia Covini, *Donne, emozioni e potere alla corte degli Sforza: Da Bianca Maria a Cecilia Gallerani* (Milan, 2012), pp. 47–9, 54–5.

24 Shell and Sironi, 'Cecilia Gallerani', pp. 56, 60–63.

25 Anthony Molho, 'Deception and Marriage Strategy in Renaissance Florence: The Case of Women's Ages', *Renaissance Quarterly*, XLI/2 (1988), pp. 193–217; Pini, 'Presenza della "magnifica et generosa Cecilia"', pp. 34, 36–7, 40–42.

26 Guido Ruggiero, *The Boundaries of Eros: Sex Crime and Sexuality in Renaissance Venice* (Oxford, 1985), pp. 148–54; Stanley Chojnacki, 'Measuring Adulthood: Adolescence and Gender in Renaissance Venice', *Journal of Family History*, XVII/4 (1992), pp. 372–5; Shell and Sironi, 'Cecilia Gallerani', p. 56; P. Renée Baernstein and John Christopoulos, 'Interpreting the Body in Early Modern Italy: Pregnancy, Abortion and Adulthood', *Past and Present*, CCXXIII (2014), pp. 41–75.

27 Elizabeth S. Cohen and Margaret Reeves, 'Introduction', in *The Youth of Early Modern Women*, ed. Elizabeth S. Cohen and Margaret Reeves (Amsterdam, 2018), pp. 17, 21, 26.

28 Ruggiero, *The Boundaries of Eros*, pp. 150–51; Michael Rocke, 'Gender and Sexual Culture in Renaissance Italy', in *Gender and Society in Renaissance Italy*, ed. Judith C. Brown and Robert C. Davis (London, 1998), p. 163.

29 Daniela Pizzagalli, *La dama con l'ermellino. Vita e passioni di Cecilia Gallerani nella Milano di Ludovico il Moro*, 4th edn (Milan, 2015), p. 77.

30 Léon-G. Pélissier, 'Les relations de François de Gonzague, marquis de Mantoue, avec Ludovic Sforza et Louis XII: Notes additionnelles et documents', *Annales de la Faculté des lettres de Bordeaux*, XV (1893), pp. 77–9; Francesco Malaguzzi Valeri, *La corte di Lodovico il Moro* (Milan, 1913–23), vol. I, p. 501; Ballarin, 'Nota sul *Ritratto*', pp. 246–8.

31 Covini, *Donne, emozioni e potere*, pp. 57–60. For Galeazzo's benefices and those of their brother (Giovanni) Stefano: Pini, 'Presenza della "magnifica et generosa Cecilia"', pp. 15–16, 44–8, 60.

32 Vincent Ilardi, 'Crosses and Carets: Renaissance Patronage and Coded Letters of Recommendation', *American Historical Review*, XCII/5 (1987), pp. 1127–49; Francesco Senatore, 'Falsi e "lettere reformate" nella diplomazia

sforzesca', *Bullettino dell'Istituto storico italiano per il Medio Evo*, XCIX (1993), pp. 221–78.

33 Melissa Meriam Bullard, *Lorenzo il Magnifico: Image and Anxiety, Politics and Finance* (Florence, 1994), p. 30; Lorenzo de' Medici, *Lettere*, vol. X: *1486–1487*, ed. Melissa Meriam Bullard (Florence, 2003), pp. 157–8; Ballarin, 'Nota sul *Ritratto*', pp. 245–6; Isabella Lazzarini, *Communication and Conflict: Italian Diplomacy in the Early Renaissance, 1350–1520* (Oxford, 2015), p. 209.

34 Shell and Sironi, 'Cecilia Gallerani', pp. 56, 62; Pini, 'Presenza della "magnifica et generosa Cecilia"', pp. 34, 38–9; Ballarin, 'Nota sul *Ritratto*', p. 244.

35 Colli, 'Cecilia Gallerani e Giulia Farnese', p. 26.

36 Shell and Sironi, 'Cecilia Gallerani', p. 61; Covini, *Donne, emozioni e potere*, pp. 49–56.

37 Shell and Sironi, 'Cecilia Gallerani', pp. 56–7, 62; Pini, 'Presenza della "magnifica et generosa Cecilia"', pp. 14, 40–42; Edoardo Rossetti, 'Il volto di Lucia: Un ritratto ritrovato', *Storia in Martesana*, IV (2010), p. 8; Covini, *Donne, emozioni e potere*, pp. 55n36, 59.

38 Malaguzzi Valeri, *La corte di Lodovico*, vol. I, pp. 503–4; Guido Lopez, ed., *Festa di nozze per Ludovico il Moro nelle testimonianze di Tristano Calco, Giacomo Trotti, Isabella d'Este, Gian Galeazzo Sforza, Beatrice de' Contrari, e altri* (Milan, 1976), p. 28; Shell and Sironi, 'Cecilia Gallerani', p. 58; Pini, 'Presenza della "magnifica et generosa Cecilia"', pp. 5, 44–5.

39 Vittorio Pini, 'Vicende del privilegio di Saronno concesso da Ludovico il Moro a Cecilia Gallerani (1491–1513)', *Raccolta vinciana*, XXVIII (1999), pp. 39–61.

40 Evelyn Welch, *Art and Authority in Renaissance Milan* (New Haven, CT, 1995), pp. 221, 225.

41 Pietro Ghinzoni, 'Lettera inedita di Bernardo Belincioni', *Archivio storico lombardo*, 2nd series, VI/2 (1889), p. 418. For other reports to Ludovico, including one about Cesare's first teeth: Covini, *Donne, emozioni e potere*, p. 68.

42 Bernardo Bellincioni, *Le rime*, ed. Pietro Fanfani (Bologna, 1876–8), vol. I, p. 72. See also Edoardo Villata, ed., *Leonardo da Vinci: I documenti e le testimonianze contemporanee* (Milan, 1999), pp. 76–7.

43 Welch, *Shopping in the Renaissance*, p. 22; Jacqueline Marie Musacchio, 'Wives, Lovers, and Art in Italian Renaissance Courts', in *Art and Love in Renaissance Italy*, ed. Andrea Bayer (New York, 2008), p. 33; Covini, *Donne, emozioni e potere*, p. 63.

44 Gustavo Uzielli, *Leonardo da Vinci e tre gentildonne milanesi del secolo XV* (Pinerolo, 1890), p. 26.

45 Adolfo Venturi, 'L'arte ferrarese nel periodo di Ercole I d'Este, II', *Atti e memorie della Regia Deputazione di storia patria per le provincie di Romagna*, VI/4–6 (1888), pp. 365–6.

46 Carolyn James, *A Renaissance Marriage: The Political and Personal Alliance of Isabella d'Este and Francesco Gonzaga, 1490–1519* (Oxford, 2020), pp. 32–3.

47 Uzielli, *Leonardo da Vinci*, pp. 21, 27–8; Lopez, ed., *Festa di nozze*, pp. 98–102; Pizzagalli, *La dama con l'ermellino*, pp. 121–4.

48 Uzielli, *Leonardo da Vinci*, appendix, n.p.; Shell and Sironi, 'Cecilia Gallerani', p. 58.

49 Rosina, 'Tre corredi inediti', pp. 67–8; Venturelli, *La moda alla corte*, pp. 46–7, 73–4. For lapis: Cotte, *Lumière on The Lady with an Ermine*, pp. 243, 247.

50 Most recently in Cammy Brothers, 'Portrait of a Portrait', *Wall Street Journal* (14 May 2022).

51 Carlo Pedretti, *Leonardo architetto* (Milan, 1978), pp. 80–85; Shell and Sironi, 'Cecilia Gallerani', p. 58; Covini, *Donne, emozioni e potere*, p. 18.

52 Colli, 'Cecilia Gallerani e Giulia Farnese', pp. 27, 30.

53 Malaguzzi Valeri, *La corte di Lodovico*, vol. I, p. 504.

54 Bernardino Corio, *Storia di Milano*, ed. Anna Morisi Guerra (Turin, 1978), vol. II, p. 1562; Silvana Aldeni, 'Il "Libellus Sepulchrorum" e il piano progettuale di S. Maria delle Grazie', *Arte lombarda*, LXVII (1983), pp. 78, 89; John Gagné, *Milan Undone: Contested Sovereignties in the Italian Wars* (Cambridge, MA, 2021), pp. 81, 97, 155 (and on the other hand, p. 93). For white brocades, see McCall, *Brilliant Bodies*, pp. 39, 41.

55 Krystyna Moczulska, 'The Most Graceful Gallerani and the Most Exquisite ΓΑΛΈΗ in the Portrait of Leonardo da Vinci', *Folia historiae artium*, I (1995), p. 83.

56 This homology was proposed by Charles J. Holmes, as an editor's note, in A. Edith Hewett, 'A Newly Discovered Portrait by Ambrogio de Predis', *Burlington Magazine*, X/47 (1907), p. 310n7. See, further, Paul Barolsky, 'La Gallerani's *Galée*', *Source*, XII/1 (1992), pp. 13–14; Musacchio, 'Wives, Lovers, and Art', p. 40; Syson, *Leonardo da Vinci*, p. 113; François Quiviger, *Leonardo da Vinci: Self, Art and Nature* (London, 2019), pp. 90–91. For Isabella Boschetto: Stephen J. Campbell, *The Cabinet of Eros: Renaissance Mythological Painting and the Studiolo of Isabella d'Este* (New Haven, CT, 2006), p. 189.

57 Patricia Simons, 'Portraiture, Portrayal, and Idealization: Ambiguous Individualism in Representations of Renaissance Women', in *Language and Images of Renaissance Italy*, ed. Alison Brown (Oxford, 1995), pp. 279–83; Adrian W. B. Randolph, *Touching Objects: Intimate Experiences of Italian Fifteenth-Century Art* (New Haven, CT, 2014), pp. 57–63; Bambach, *Leonardo da Vinci Rediscovered*, vol. I, p. 117.

58 For contemporary ideologies of whiteness and nobility: McCall, *Brilliant Bodies*, pp. 119–44 (and, for hands in particular, pp. 137–8).

59 Cicco Simonetta, *I diari di Cicco Simonetta*, ed. Alfio Rosario Natale (Milan, 1962), p. III; Evelyn Welch, 'Between Italy and Moscow: Cultural Crossroads and the Culture of Exchange', in *Cultural Exchange in Early Modern Europe*, vol. IV: *Forging European Identities, 1400–1700*, ed. Herman Roodenburg (Cambridge, 2007), pp. 76–7, 81–2; Elizabeth Horodowich, 'The Wider World: Foreigners, Travels, and Geography', in *Italian Renaissance Diplomacy*, ed. Azzolini and Lazzarini, p. 204.

60 Pedretti, 'La dama dell'ermellino', p. 178.

61 Nerida Newbigin, ed., '*Le onoranze fiorentine del 1459*. Poema anonimo', *Letteratura italiana antica*, XII (2011), p. 99.

62 Verga, 'Le leggi suntuarie milanesi', p. 17; Giustiniana Migliardi O'Riordan, 'Per una ricerca sulle pelli di ermellino e zibellino nelle fonti dell'Archivio di Stato di Venezia', *Византийский временник*, LVII/2 (1997), pp. 19–22.

63 Isabella d'Este, *Selected Letters*, ed. and trans. Deanna Shemek (Toronto, 2017), p. 186.

64 McCall, *Brilliant Bodies*, p. 12.

65 Bellincioni, *Le rime*, vol. I, p. 147.

66 Cotte, *Lumière on The Lady with an Ermine*, pp. 156, 200.

67 Clark, *Collecting Art*, p. 167.

68 Cotte, *Lumière on The Lady with an Ermine*, pp. 148, 151.

69 Arturo Galansino in Syson, *Leonardo da Vinci*, pp. 120–21; Bambach, *Leonardo da Vinci Rediscovered*, vol. I, pp. 274–7.

70 Francesco Malaguzzi Valeri, 'Il ritratto femminile del Boltraffio', *Rassegna d'arte*, XII (1912), pp. 9–11.

71 Moczulska, 'The Most Graceful Gallerani', pp. 84–5; Jacqueline Marie Musacchio, 'Weasels and Pregnancy in Renaissance Italy', *Renaissance Studies*, XV/2 (2001), pp. 172–87; Musacchio, 'Wives, Lovers, and Art', p. 33.

72 Musacchio, 'Weasels and Pregnancy'.

73 Bestor, 'Bastardy and Legitimacy'; Timothy McCall, 'Pier Maria's Legacy: (Il)legitimacy, Inheritance, and Rule of Parma's Rossi Dynasty', in *Wives, Widows, Mistresses, and Nuns in Early Modern Italy: Making the Invisible Visible through Art and Patronage*, ed. Katherine A. McIver (Farnham, 2012), pp. 33–54.

74 Barbara Fabjan, 'In margine all'ermellino', in *Leonardo*, ed. Fabjan and Marani, p. 73. For Leonardo's ownership of the text, see Martin Kemp, *Leonardo da Vinci: The Marvellous Works of Nature and Man* (Oxford, 2006), p. 140.

75 Bellincioni, *Le rime*, vol. I, pp. 55–6, 178–9; Elizabeth McGrath, 'Ludovico il Moro and His Moors', *Journal of the Warburg and Courtauld Institutes*, LXV (2002), pp. 67–94; McCall, *Brilliant Bodies*, pp. 125–33.

76 Luciano Cheles, *The Studiolo of Urbino: An Iconographic Investigation* (University Park, PA, 1986), pp. 78, 81; Paola Venturelli, *Gioielli e gioiellieri milanesi: Storia, arte, moda (1450–1630)* (Cinisello Balsamo, 1996), p. 80; Kathleen Wren Christian, 'Petrarch's *Triumph of Chastity* in Leonardo's *Lady with an Ermine*', in *Coming About . . . A Festschrift for John Shearman*, ed. Lars R. Jones and Louisa C. Matthew (Cambridge, MA, 2001), pp. 33–40; Patricia Phillippy, *Painting Women: Cosmetics, Canvases, and Early Modern Culture* (Baltimore, MD, 2006), pp. 124–5; Cristelle Baskins, *The Triumph of Marriage: Painted Cassoni of the Renaissance* (Pittsburgh, PA, 2008), pp. 105, 114.

77 Pedretti, 'La dama dell'ermellino', pp. 167–8, 177–8; Ballarin, 'Nota sul Ritratto', pp. 238–40; Pietro C. Marani, 'Leonardo e i prìncipi invisibili: Allegorie figurate e fortezze come allegorie politiche per Ludovico il Moro e Cesare Borgia', in *Il Principe inVisibile: La rappresentazione e la riflessione sul potere tra Medioevo e Rinascimento*, ed. Lucia Bertolini, Arturo Calzona, Glauco Cantarella and Stefano Caroti (Turnhout, 2015), pp. 273–4; Bambach, *Leonardo da Vinci Rediscovered*, vol. I, pp. 493–5. For related ermine-lore in Leonardo's notebooks, see Götz Pochat, 'The Ermine: A Metaphor in Renaissance Poetry and a Portrait by Leonardo da Vinci', *Tidskrift för litteraturvetenskap*, III (1974), pp. 140–58; Pier Luigi Mulas, 'Le allegorie di Leonardo', in *Ludovicus Dux*, ed. Luisa Giordano (Vigevano, 1995), pp. 118–21.

78 Clark, *Collecting Art*, pp. 190–92.

79 Simons, 'Portraiture, Portrayal, and Idealization', pp. 279–80.

80 Rachele Magnani, *Relazioni private tra la corte sforzesca di Milano e casa Medici, 1450–1500* (Milan, 1910), p. 46n1; Franca Leverotti, 'Lucia Marliani

e la sua famiglia: Il potere di una donna amata', in *Donne di potere nel Rinascimento*, ed. Letizia Arcangeli and Susanna Peyronel (Rome, 2008), pp. 282n3, 285. See too Gayle Rubin, 'The Traffic in Women: Notes on the "Political Economy" of Sex', in *Toward an Anthropology of Women*, ed. Rayna R. Reiter (New York, 1975), pp. 157–210.

81 P. J. Jones, *The Malatesta of Rimini and the Papal State: A Political History* (Cambridge, 1974), pp. 241–6; Alan Ryder, *Alfonso the Magnanimous: King of Aragon, Naples and Sicily, 1396–1458* (Oxford, 1990), pp. 398–9; Leverotti, 'Lucia Marliani'.

82 Toril Moi, 'Desire in Language: Andreas Capellanus and the Controversy of Courtly Love', in *Medieval Literature: Criticism, Ideology and History*, ed. David Aers (Brighton, 1986), pp. 22–5. See too E. Jane Burns, 'Courtly Love: Who Needs It? Recent Feminist Work in the Medieval French Tradition', *Signs*, XXVII/1 (2001), pp. 23–57.

83 Musacchio, 'Wives, Lovers, and Art', p. 33.

84 Shell and Sironi, 'Cecilia Gallerani', pp. 49–50; Villata, *Leonardo da Vinci*, pp. 112–15; Ballarin, 'Nota sul *Ritratto*', p. 257; Francis Ames-Lewis, *Isabella and Leonardo: The Artistic Relationship between Isabella d'Este and Leonardo da Vinci, 1500–1506* (New Haven, CT, 2012), pp. 110–19, 156–60, 223–5; Isabella d'Este, *Selected Letters*, p. 122.

85 Pini, 'Presenza della "magnifica et generosa Cecilia"', p. 78; Musacchio, 'Wives, Lovers, and Art', pp. 33–4; Gagné, *Milan Undone*, p. 188.

86 Adelin Charles Fiorato, *Bandello entre l'histoire et l'écriture: La vie, l'expérience sociale, l'évolution culturelle d'un conteur de la Renaissance* (Florence, 1979), pp. 200–201, 212–13, 231–4.

87 A notary document of 22 February 1533 involving Cecilia and Ludovico Bergamino's sons Giovanni Pietro and Francesco refers to their mother as 'quondam … magnifice domine Cecilie Gallerane': Pini, 'Presenza della "magnifica et generosa Cecilia"', pp. 6, 103.

88 Virginia Cox, *Women's Writing in Italy, 1400–1650* (Baltimore, MD, 2008), pp. 46, 51; Sarah Gwyneth Ross, *The Birth of Feminism: Woman as Intellect in Renaissance Italy and England* (Cambridge, MA, 2009).

89 Cox, *Women's Writing*, pp. 38–53.

90 Colli, 'Cecilia Gallerani e Giulia Farnese', p. 28; Antonio Tebaldeo, *Rime*, vol. III, pt II: *Rime estravaganti*, ed. Jean-Jacques Marchand (Ferrara, 1992), pp. 1050–53; Jean-Jacques Marchand, 'I sonetti del Tebaldeo in morte di Serafino', in *Studi in onore di Pier Vincenzo Mengaldo per i suoi settant'anni*, vol. II (Florence, 2007), pp. 423–34; Ballarin, 'Nota sul *Ritratto*', pp. 253–5.

91 Giulio Cesare Scaligero, *Poemata in duas partes divisa* (Geneva, 1591), vol. I, pp. 379–80; Bernardo Morsolin, *Giangiorgio Trissino: O, monografia di un letterato nel secolo XVI* (Vicenza, 1878), pp. 453–4; Uzielli, *Leonardo da Vinci*, p. 13.

92 Matteo Bandello, *Tutte le opere di Matteo Bandello*, ed. Francesco Flora, 4th edn (Milan, 1966), vol. I, pp. 7, 44, 263 and vol. II, pp. 750, 1180; Carlo Pedretti, 'Gleanings: An Ermine for Lady Purity', *Achademia Leonardi Vinci*, X (1997), pp. 233–4; Cox, *Women's Writing*, pp. 46, 284n67.

93 Cox, *Women's Writing*, pp. 48–9, 77. See too Campbell, *The Cabinet of Eros*, pp. 199–204.

94 Bandello, *Tutte le opere*, vol. I, p. 263.

95 Ibid., pp. 116, 241–2, 263–4 and vol. II, p. 396; Fiorato, *Bandello entre l'histoire*, p. 212.

96 This claim is true whether Ginevra or Bernardo commissioned the painting: Mary D. Garrard, 'Who Was Ginevra de' Benci? Leonardo's Portrait and Its Sitter Recontextualized', *Artibus et Historiae*, XXVII/53 (2006), pp. 23–56; Cox, *Women's Writing*, p. 45; Judith Bryce, 'The Faces of Ginevra de' Benci: Homosocial Agendas and Female Subjectivity in Later Quattrocento Florence', in *Masculinities and Femininities in the Middle Ages and Renaissance*, ed. Frederick Kiefer (Turnhout, 2009), pp. 131–58; Quiviger, *Leonardo da Vinci*, pp. 35–42.

5 Borso d'Este and the History of Lordly Sexuality

1 Pius II, *Commentaries*, ed. Margaret Meserve and Marcello Simonetta (Cambridge, MA, 2003–7), vol. II, pp. 84–7; Marco Folin, 'Modelli internazionali e tradizioni signorili: Mausolei estensi tra tardo Medioevo e prima età moderna', in *Il Principe inVisibile: La rappresentazione e la riflessione sul potere tra Medioevo e Rinascimento*, ed. Lucia Bertolini, Arturo Calzona, Glauco Maria Cantarella and Stefano Caroti (Turnhout, 2015), p. 185.

2 Stefania Buganza, 'Intorno a Baldassarre d'Este e al suo soggiorno lombardo', *Solchi*, IX/1–3 (2007), pp. 14, 58–9; Marcello Toffanello, *Le arti a Ferrara nel Quattrocento: Gli artisti e la corte* (Ferrara, 2010), pp. 72–6, 234.

3 Timothy McCall, *Brilliant Bodies: Fashioning Courtly Men in Early Renaissance Italy* (University Park, PA, 2022), pp. 8–9, 120–22.

4 Werner L. Gundersheimer, 'Clarity and Ambiguity in Renaissance Gesture: The Case of Borso d'Este', *Journal of Medieval and Renaissance Studies*, XXIII/1 (1993), p. 11.

5 Lewis Lockwood, *Music in Renaissance Ferrara, 1400–1505: The Creation of a Musical Center in the Fifteenth Century* (Cambridge, MA, 1984), p. 89n10; Emanuele Mattaliano, '"Le donne, i cavallier, l'arme, gli amori" estensi nel Cinquecento a Ferrara', in *Da Borso a Cesare d'Este. La scuola di Ferrara, 1450–1628* (Ferrara, 1985), pp. 39–40; Gundersheimer, 'Clarity and Ambiguity', pp. 13–17; Folin, 'Modelli internazionali', p. 185. Contrarily, see Micaela Torboli, *Il duca Borso d'Este e la politica delle immagini nella Ferrara del Quattrocento* (Ferrara, 2007), pp. 24–9.

6 The translations derive from the English-language catalogue. For the Italian, see Mattaliano, '"Le donne, i cavallier"', pp. 39–40. Renaissance men's *calze* and sequins are historicized in McCall, *Brilliant Bodies*, pp. 66–74, 106–16.

7 Luke Syson, 'Lo stile di una signoria: Il mecenatismo di Borso d'Este', in *Cosmè Tura e Francesco del Cossa: L'arte a Ferrara nell'età di Borso d'Este*, ed. Mauro Natale (Ferrara, 2007), pp. 76, 84–5.

8 James A. Schultz, 'Heterosexuality as a Threat to Medieval Studies', *Journal of the History of Sexuality*, XV/1 (2006), pp. 17, 20, 29.

9 Judith Butler, *Gender Trouble: Feminism and the Subversion of Identity* (London, 1990), pp. 143–63; Karma Lochrie, *Covert Operations: The Medieval Uses of Secrecy* (Philadelphia, PA, 1999), pp. 199–227. For the construction of heterosexuality generally, see Jonathan Ned Katz, *The Invention of Heterosexuality*, 2nd edn (Chicago, IL, 2007).

10 Karma Lochrie, *Heterosyncrasies: Female Sexuality When Normal Wasn't* (Minneapolis, MN, 2005); Schultz, 'Heterosexuality as a Threat'.

11 Kenneth Borris, 'Introduction: The Prehistory of Homosexuality in the Early Modern Sciences', in *The Sciences of Homosexuality in Early Modern Europe*, ed. Kenneth Borris and George Rousseau (London, 2006), p. 28. For gay genealogies, see James Saslow, 'Gianantonio Bazzi, called "Il Sodoma": Homosexuality in Art, Life, and History', in *Sex, Gender and Sexuality in Renaissance Italy*, ed. Jacqueline Murray and Nicholas Terpstra (London, 2019), pp. 183–210.

12 David Halperin, *How to Do the History of Homosexuality* (Chicago, IL, 2002), pp. 3, 17, 116, 134, 154.

13 Lochrie, *Heterosyncrasies*; Halperin, *How to Do*, p. 43.

14 Syson, 'Lo stile', pp. 79, and 76–7, 84 for criticism of scholars insisting upon Borso's heterosexuality. Though Werner Gundersheimer suggested that 'the complicated marital and extramarital alliances of Niccolò III and the peculiarities of his sons had disrupted the standard procedure', Jane Fair Bestor has persuasively shown that such pragmatic 'peculiarities' had for well over a century been standard operating procedure for Este lords: Werner L. Gundersheimer, 'Women, Learning, and Power: Eleonora of Aragon and the Court of Ferrara', in *Beyond Their Sex: Learned Women of the European Past*, ed. Patricia H. Labalme (New York, 1980), p. 45; Jane Fair Bestor, 'Bastardy and Legitimacy in the Formation of a Regional State in Italy: The Estense Succession', *Comparative Studies in Society and History*, XXXVIII/3 (1996), pp. 549–85.

15 Patricia Simons, 'Homosociality and Erotics in Italian Renaissance Portraiture', in *Portraiture: Facing the Subject*, ed. Joanna Woodall (Manchester, 1997), pp. 32, 42; Will Fisher, 'Peaches and Figs: Bisexual Eroticism in the Paintings and Burlesque Poetry of Bronzino', in *Sex Acts in Early Modern Italy: Practice, Performance, Perversion, Punishment*, ed. Allison Levy (Farnham, 2010), p. 162n8.

16 For the pleasures and pitfalls of locating gay forebearers in the past, see Halperin, *How to Do*, pp. 15–17.

17 Simons, 'Homosociality and Erotics'; Helmut Puff, 'After the History of (Male) Homosexuality', in *After the History of Sexuality: German Genealogies with and beyond Foucault*, ed. Scott Spector, Helmut Puff and Dagmar Herzog (New York, 2012), pp. 17–30; Roland Betancourt, *Byzantine Intersectionality: Sexuality, Gender, and Race in the Middle Ages* (Princeton, NJ, 2020), pp. 130–31.

18 Gregory Lubkin, *A Renaissance Court: Milan under Galeazzo Maria Sforza* (Berkeley, CA, 1994), p. 202.

19 Michael Rocke, *Forbidden Friendships: Homosexuality and Male Culture in Renaissance Florence* (Oxford, 1996). See too Stephen J. Campbell, *Cosmè Tura of Ferrara: Style, Politics, and the Renaissance City, 1450–1495* (New Haven, CT, 1997), pp. 53–61; Maya Corry, 'The Homoerotics of Power: Art and Desire in Leonardo's Milan', in *The Male Body and Social Masculinity in Premodern Europe*, ed. Jacqueline Murray (Toronto, 2022), pp. 193–227.

20 For the menace of respectability politics: Betancourt, *Byzantine Intersectionality*. Most insightful, in relation to genders and sexes of

past and present, is Leah DeVun, *The Shape of Sex: Nonbinary Gender from Genesis to the Renaissance* (New York, 2021), pp. 159–62, 201–7.

21 Pier Candido Decembrio, *Lives of the Milanese Tyrants*, trans. Gary Ianziti and ed. Massimo Zaggia (Cambridge, MA, 2019), pp. 82–5, 250–55; Gary Ianziti, 'The Life of the Last Visconti: A Study in Tyranny?', *Renaissance Quarterly*, LXXV/3 (2022), pp. 759–61.

22 Bestor, 'Bastardy and Legitimacy', pp. 559–68; Jane Fair Bestor, 'Marriage and Succession in the House of Este: A Literary Perspective', in *Phaethon's Children: The Este Court and Its Culture in Early Modern Ferrara*, ed. Dennis Looney and Deanna Shemek (Tempe, AZ, 2005), pp. 54, 71–4.

23 Antonio Cappelli, 'Notizie di Ugo Caleffini notaro ferrarese del secolo XV con la sua Cronaca in rima di Casa d'Este', *Atti e memorie delle Regie Deputazioni di storia patria per le provincie modenesi e parmensi*, II (1864), p. 286; Matteo Bandello, *Tutte le opere di Matteo Bandello*, ed. Francesco Flora, 4th edn (Milan, 1966), vol. I, p. 518. For *pater patriae*: Werner L. Gundersheimer, *Ferrara: The Style of a Renaissance Despotism* (Princeton, NJ, 1973), pp. 67–9.

24 For another joke about Niccolò's children: Ludovico Carbone, *Facezie e dialogo de la partita soa*, ed. Gino Ruozzi (Bologna, 1989), p. 9. For an additional saying ('Dietro al fiume del Po, trecento figliuoli del marchese Niccolò hanno tirata l'altana de le navi'): Bandello, *Tutte le opere*, vol. I, p. 517.

25 Bestor, 'Bastardy and Legitimacy', pp. 571–2; Charles M. Rosenberg, *The Este Monuments and Urban Development in Renaissance Ferrara* (Cambridge, 1997), p. 52; Pius II, *Commentaries*, vol. I, pp. 360–61.

26 Alfonso Lazzari, *Il primo duca di Ferrara, Borso d'Este* (Ferrara, 1945), pp. II, 21; Rosenberg, *The Este Monuments*, pp. 80–82.

27 Cappelli, 'Notizie di Ugo Caleffini', p. 289; Antonio Cappelli, 'Niccolò di Lionello d'Este', *Atti e memorie delle Regie Deputazioni di storia patria per le provincie modenesi e parmensi*, V (1870), pp. 415–18; Giuseppe Pardi, ed., *Diario ferrarese dall'anno 1409 sino al 1502* (Bologna, 1928–33), p. 64; Richard M. Tristano, 'Ferrara in the Fifteenth Century: Borso d'Este and the Development of a New Nobility', PhD thesis, New York University, 1983, pp. 196–7; Federica Toniolo, 'Un Libro d'Ore di Nicolò di Leonello d'Este', *Musei ferraresi*, XVII (1990–91), pp. 77–81; Adriano Franceschini, *Artisti a Ferrara in età umanistica e rinascimentale: Testimonianze archivistiche* (Ferrara, 1993), vol. I, pp. 625–6, 732, 737, 762–5; Maria Nadia Covini, *Donne, emozioni e potere alla corte degli Sforza: Da Bianca Maria a Cecilia Gallerani* (Milan, 2012), p. 79.

28 Cappelli, 'Niccolò di Lionello', pp. 418–21; Pardi, ed., *Diario ferrarese dall'anno 1409*, pp. 71, 75–8; Thomas Tuohy, *Herculean Ferrara: Ercole d'Este, 1471–1505, and the Invention of a Ducal Capital* (Cambridge, 1996), p. 405; Marco Folin, 'Borso a Schifanoia: Il Salone dei Mesi come *speculum principis*', in *Il Palazzo Schifanoia a Ferrara / The Palazzo Schifanoia in Ferrara*, ed. Salvatore Settis and Walter Cupperi, vol. I (Modena, 2007), p. 27.

29 For the famous, but spurious etymological connection between gifts and poison: Marcel Mauss, *The Gift: The Form and Reason for Exchange in Archaic Societies*, trans. W. D. Halls (New York, 1990), p. 63.

30 Cappelli, 'Niccolò di Lionello', pp. 421–2, 436–7.

31 David Chambers and Trevor Dean, *Clean Hands and Rough Justice: An Investigating Magistrate in Renaissance Italy* (Ann Arbor, MI, 1997),

pp. 116–17. Cesare's brother was also beheaded and quartered: Pardi, ed.,
Diario ferrarese dall'anno 1409, p. 77.

32 For the dramatic events, see Cappelli, 'Niccolò di Lionello', pp. 424–7; Pardi,
ed., *Diario ferrarese dall'anno 1409*, pp. 91–3; Bernardino Zambotti, *Diario
ferrarese dall'anno 1476 sino al 1504*, ed. Giuseppe Pardi (Bologna, 1934–7),
pp. 15–21; Ugo Caleffini, *Croniche, 1471–1494* (Ferrara, 2006), pp. 180–88;
Bestor, 'Bastardy and Legitimacy', pp. 574–6; Folin, 'Borso a Schifanoia',
p. 27; Isabella Lazzarini, 'L'âge des conjurations: Violence, dynamiques
politiques et ritualités sociales dans les cours de l'Italie du Nord à la fin
du xve siècle', in *Passions et pulsions à la cour (Moyen Âge - Temps modernes)*,
ed. Bernard Andenmatten, Armand Jamme, Laurence Moulinier-Brogi
and Marilyn Nicoud (Florence, 2015), pp. 324–8.

33 Pardi, ed., *Diario ferrarese dall'anno 1409*, pp. 77, 92–3; Zambotti, *Diario
ferrarese dall'anno 1476*, p. 19; Giovanni Ricci, *Il principe e la morte: Corpo,
cuore, effigie nel Rinascimento* (Bologna, 1998), pp. 111–13; McCall, *Brilliant
Bodies*, p. 78.

34 Pardi, ed., *Diario ferrarese dall'anno 1409*, p. 92; Zambotti, *Diario ferrarese
dall'anno 1476*, p. 19; Bernardino Corio, *Storia di Milano*, ed. Anna Morisi
Guerra (Turin, 1978), vol. II, p. 1395; Caleffini, *Croniche, 1471–1494*, pp. 185–6.
For Este burials here: Folin, 'Modelli internazionali', pp. 173–5.

35 Bestor, 'Bastardy and Legitimacy', p. 567; Folin, 'Borso a Schifanoia', p. 26.

36 Giuseppe Pardi, *Leonello d'Este, marchese di Ferrara* (Bologna, 1904), p. 45;
Bestor, 'Bastardy and Legitimacy', pp. 570, 576–7; Caleffini, *Croniche,
1471–1494*, p. 188; Lazzarini, 'L'âge des conjurations', pp. 327–8.

37 Timothy McCall, 'Visual Imagery and Historical Invisibility: Antonia
Torelli, Her Husband, and His Mistress in Fifteenth-Century Parma',
Renaissance Studies, XXIII/3 (2009), pp. 284–5.

38 Niccolò di Leonello never married; for rumours about his children, see
Caleffini, *Croniche, 1471–1494*, p. 188.

39 Carbone, *Facezie e dialogo*, p. 16.

40 Gino Franceschini, 'Notizie su Oddantonio da Montefeltro primo duca
d'Urbino (20 febbraio 1443–22 luglio 1444)', *Atti e memorie della Regia
Deputazione di storia patria per le Marche*, I (1946), pp. 86–7. For the medal,
see Luke Syson and Dillian Gordon, *Pisanello: Painter to the Renaissance
Court* (London, 2001), pp. 116–17; Stephen J. Campbell in *The Renaissance
Nude*, ed. Thomas Kren with Jill Burke and Stephen J. Campbell (Los
Angeles, CA, 2018), pp. 325–6.

41 Franceschini, *Artisti a Ferrara*, vol. I, p. 355.

42 Costantino Corvisieri, 'Il trionfo romano di Eleonora d'Aragona nel
giugno del 1473', *Archivio della Regia società romana di storia patria*, I (1878),
p. 651.

43 Campbell, *Cosmè Tura of Ferrara*, pp. 35–8; Natale, ed., *Cosmè Tura e Francesco
del Cossa*, pp. 203, 272–3; Torboli, *Il duca Borso*, pp. 16–23. For Schifanoia's
portal, see Walter Cupperi, 'Esterno', in *Il Palazzo Schifanoia*, ed. Settis and
Cupperi, pp. 197–209; Toffanello, *Le arti a Ferrara*, pp. 328–32.

44 Chris Lavers, 'Origin of Myths Related to Curative, Antidotal and Other
Medicinal Properties of Animal "Horns" in the Middle Ages', in *Toxicology
in the Middle Ages and Renaissance*, ed. Philip Wexler (London, 2017),
pp. 101–14; McCall, *Brilliant Bodies*, p. 123.

45 Cesare Foucard, *Relazioni dei duchi di Ferrara e di Modena coi re di Tunisi* (Modena, 1881), p. 11; Elizabeth Horodowich, 'The Wider World: Foreigners, Travels, and Geography', in *Italian Renaissance Diplomacy: A Sourcebook*, ed. Monica Azzolini and Isabella Lazzarini (Toronto, 2017), p. 197.

46 Giuliano Antigini, *Annali di Ferrara* (Ferrara, Biblioteca Comunale Ariostea, Classe I, MS 757), published in Folin, 'Borso a Schifanoia', p. 40; Kristen Lippincott, 'The Neo-Latin Historical Epics of the North Italian Courts: An Examination of "Courtly Culture" in the Fifteenth Century', *Renaissance Studies*, III/4 (1989), pp. 422–5; Bestor, 'Marriage and Succession'.

47 *Chronicon Estense, gesta Marchionum Estensium complectens ab anno 1101 usque ad annum 1354, per anonymos scriptores synchronos deductum, et ab aliis auctoribus continuatum usque ad annum 1393*, ed. Lodovico Muratori (Milan, 1729), column 543; Ricci, *Il principe e la morte*, pp. 87, 100, 110, 131–2.

48 *Genealogia dei Signori d'Este*, Biblioteca Estense Universitaria, Modena, MS Ital. 730=α.L.5.16, fol. 3r; Folin, 'Borso a Schifanoia', p. 42.

49 Carbone, *Facezie e dialogo*, p. 16.

50 Alfonso Lazzari, 'Un dialogo di Lodovico Carbone in lode del Duca Borso', *Atti e memorie della Deputazione ferrarese di storia patria*, XXVII (1929), pp. 144–5; Folin, 'Borso a Schifanoia', p. 26.

51 Antonio Cappelli, 'La congiura dei Pio signori di Carpi contro Borso d'Este, marchese di Ferrara, duca di Modena e Reggio, scritta nel 1469 da Carlo da San Giorgio Bolognese con aggiunta di osservazioni e documenti', *Atti e memorie delle Regie Deputazioni di storia patria per le provincie modenesi e parmensi*, II (1864), p. 386. See also Guido Antonioli, 'La caccia nel pensiero degli umanisti della corte estense (XV secolo)', *F.D. Bollettino della 'Ferrariae Decus'*, XX (2003), pp. 40–41; Pius II, *Commentaries*, vol. I, pp. 361–3.

52 Pardi, ed., *Diario ferrarese dall'anno 1409*, p. 66; Antigini, *Annali di Ferrara*, in Folin, 'Borso a Schifanoia', p. 40.

53 *Genealogia dei Signori d'Este*, fol. 3r; Folin, 'Borso a Schifanoia', p. 42.

54 Helen S. Ettlinger, 'Visibilis et Invisibilis: The Mistress in Italian Renaissance Court Society', *Renaissance Quarterly*, XLVII/4 (1994), pp. 770–92.

55 Adriano Franceschini, *Giurisdizione episcopale e comunità rurali altopolesane: Bergantino, Melara, Bariano tra Gonzaga, vescovi ed Estensi (1393–1458)* (Bologna, 1999), p. 80n244; Luciano Chiappini, *Gli Estensi: Mille anni di storia* (Ferrara, 2001), pp. 158, 616; Torboli, *Il duca Borso*, p. 25.

56 Pardi, ed., *Diario ferrarese dall'anno 1409*, p. 73; Antigini, *Annali di Ferrara*, in Folin, 'Borso a Schifanoia', p. 40; Hondedio di Vitale, *Cronaca* (Ferrara, Biblioteca Comunale Ariostea, Collezione Antonelli, MS 257), published in Folin, 'Borso a Schifanoia', p. 42.

57 Cappelli, 'La congiura dei Pio', pp. 381–3, 393.

58 Ibid.; Pardi, ed., *Diario ferrarese dall'anno 1409*, pp. 39, 43–4, 60–63; Lazzari, *Il primo duca*, pp. 23–4, 62–5, 87–8; Gundersheimer, *Ferrara*, pp. 177–9. For the melon: Domenico Malipiero, 'Annali veneti dall'anno 1457 al 1500 del Senatore Domenico Malipiero', *Archivio storico italiano*, VII (1843), p. 240.

59 Pardi, ed., *Diario ferrarese dall'anno 1409*, pp. 38–42; Aeneas Silvius Piccolomini, *De viris illustribus*, ed. Adrianus van Heck (Vatican City, 1991), p. 23; Pius II, *Commentaries*, vol. I, pp. 120–23, 204–5, 358–65.

60 Pius II, *Commentaries*, vol. I, pp. 360–63 and vol. II, pp. 82–7, 198–9, 212–13. Also, Lazzari, *Il primo duca*, pp. 38–40; Emily O'Brien, *The Commentaries of Pope Pius II (1458–1464) and the Crisis of the Fifteenth-Century Papacy* (Toronto, 2015), pp. 163–4; Richard M. Tristano, '"Lo amore deli subditi": The Statecraft of Borso d'Este', *Studies in Medieval and Renaissance History*, XV (2018), pp. 269–71. For additional criticisms of Borso's obsession with hunting: Antonioli, 'La caccia nel pensiero', p. 41.

61 Torboli, *Il duca Borso*, pp. 54–7. For woad's economic importance: Franco Borlandi, 'Il commercio del guado nel Medioevo', in *Storia dell'economia italiana: Saggi di storia economica*, ed. Carlo M. Cipolla (Turin, 1959), pp. 263–84.

62 Emilio Motta, 'Il pittore Baldassare da Reggio (1461–1471)', *Archivio storico lombardo*, 2nd series, VI/2 (1889), pp. 407–8; Buganza, 'Intorno a Baldassarre d'Este', pp. 14–15, 56.

63 Gundersheimer, 'Clarity and Ambiguity', p. 11. As Patricia Simons argued, however, only if Borso's gesture is 'read through the lens of a much later Camp style, and with the assumption that both heterosexuality and masculinity only operate within a narrow register', can it, or he, be seen as problematically effeminate: Simons, 'Homosociality and Erotics', p. 32.

64 Carlo Morbio, *Codice visconteo-sforzesco, ossia raccolta di leggi, decreti e lettere famigliari dei duchi di Milano* (Milan, 1846), pp. 462–3; Adolfo Venturi, 'Relazioni artistiche tra le corti di Milano e Ferrara nel secolo XV', *Archivio storico lombardo*, 2nd series, II/2 (1885), p. 247; Eugenio Casanova, 'L'astrologia e la consegna del bastone al capitano generale della Repubblica fiorentina', *Archivio storico italiano*, 5th series, VII/181 (1891), pp. 134–44; Covini, *Donne, emozioni e potere*, p. 51; Alison Brown, 'Piero in Power, 1492–1494: A Balance Sheet for Four Generations of Medici Control', in *The Medici: Citizens and Masters*, ed. Robert Black and John E. Law (Settignano, 2015), pp. 115–16.

65 Cappelli, 'Niccolò di Lionello', pp. 420, 436; Rachele Magnani, *Relazioni private tra la corte sforzesca di Milano e casa Medici, 1450–1500* (Milan, 1910), pp. 43, xxxiv; Pier Luigi Mulas, 'L'effimero e la memoria. L'investitura ducale', in *Ludovicus Dux*, ed. Luisa Giordano (Vigevano, 1995), p. 175; Jane Black, *Absolutism in Renaissance Milan: Plenitude of Power under the Visconti and the Sforza, 1329–1535* (Oxford, 2009), pp. 86–7.

66 Michele Savonarola, *Del felice progresso di Borso d'Este*, ed. Maria Aurelia Mastronardi (Bari, 1996), pp. 155, 197; Rosenberg, *The Este Monuments*, pp. 36, 43, 53, 72–3, 78, 81; Folin, 'Borso a Schifanoia', pp. 17–19.

67 Girolamo Baruffaldi, *Vite de' pittori e scultori ferraresi* (Ferrara, 1844), vol. I, p. 72; Marco Bertozzi, *La tirannia degli astri: Gli affreschi astrologici di Palazzo Schifanoia* (Livorno, 1999), pp. 51, 54.

68 Pardi, ed., *Diario ferrarese dall'anno 1409*, p. 38; Rosenberg, *The Este Monuments*, pp. 28–9, 32, 36, 40, 68, 71–2, 88–97, 100, 106–7.

69 Andrea Pannonio, *De origine clarissime illustrissimeque domus Estensis e super decessu Divi Borsii Ducis*, Biblioteca Estense Universitaria, Modena, MS Lat.108=α.Q.9.12, fol. 1r.

70 Adolfo Levi, *Le poesie latine e italiane di Malatesta Ariosti* (Florence, 1904), pp. 27–8, 34; Ken Mondschein, *The Knightly Art of Battle* (Los Angeles, CA, 2011), p. 32.

71 Giuseppe Campori, ed., *Raccolta di cataloghi ed inventarii inediti di quadri, statue, disegni, bronzi, dorerie, smalti, medaglie, avorii, ecc.: Dal secolo XV al secolo XIX* (Modena, 1870), pp. 12–13; Enrico Celani, 'La venuta di Borso d'Este in Roma. L'anno 1471', *Archivio della Regia società romana di storia patria*, XIII/3–4 (1890), pp. 374n1, 429; Pardi, ed., *Diario ferrarese dall'anno 1409*, p. 67; Caleffini, *Croniche, 1471–1494*, p. 5; McCall, *Brilliant Bodies*, p. 79.

72 Mario Tabanelli, *Sigismondo Pandolfo Malatesta, signore del Medioevo e del Rinascimento* (Faenza, 1977), p. 391.

73 Testimony of Giacopino Zacchinardi: Archivio di Stato di Parma, Feudi e Comunità, Roccabianca, busta 186, Processo de testimonii essaminate sopra l'edificatione di Roccabianca, nel qual si prova la descendentia da Pietro Maria p.o sino a Pietro Maria 2.o, fol. 30r–31v.

74 Gundersheimer ultimately concluded that Borso's image could be interpreted as 'desexualized'. But aristocratic, Renaissance male bodies on display were never desexualized, even if they fail to meet modern expectations of normative masculinity or sexuality. The claim seems symptomatic of the persistent assumption that only women are gendered or sexed and that men have standard, essentially human bodies: Gundersheimer, 'Clarity and Ambiguity', p. 17. Pat Simons excoriates 'the heterosexist assumption that any element of femininity makes a figure sexual but that its absence renders a body sexless': Simons, 'Homosociality and Erotics', p. 49n10.

75 Benvenuto Cellini, *Autobiography*, trans. George Bull (Harmondsworth, 1956), p. 360; Simons, 'Homosociality and Erotics', p. 42.

76 Bandello, *Tutte le opere*, vol. 1, p. 518. For historical constructions of effeminacy: Halperin, *How to Do*, pp. 111–13; Gerry Milligan, 'The Politics of Effeminacy in "Il cortegiano"', *Italica*, LXXXIII/3–4 (2006), pp. 345–66; Elizabeth Currie, *Fashion and Masculinity in Renaissance Florence* (London, 2016), pp. 116–27.

77 Giovanni Pontano, *I libri delle virtù sociali*, ed. Francesco Tateo (Rome, 1999), p. 178; Stephen J. Campbell, *The Cabinet of Eros: Renaissance Mythological Painting and the Studiolo of Isabella d'Este* (New Haven, CT, 2006), p. 37.

78 Pietro Aretino, *Tutte le commedie*, ed. G. B. De Sanctis (Milan, 1968), p. 36. For the comedy's reckoning with alternatives between sex with boys and marriage: Deanna Shemek, 'Aretino's *Marescalco*: Marriage Woes and the Duke of Mantua', *Renaissance Studies*, XVI/3 (2002), pp. 366–80. For the Wars of Italy and unmanliness, see Milligan, 'The Politics of Effeminacy'.

79 Battista Guarino, *Sermone del cane e del cavallo*, ed. Gianluca Valenti (Rome, 2016); Marco Veneziale, 'Per la biblioteca di Teofilo Calcagnini, "compagno" di Borso d'Este', *La Bibliofilía*, CXX/1 (2018), pp. 5–26.

80 Tristano, 'Ferrara in the Fifteenth Century', pp. 239–45; Giovanni Sassu, 'Una scultura per Borso d'Este (parte seconda)', *MuseoinVita*, II (2015).

81 Alfonso Maresti, *Teatro geneologico et istorico dell'antiche, et illustri famiglie di Ferrara* (Ferrara, 1678–1708), vol. II, pp. 18–20; Sassu, 'Una scultura per Borso d'Este'. For the sculpture generally: Cupperi, 'Esterno', p. 199.

82 Marco Folin in Settis and Cupperi, eds, *Il Palazzo Schifanoia*, pp. 254–7. The evidence that Folin provides for Borso's sexual identity is Micaela Torboli's study, which wholly discounts it: Torboli, *Il duca Borso*, pp. 24–9; Folin,

'Modelli internazionali', p. 185. For the monkey and page in the context of erotic male legs: McCall, *Brilliant Bodies*, p. 115.

83 Sassu, 'Una scultura per Borso d'Este'; Marco Folin in Settis and Cupperi, eds, *Il Palazzo Schifanoia*, pp. 244–5.

84 Eve Kosofsky Sedgwick, *Between Men: English Literature and Male Homosocial Desire* (New York, 1985); Corry, 'The Homoerotics of Power'.

85 Rocke, *Forbidden Friendships*. See also Lubkin, *A Renaissance Court*, pp. 201–2.

86 Arnold Victor Coonin, 'The Most Elusive Woman in Renaissance Art: A Portrait of Marietta Strozzi', *Artibus et Historiae*, xxx/59 (2009), pp. 41–64.

87 Tristano, 'Ferrara in the Fifteenth Century', pp. 117–23, 170, 203–4, 230–49.

88 Tuohy, *Herculean Ferrara*; Anthony Colantuono, 'Estense Patronage and the Construction of the Ferrarese Renaissance, *c.* 1395–1598', in *The Court Cities of Northern Italy: Milan, Parma, Piacenza, Mantua, Ferrara, Bologna, Urbino, Pesaro, and Rimini*, ed. Charles M. Rosenberg (Cambridge, 2010), pp. 216–20.

89 For Savenuzzo, see Franceschini, *Artisti a Ferrara*, vol. I, pp. 318–19, 338, 434, 436–7. For Folco's lavish clothing produced at Leonello's expense, see Franceschini, *Artisti a Ferrara*, vol. I, pp. 265, 298, 301–2, 342, 403. For Mantegna's double portrait, see Ronald Lightbown, *Mantegna: With a Complete Catalogue of the Paintings, Drawings and Prints* (Oxford, 1986), p. 457; Toffanello, *Le arti a Ferrara*, pp. 28, 221, 245.

90 Tristano, 'Ferrara in the Fifteenth Century', pp. 254–68; Marco Folin, 'Le residenze di corte e il sistema delle delizie fra Medioevo ed età moderna', in *Delizie estensi: Architetture di villa nel Rinascimento italiano ed europeo*, ed. Francesco Ceccarelli and Marco Folin (Florence, 2009), p. 114.

91 Pardi, ed., *Diario ferrarese dall'anno 1409*, pp. 20, 36, 42, 50, 53–4, 56, 59, 71–2, 74, 76–7, 80–81, 85.

92 Cappelli, 'Notizie di Ugo Caleffini', pp. 282, 286, 292; Piccolomini, *De viris illustribus*, p. 23; Caleffini, *Croniche, 1471–1494*, p. 6.

93 Incisive here is Betancourt, *Byzantine Intersectionality*, pp. 121–31.

Alexander, Jonathan J. G., *The Painted Book in Renaissance Italy, 1450–1600* (New Haven, CT, 2016)

Antonioli, Guido, 'La caccia nel pensiero degli umanisti della corte estense (xv secolo)', *F.D. Bollettino della 'Ferrariae Decus'*, xx (2003), pp. 36–48

Arrighi, Gino, 'Canzone per Leonello d'Este raccolta da Felino Sandei dello studio di Ferrara in un codice lucchese del '400', *Rinascimento*, ii/2 (1962), pp. 203–10

Arrigoni Martelli, Cristina, 'Ducks and Deer, Profit and Pleasure: Hunters, Game and the Natural Landscapes of Medieval Italy', PhD thesis, York University, 2015

Avril, François, and Yolanta Załuska, eds, *Dix siècles d'enluminure italienne: vie–xvie siècles* (Paris, 1984)

Ballarin, Alessandro, 'Nota sul *Ritratto di Cecilia Gallerani*', in *Leonardo a Milano: Problemi di leonardismo milanese fra '400 e '500: Giovanni Antonio Boltraffio prima della Pala Casio*, vol. i (Verona, 2010), pp. 233–57

Bambach, Carmen C., *Leonardo da Vinci Rediscovered*, 4 vols (New Haven, CT, 2019), vol. i

Bandello, Matteo, *Tutte le opere di Matteo Bandello*, ed. Francesco Flora, 2 vols, 4th edn (Milan, 1966)

Baskins, Cristelle, *The Triumph of Marriage: Painted Cassoni of the Renaissance* (Pittsburgh, PA, 2008)

Bayer, Andrea, ed., *Art and Love in Renaissance Italy* (New York, 2008)

Bellincioni, Bernardo, *Le rime*, ed. Pietro Fanfani, 2 vols (Bologna, 1876–8), vol. i

Belotti, Bortolo, *Storia di una congiura* (Milan, 1950)

Bertoni, Giulio, and Emilio Paolo Vicini, *Il castello di Ferrara ai tempi di Niccolò iii: Inventario della suppellettile del castello, 1436* (Bologna, 1907)

Bestor, Jane Fair, 'Bastardy and Legitimacy in the Formation of a Regional State in Italy: The Estense Succession', *Comparative Studies in Society and History*, xxxviii/3 (1996), pp. 549–85

——, 'Marriage and Succession in the House of Este: A Literary Perspective', in *Phaethon's Children: The Este Court and Its Culture in Early Modern Ferrara*, ed. Dennis Looney and Deanna Shemek (Tempe, AZ, 2005), pp. 49–85

Betancourt, Roland, *Byzantine Intersectionality: Sexuality, Gender, and Race in the Middle Ages* (Princeton, NJ, 2020)

Black, Jane, *Absolutism in Renaissance Milan: Plenitude of Power under the Visconti and the Sforza, 1329–1535* (Oxford, 2009)

Borgo, Francesca, 'Leonardo's Hunts: Metaphors for the Physiology of Perception', in *Hunting without Weapons: On the Pursuit of Images*, ed. Maurice Saß (Berlin, 2017), pp. 19–44

Borsa, Mario, *La caccia nel milanese: Dalle origini ai giorni nostri* (Milan, 1924)

Bourne, Molly, *Francesco II Gonzaga: The Soldier-Prince as Patron* (Rome, 2008)

Brenker, Fabian, *Turniere und Lanzenspiele in Bildern aus dem Mittelalter und der frühen Neuzeit: Orte, Auftraggeber und soziale Funktionen* (Petersberg, 2021)

Bridgeman, Jane, ed., *A Renaissance Wedding: The Celebrations at Pesaro for the Marriage of Costanzo Sforza and Camilla Marzano d'Aragona, 26–30 May 1475* (London, 2013)

Buganza, Stefania, 'Intorno a Baldassarre d'Este e al suo soggiorno lombardo', *Solchi*, IX/1–3 (2007), pp. 3–69

Burns, E. Jane, 'Courtly Love: Who Needs It? Recent Feminist Work in the Medieval French Tradition', *Signs*, XXVII/1 (2001), pp. 23–57

Butler, Judith, *Bodies That Matter: On the Discursive Limits of Sex* (London, 1996)

——, *Gender Trouble: Feminism and the Subversion of Identity* (London, 1990)

Calco, Tristano, *Mediolanensis historiographi, Residua e bibliotheca patricij nobilissimi* (Milan, 1644)

Caleffini, Ugo, *Croniche, 1471–1494* (Ferrara, 2006)

Campbell, C. Jean, 'Pier Maria Rossi's Treasure: Love, Knowledge and the Invention of the Source in the Camera d'Oro at Torrechiara', in *Emilia e Marche nel Rinascimento: L'identità visiva della 'periferia'*, ed. Giancarla Periti (Azzano San Paolo, 2005), pp. 63–88

Campbell, Stephen J., *The Cabinet of Eros: Renaissance Mythological Painting and the Studiolo of Isabella d'Este* (New Haven, CT, 2006)

——, *Cosmè Tura of Ferrara: Style, Politics, and the Renaissance City, 1450–1495* (New Haven, CT, 1997)

Cappelli, Adriano, 'Guiniforte Barzizza, maestro di Galeazzo Maria Sforza', *Archivio storico lombardo*, 3rd series, I/2 (1894), pp. 399–442

Cappelli, Antonio, 'Niccolò di Lionello d'Este', *Atti e memorie delle Regie Deputazioni di storia patria per le provincie modenesi e parmensi*, V (1870), pp. 413–38

——, 'Notizie di Ugo Caleffini notaro ferrarese del secolo XV con la sua Cronaca in rima di Casa d'Este', *Atti e memorie delle Regie Deputazioni di storia patria per le provincie modenesi e parmensi*, II (1864), pp. 267–312

Carbone, Ludovico, *Facezie e dialogo de la partita soa*, ed. Gino Ruozzi (Bologna, 1989)

Carrari, Vincenzo, *Historia de' Rossi parmigiani* (Ravenna, 1583)

Carteggio degli oratori mantovani alla corte sforzesca (1450–1500), vol. I: *1450–1459*, ed. Isabella Lazzarini (Rome, 1999)

Carteggio degli oratori mantovani alla corte sforzesca (1450–1500), vol. V: *1463*, ed. Marco Folin (Rome, 2003)

Carteggio degli oratori mantovani alla corte sforzesca (1450–1500), vol. VI: *1464–1465*, ed. Maria Nadia Covini (Rome, 2001)

Carteggio degli oratori mantovani alla corte sforzesca (1450–1500), vol. VIII: *1468–1471*, ed. Maria Nadia Covini (Rome, 2000)

Caviceo, Jacopo, *Maximo humanae imbecilitatis simulachro fortunae bifronti vita Petrimariae de Rubeis viri illustris* (Venice, *c.* 1490)

Celani, Enrico, 'La venuta di Borso d'Este in Roma. L'anno 1471', *Archivio della Regia società romana di storia patria*, XIII/3–4 (1890), pp. 361–450

Chambers, David, and Trevor Dean, *Clean Hands and Rough Justice: An Investigating Magistrate in Renaissance Italy* (Ann Arbor, MI, 1997)

Christiansen, Keith, and Stefan Weppelmann, eds, *The Renaissance Portrait from Donatello to Bellini* (New York, 2011)

Cittadella, Luigi Napoleone, *Notizie amministrative, storiche, artistiche relative a Ferrara*, 2 vols (Ferrara, 1868), vol. 1

Clark, Leah R., *Collecting Art in the Italian Renaissance Court: Objects and Exchanges* (Cambridge, 2018)

Cockram, Sarah, 'Interspecies Understanding: Exotic Animals and Their Handlers at the Italian Renaissance Court', *Renaissance Studies*, XXXI/2 (2017), pp. 277–96

——, 'Sleeve Cat and Lap Dog: Affection, Aesthetics and Proximity to Companion Animals in Renaissance Mantua', in *Interspecies Interactions: Animals and Humans between the Middle Ages and Modernity*, ed. Sarah Cockram and Andrew Wells (London, 2017), pp. 34–65

Coerver, Chad, '*Donna/Dono*: Chivalry and Adulterous Exchange in the Quattrocento', in *Picturing Women in Renaissance and Baroque Italy*, ed. Geraldine A. Johnson and Sara F. Matthews Grieco (Cambridge, 1997), pp. 196–221

Colli, Vincenzo, 'Cecilia Gallerani e Giulia Farnese', in *Prose e lettere edite e inedite*, ed. Cecil Grayson (Bologna, 1959), pp. 26–31

Connell, R. W., *Masculinities*, 2nd edn (Berkeley, CA, 2005)

——, and James W. Messerschmidt, 'Hegemonic Masculinity: Rethinking the Concept', *Gender and Society*, XIX/6 (2005), pp. 829–59

Corio, Bernardino, *Storia di Milano*, ed. Anna Morisi Guerra, 2 vols (Turin, 1978), vol. II

Corry, Maya, 'The Homoerotics of Power: Art and Desire in Leonardo's Milan', in *The Male Body and Social Masculinity in Premodern Europe*, ed. Jacqueline Murray (Toronto, 2022), pp. 193–227

Cotte, Pascal, *Lumière on The Lady with an Ermine by Leonardo da Vinci: Unprecedented Discoveries* (Saint-Fargeau-Ponthierry, 2014)

Covini, Maria Nadia, *Donne, emozioni e potere alla corte degli Sforza: Da Bianca Maria a Cecilia Gallerani* (Milan, 2012)

Cox, Virginia, *Women's Writing in Italy, 1400–1650* (Baltimore, MD, 2008)

Currie, Elizabeth, *Fashion and Masculinity in Renaissance Florence* (London, 2016)

dal Conte, Luchino, 'Viaggio a Gerusalemme di Nicolò da Este', ed. Giovanni Ghinassi, in *Miscellanea di opuscoli inediti o rari dei secoli XIV e XV* (Turin, 1861), pp. 99–160

Dean, Trevor, *Crime and Justice in Late Medieval Italy* (Cambridge, 2007)

Decembrio, Pier Candido, *Lives of the Milanese Tyrants*, trans. Gary Ianziti and ed. Massimo Zaggia (Cambridge, MA, 2019)

D'Elia, Anthony F., *Pagan Virtue in a Christian World: Sigismondo Malatesta and the Italian Renaissance* (Cambridge, MA, 2016)

DeVun, Leah, *The Shape of Sex: Nonbinary Gender from Genesis to the Renaissance* (New York, 2021)

Dijk, Sara van, '"Beauty adorns virtue": Dress in Portraits of Women by
  Leonardo da Vinci', PhD thesis, University of Leiden, 2015
Dunlop, Anne, *Painted Palaces: The Rise of Secular Art in Early Renaissance Italy*
  (University Park, PA, 2009)
d'Este, Isabella, *Selected Letters*, ed. and trans. Deanna Shemek (Toronto, 2017)
Ettlinger, Helen S., 'Visibilis et Invisibilis: The Mistress in Italian Renaissance
  Court Society', *Renaissance Quarterly*, XLVII/4 (1994), pp. 770–92
Fabjan, Barbara, and Pietro C. Marani, eds, *Leonardo: La dama con l'ermellino*
  (Cinisello Balsamo, 1998)
Ferrari, Monica, 'Lettere di principi bambini del Quattrocento lombardo',
  Mélanges de l'Ecole française de Rome, CIX/1 (1997), pp. 339–54
——, *'Per non manchare in tuto del debito mio.' L'educazione dei bambini Sforza nel
  Quattrocento* (Milan, 2000)
Fiorato, Adelin Charles, *Bandello entre l'histoire et l'écriture: La vie, l'expérience
  sociale, l'évolution culturelle d'un conteur de la Renaissance* (Florence, 1979)
Folin, Marco, 'Borso a Schifanoia: Il Salone dei Mesi come *speculum principis*',
  in *Il Palazzo Schifanoia a Ferrara / The Palazzo Schifanoia in Ferrara*, ed.
  Salvatore Settis and Walter Cupperi, vol. 1 (Modena, 2007), pp. 9–50
——, 'Le residenze di corte e il sistema delle delizie fra Medioevo ed età
  moderna', in *Delizie estensi: Architetture di villa nel Rinascimento italiano
  ed europeo*, ed. Francesco Ceccarelli and Marco Folin (Florence, 2009),
  pp. 79–135
——, 'Modelli internazionali e tradizioni signorili: Mausolei estensi tra tardo
  Medioevo e prima età moderna', in *Il Principe inVisibile: La rappresentazione
  e la riflessione sul potere tra Medioevo e Rinascimento*, ed. Lucia Bertolini,
  Arturo Calzona, Glauco Maria Cantarella and Stefano Caroti (Turnhout,
  2015), pp. 173–99
Foucard, Cesare, *Relazioni dei duchi di Ferrara e di Modena coi re di Tunisi*
  (Modena, 1881)
Franceschini, Adriano, *Artisti a Ferrara in età umanistica e rinascimentale:
  Testimonianze archivistiche*, 3 vols (Ferrara, 1993), vol. I and vol. II (pt I of II)
Fudge, Erica, *Animal* (London, 2002)
——, 'Renaissance Animal Things', *New Formations*, LXXVI (2012), pp. 86–100
Fumagalli, Edoardo, 'Nuovi documenti su Lorenzo e Giuliano de' Medici', *Italia
  medioevale e umanistica*, XXIII (1980), pp. 115–64
Gagné, John, 'Collecting Women: Three French Kings and Manuscripts of
  Empire in the Italian Wars', *I Tatti Studies in the Italian Renaissance*, XX/1
  (2017), pp. 127–84
——, *Milan Undone: Contested Sovereignties in the Italian Wars* (Cambridge, MA,
  2021)
Gandini, Luigi Alberto, 'Viaggi, cavalli, bardature e stalle degli Estensi nel
  Quattrocento', *Atti e memorie della Regia Deputazione di storia patria per le
  provincie di Romagna*, X (1892), pp. 41–94
Griffin, Ben, 'Hegemonic Masculinity as a Historical Problem', *Gender and
  History*, XXX/2 (2018), pp. 377–400
Guarino, Battista, *Sermone del cane e del cavallo*, ed. Gianluca Valenti (Rome,
  2016)
Gundersheimer, Werner L., *Art and Life at the Court of Ercole I d'Este: The 'De
  triumphis religionis' of Giovanni Sabadino degli Arienti* (Geneva, 1972)

——, 'Clarity and Ambiguity in Renaissance Gesture: The Case of
  Borso d'Este', *Journal of Medieval and Renaissance Studies*, XXIII/1 (1993),
  pp. 1–17
——, *Ferrara: The Style of a Renaissance Despotism* (Princeton, NJ, 1973)
——, 'Women, Learning, and Power: Eleonora of Aragon and the Court
  of Ferrara', in *Beyond Their Sex: Learned Women of the European Past*,
  ed. Patricia H. Labalme (New York, 1980), pp. 43–65
Halberstam, Jack, *Female Masculinity* (Durham, NC, 1998)
Halperin, David, *How to Do the History of Homosexuality* (Chicago, IL, 2002)
Horodowich, Elizabeth, 'The Wider World: Foreigners, Travels, and Geography',
  in *Italian Renaissance Diplomacy: A Sourcebook*, ed. Monica Azzolini and
  Isabella Lazzarini (Toronto, 2017), pp. 190–213
Ianziti, Gary, 'The Life of the Last Visconti: A Study in Tyranny?', *Renaissance
  Quarterly*, LXXV/3 (2022), pp. 753–95
James, Carolyn, *A Renaissance Marriage: The Political and Personal Alliance of
  Isabella d'Este and Francesco Gonzaga, 1490–1519* (Oxford, 2020)
Jaser, Christian, 'Beyond Siena: The Palio Culture of Renaissance Italy', *Ludica*,
  XXIII (2017), pp. 24–34
Kaeuper, Richard W., *Chivalry and Violence in Medieval Europe* (Oxford, 1999)
Karras, Ruth Mazo, *From Boys to Men: Formations of Masculinity in Late Medieval
  Europe* (Philadelphia, PA, 2003)
Lazzari, Alfonso, 'Il "Barco" di Lodovico Carbone', *Atti e memorie della
  Deputazione ferrarese di storia patria*, XXIV (1919), pp. 5–44
——, *Il primo duca di Ferrara, Borso d'Este* (Ferrara, 1945)
——, *Parisina* (Florence, 1949)
Leverotti, Franca, *'Governare a modo e stillo de' Signori … ' Osservazioni in margine
  all'amministrazione della giustizia al tempo di Galeazzo Maria Sforza duca di
  Milano (1466–76)* (Florence, 1994)
——, 'Lucia Marliani e la sua famiglia: Il potere di una donna amata', in *Donne di
  potere nel Rinascimento*, ed. Letizia Arcangeli and Susanna Peyronel (Rome,
  2008), pp. 281–311
Lloyd, Joan Barclay, *African Animals in Renaissance Literature and Art* (Oxford,
  1971)
Lochrie, Karma, *Heterosyncrasies: Female Sexuality When Normal Wasn't*
  (Minneapolis, MN, 2005)
Lubkin, Gregory, *A Renaissance Court: Milan under Galeazzo Maria Sforza*
  (Berkeley, CA, 1994)
McCall, Timothy, *Brilliant Bodies: Fashioning Courtly Men in Early Renaissance
  Italy* (University Park, PA, 2022)
——, 'Galeazzo's Gem and *Ghellero* in the Uffizi Portrait by Piero Pollaiuolo',
  Source: Notes in the History of Art, XXXIX/3 (2020), pp. 150–61
——, 'Male Dress', in *Early Modern Court Culture*, ed. Erin Griffey (London,
  2021), pp. 376–89
——, 'Pier Maria's Legacy: (Il)legitimacy, Inheritance, and Rule of Parma's Rossi
  Dynasty', in *Wives, Widows, Mistresses, and Nuns in Early Modern Italy:
  Making the Invisible Visible through Art and Patronage*, ed. Katherine
  A. McIver (Farnham, 2012), pp. 33–54
——, '"Questo misto di profano e di sacro": The *Studiolo Oratorio* of Torrechiara',
  Predella, 47 (2020), pp. 165–83

——, 'Secrecy and the Production of Seignorial Space: The *Coretto* of Torrechiara',
   in *Visual Cultures of Secrecy in Early Modern Europe*, ed. Timothy McCall,
   Sean Roberts and Giancarlo Fiorenza (Kirksville, MO, 2013), pp. 76–104
——, 'Traffic in Mistresses: Sexualized Bodies and Systems of Exchange in
   the Early Modern Court', in *Sex Acts in Early Modern Italy: Practice,
   Performance, Perversion, Punishment*, ed. Allison Levy (Farnham, 2010),
   pp. 125–36
——, 'Visual Imagery and Historical Invisibility: Antonia Torelli, Her Husband,
   and His Mistress in Fifteenth-Century Parma', *Renaissance Studies*, XXIII/3
   (2009), pp. 269–87
——, and Sean Roberts, 'Art and the Material Culture of Diplomacy', in *Italian
   Renaissance Diplomacy: A Sourcebook*, ed. Monica Azzolini and Isabella
   Lazzarini (Toronto, 2017), pp. 214–33
——,——, 'Introduction: Revealing Early Modern Secrecy', in *Visual Cultures of
   Secrecy in Early Modern Europe*, ed. Timothy McCall, Sean Roberts and
   Giancarlo Fiorenza (Kirksville, MO, 2013), pp. 1–23
——, —— and Giancarlo Fiorenza, eds, *Visual Cultures of Secrecy in Early Modern
   Europe* (Kirksville, MO, 2013)
Magenta, Carlo, *I Visconti e gli Sforza nel castello di Pavia e loro attinenze con la
   Certosa e la storia cittadina*, 2 vols (Milan, 1883)
Magnani, Rachele, *Relazioni private tra la corte sforzesca di Milano e casa Medici,
   1450–1500* (Milan, 1910)
Malacarne, Giancarlo, *Le cacce del principe: L'ars venandi nella terra dei Gonzaga*
   (Modena, 1998)
Malaguzzi Valeri, Francesco, *La corte di Lodovico il Moro*, 4 vols (Milan, 1913–23),
   vol. I
Maresti, Alfonso, *Teatro geneologico et istorico dell'antiche, et illustri famiglie di
   Ferrara*, 3 vols (Ferrara, 1678–1708), vol. II
Masseti, Marco, 'Pictorial Evidence from Medieval Italy of Cheetahs and
   Caracals, and Their Use in Hunting', *Archives of Natural History*, XXXVI/1
   (2009), pp. 37–47
Mattaliano, Emanuele, '"Le donne, i cavallier, l'arme, gli amori" estensi nel
   Cinquecento a Ferrara', in *Da Borso a Cesare d'Este. La scuola di Ferrara,
   1450–1628* (Ferrara, 1985), pp. 39–43
Medici, Lorenzo de', *Lettere*, vol. I: *1460–1474*, ed. Riccardo Fubini (Florence,
   1977)
——, *Lettere*, vol. II: *1474–1478*, ed. Riccardo Fubini (Florence, 1977)
——, *Lettere*, vol. X: *1486–1487*, ed. Melissa Meriam Bullard (Florence, 2003)
Milligan, Gerry, 'The Politics of Effeminacy in "Il cortegiano"', *Italica*,
   LXXXIII/3–4 (2006), pp. 345–66
Moczulska, Krystyna, 'The Most Graceful Gallerani and the Most Exquisite
   ΓΑΛΕΗ in the Portrait of Leonardo da Vinci', *Folia historiae artium*, I (1995),
   pp. 77–86
Mondschein, Ken, *The Knightly Art of Battle* (Los Angeles, CA, 2011)
Morbio, Carlo, *Codice visconteo-sforzesco, ossia raccolta di leggi, decreti e lettere
   famigliari dei duchi di Milano* (Milan, 1846)
Murray, Jacqueline, 'Reflections on the Male Body and Social Masculinity', in
   The Male Body and Social Masculinity in Premodern Europe, ed. Jacqueline
   Murray (Toronto, 2022), pp. 9–21

Musacchio, Jacqueline Marie, 'Weasels and Pregnancy in Renaissance Italy', *Renaissance Studies*, xv/2 (2001), pp. 172–87

——, 'Wives, Lovers, and Art in Italian Renaissance Courts', in *Art and Love in Renaissance Italy*, ed. Andrea Bayer (New York, 2008), pp. 29–41

Neuschel, Kristen B., *Living by the Sword: Weapons and Material Culture in France and Britain, 600–1600* (Ithaca, NY, 2020)

Newbigin, Nerida, ed., '*Le onoranze fiorentine del 1459*. Poema anonimo', *Letteratura italiana antica*, XII (2011), pp. 17–135

Nogueira, Alison Manges, 'An Illuminated Schoolbook for Ludovico Sforza: Portraiture in Educational Manuscripts at the Court of Milan', *Manuscripta*, LIX/2 (2015), pp. 187–222

Paolini, Claudio, Daniela Parenti and Ludovica Sebregondi, eds, *Virtù d'amore: Pittura nuziale nel Quattrocento fiorentino* (Florence, 2010)

Pardi, Giuseppe, ed., *Diario ferrarese dall'anno 1409 sino al 1502* (Bologna, 1928–33)

——, *Leonello d'Este, marchese di Ferrara* (Bologna, 1904)

Pedretti, Carlo, 'La dama dell'ermellino come allegoria politica', in *Studi politici in onore di Luigi Firpo*, ed. Silvia Rota Ghibaudi and Franco Barcia, vol. I (Milan, 1990), pp. 161–81

Pélissier, Léon-G., 'Les relations de François de Gonzague, marquis de Mantoue, avec Ludovic Sforza et Louis XII: Notes additionnelles et documents', *Annales de la Faculté des lettres de Bordeaux*, XV (1893), pp. 50–95

Pezzana, Angelo, *Storia della città di Parma*, 5 vols (Parma, 1837–59), vol. II, III and IV

Pfisterer, Ulrich, 'Die Erotik der Macht: Visualisierte Herrscher-Potenz in der Renaissance', in *Menschennatur und politische Ordnung*, ed. Andreas Höfele and Beate Kellner (Paderborn, 2016), pp. 177–201

Pini, Vittorio, 'Presenza della "magnifica et generosa Cecilia" Gallerani, nonché delle famiglie paterna, materna e maritale in imbreviature notarili dal 1407 al 1573, all'Archivio di Stato di Milano', *Raccolta vinciana*, XXXI (2005), pp. 3–110

Pius II, *Commentaries*, ed. Margaret Meserve and Marcello Simonetta, 2 vols (Cambridge, MA, 2003–7)

Porro Lambertenghi, Giulio, 'Lettere di Galeazzo Maria Sforza, duca di Milano', *Archivio storico lombardo*, V (1878), pp. 107–29, 254–74, 637–68

Provasi, Matteo, *Il popolo ama il duca? Rivolta e consenso nella Ferrara estense* (Rome, 2011)

Quiviger, François, *Leonardo da Vinci: Self, Art and Nature* (London, 2019)

Randolph, Adrian W. B., *Engaging Symbols: Gender, Politics, and Public Art in Fifteenth-Century Florence* (New Haven, CT, 2002)

Ricci, Giovanni, *Il principe e la morte: Corpo, cuore, effigie nel Rinascimento* (Bologna, 1998)

Ricciardi, Lucia, *'Col senno, col tesoro e colla lancia': Riti e giochi cavallereschi nella Firenze del Magnifico Lorenzo* (Florence, 1992)

Rocke, Michael, *Forbidden Friendships: Homosexuality and Male Culture in Renaissance Florence* (Oxford, 1996)

Rosenberg, Charles M., *The Este Monuments and Urban Development in Renaissance Ferrara* (Cambridge, 1997)

Rosmini, Carlo de', *Dell'istoria di Milano*, 4 vols (Milan, 1820), vol. IV

Rossetti, Edoardo, 'Il volto di Lucia: Un ritratto ritrovato', *Storia in Martesana*, IV (2010), pp. 1–22

Rubin, Gayle, 'The Traffic in Women: Notes on the "Political Economy" of Sex', in *Toward an Anthropology of Women*, ed. Rayna R. Reiter (New York, 1975), pp. 157–210

Ruggiero, Guido, *The Boundaries of Eros: Sex Crime and Sexuality in Renaissance Venice* (Oxford, 1985)

Rustici, Gerardo, *Cantilena pro potenti D. Petro Maria Rubeo Berceti comite magnifico et Noceti domino*, Parma, Biblioteca Palatina, MS Parm. 1992

Ryder, Alan, *Alfonso the Magnanimous: King of Aragon, Naples and Sicily, 1396–1458* (Oxford, 1990)

Sassu, Giovanni, 'Una scultura per Borso d'Este (parte seconda)', *MuseoinVita*, II (2015), n.p. online journal

Schiaparelli, Attilio, *Leonardo ritrattista* (Milan, 1921)

Schultz, James A., *Courtly Love, the Love of Courtliness, and the History of Sexuality* (Chicago, IL, 2006)

——, 'Heterosexuality as a Threat to Medieval Studies', *Journal of the History of Sexuality*, XV/1 (2006), pp. 14–29

Sedgwick, Eve Kosofsky, *Between Men: English Literature and Male Homosocial Desire* (New York, 1985)

Settis, Salvatore, and Walter Cupperi, eds, *Il Palazzo Schifanoia a Ferrara / The Palazzo Schifanoia in Ferrara*, 2 vols (Modena, 2007), vol. I

Sforza, Ippolita Maria, *Duchess and Hostage in Renaissance Naples: Letters and Orations*, ed. and trans. Diana Robin and Lynn Lara Westwater (Toronto, 2017)

Shell, Janice, and Grazioso Sironi, 'Cecilia Gallerani: Leonardo's Lady with an Ermine', *Artibus et Historiae*, XIII/25 (1992), pp. 47–66

Shemek, Deanna, 'Aretino's *Marescalco*: Marriage Woes and the Duke of Mantua', *Renaissance Studies*, XVI/3 (2002), pp. 366–80

——, 'Circular Definitions: Configuring Gender in Italian Renaissance Festival', *Renaissance Quarterly*, XLVIII/1 (1995), pp. 1–40

Shepard, Alexandra, 'Manhood, Patriarchy, and Gender in Early Modern History', in *Masculinities, Childhood, Violence: Attending to Early Modern Women and Men*, ed. Amy E. Leonard and Karen L. Nelson (Newark, DE, 2010), pp. 77–95

Shephard, Tim, *Echoing Helicon: Music, Art and Identity in the Este Studioli, 1440–1530* (Oxford, 2014)

Simonetta, Cicco, *I diari di Cicco Simonetta*, ed. Alfio Rosario Natale (Milan, 1962)

Simonetta, Marcello, *Rinascimento segreto: Il mondo del segretario da Petrarca a Machiavelli* (Milan, 2004)

Simons, Patricia, 'Homosociality and Erotics in Italian Renaissance Portraiture', in *Portraiture: Facing the Subject*, ed. Joanna Woodall (Manchester, 1997), pp. 29–51

——, 'Portraiture, Portrayal, and Idealization: Ambiguous Individualism in Representations of Renaissance Women', in *Language and Images of Renaissance Italy*, ed. Alison Brown (Oxford, 1995), pp. 263–311

——, *The Sex of Men in Premodern Europe: A Cultural History* (Cambridge, 2011)

Smith, Ali, *How to Be Both* (London, 2015)

Stapleford, Richard, *Lorenzo de' Medici at Home: The Inventory of the Palazzo Medici in 1492* (University Park, PA, 2013)

Syson, Luke, *Leonardo da Vinci: Painter at the Court of Milan* (London, 2011)

——, 'Lo stile di una signoria: Il mecenatismo di Borso d'Este', in *Cosmè Tura e Francesco del Cossa: L'arte a Ferrara nell'età di Borso d'Este*, ed. Mauro Natale (Ferrara, 2007), pp. 75–88

——, and Dillian Gordon, *Pisanello: Painter to the Renaissance Court* (London, 2001)

Tabanelli, Mario, *Sigismondo Pandolfo Malatesta, signore del Medioevo e del Rinascimento* (Faenza, 1977)

Terjanian, Pierre, ed., *The Last Knight: The Art, Armor, and Ambition of Maximilian I* (New York, 2019)

Tobey, Elizabeth, 'The *Palio* Banner and the Visual Culture of Horse Racing in Renaissance Italy', *International Journal of the History of Sport*, XXVIII/8–9 (2011), pp. 1269–82

——, 'The *Palio* Horse in Renaissance and Early Modern Italy', in *The Culture of the Horse: Status, Discipline, and Identity in the Early Modern World*, ed. Karen Raber and Treva J. Tucker (New York, 2005), pp. 63–90

Toffanello, Marcello, *Le arti a Ferrara nel Quattrocento: Gli artisti e la corte* (Ferrara, 2010)

Torboli, Micaela, *Il duca Borso d'Este e la politica delle immagini nella Ferrara del Quattrocento* (Ferrara, 2007)

Tristano, Richard M., 'Ferrara in the Fifteenth Century: Borso d'Este and the Development of a New Nobility', PhD thesis, New York University, 1983

Tuohy, Thomas, *Herculean Ferrara: Ercole d'Este, 1471–1505, and the Invention of a Ducal Capital* (Cambridge, 1996)

Uzielli, Gustavo, *Leonardo da Vinci e tre gentildonne milanesi del secolo XV* (Pinerolo, 1890)

Vaglienti, Francesca M., 'Cacce e parchi ducali sul Ticino (1450–1476)', in *Vigevano e i territori circostanti alla fine del Medioevo*, ed. Giorgio Chittolini (Milan, 1997), pp. 185–260

——, 'Le cacce ducali. Politica ambientale e tutela del territorio in età sforzesca', *Natura*, LXXXVII/2 (1996), pp. 63–81

Vasari, Giorgio, *Vite de' più eccellenti pittori, scultori et architettori*, ed. Gaetano Milanesi, 9 vols (Florence, 1906), vol. V and VI

Venturelli, Paola, *La moda alla corte degli Sforza: Leonardo da Vinci tra creatività e tecnica* (Cinisello Balsamo, 2019)

Venturi, Adolfo, 'L'arte a Ferrara nel periodo di Borso d'Este', *Rivista storica italiana*, II (1885), pp. 689–749

——, 'L'arte ferrarese nel periodo di Ercole I d'Este, II', *Atti e memorie della Regia Deputazione di storia patria per le provincie di Romagna*, VI/4–6 (1888), pp. 350–422

——, 'Relazioni artistiche tra le corti di Milano e Ferrara nel secolo XV', *Archivio storico lombardo*, 2nd series, II/2 (1885), pp. 225–80

Villata, Edoardo, ed., *Leonardo da Vinci: I documenti e le testimonianze contemporanee* (Milan, 1999)

Watt, Diane, 'Why Men Still Aren't Enough', GLQ: *A Journal of Lesbian and Gay Studies*, XVI/3 (2010), pp. 451–64

Welch, Evelyn, *Art and Authority in Renaissance Milan* (New Haven, CT, 1995)

——, 'Art on the Edge: Hair and Hands in Renaissance Italy', *Renaissance Studies*, XXIII/3 (2009), pp. 241–68

——, 'Between Italy and Moscow: Cultural Crossroads and the Culture of
    Exchange', in *Cultural Exchange in Early Modern Europe*, vol. IV: *Forging
    European Identities, 1400–1700*, ed. Herman Roodenburg (Cambridge, 2007),
    pp. 59–99
——, 'Galeazzo Maria Sforza and the Castello di Pavia, 1469', *Art Bulletin*, LXXI/3
    (1989), pp. 352–75
——, 'The Image of a Fifteenth-Century Court: Secular Frescoes for the Castello
    di Porta Giovia, Milan', *Journal of the Warburg and Courtauld Institutes*, LIII
    (1990), pp. 163–84
——, 'Secular Fresco Painting at the Court of Galeazzo Maria Sforza, 1466–1476',
    PhD thesis, University of London, Warburg Institute, 1987
——, *Shopping in the Renaissance: Consumer Cultures in Italy, 1400–1600* (New
    Haven, CT, 2005)
——, 'Sight, Sound and Ceremony in the Chapel of Galeazzo Maria Sforza',
    Early Music History, XII (1993), pp. 151–90
Woods-Marsden, Joanna, *The Gonzaga of Mantua and Pisanello's Arthurian
    Frescoes* (Princeton, NJ, 1988)
Zambotti, Bernardino, *Diario ferrarese dall'anno 1476 sino al 1504*, ed. Giuseppe
    Pardi (Bologna, 1934–7)
Zanichelli, Giuseppa Z., 'La committenza dei Rossi: Immagini di potere fra
    sacro e profano', in *Le signorie dei Rossi di Parma tra XIV e XVI secolo*, ed.
    Letizia Arcangeli and Marco Gentile (Florence, 2007), pp. 187–212
Zorach, Rebecca, *Blood, Milk, Ink, Gold: Abundance and Excess in the French
    Renaissance* (Chicago, IL, 2005)

ACKNOWLEDGEMENTS

This book was supported by a great many people. I am grateful to colleagues at Villanova University including Hibba Abugideiri, Alice Dailey, Travis Foster, Lynne Hartnett, Marc Gallicchio, Judy Giesberg, Maghan Keita, Catherine Kerrison, Elizabeth Kolsky, Anthony Lagalante, Adele Lindenmeyr, Megan Quigley, Lauren Shohet, Cristina Soriano, Paul Steege and Rebecca Winer. Funding for the acquisition of images and publication of the book's spectacular colour plates was provided by the Villanova University Subvention of Publications Program; a College of Liberal Arts and Sciences Faculty Research and Development Grant; the History Department; and the Birle Professorship (with thanks to Paul Rosier).

For feedback and invitations in various venues, as these chapters were shaped in lectures, conference papers and written drafts, and for references, suggestions and assistance over many years, I thank Andrea Bayer, Nicolas Bock, Louise Bourdua, Fabian Brenker, Jill Burke, Bill Caferro, Elena Calvillo, Jean Campbell, Maya Corry, Elizabeth Currie, Gerardo de Simone, Leah DeVun, Konrad Eisenbichler, Leslie Geddes, Erin Griffey, Sarah Guérin, Emily Hage, Nick Herman, Christopher Heuer, Cecily Hilsdale, Jocelyn Karlan, Dana Katz, Jessica Keating, David Kim, Homay King, Vicky Kirkham, Kostis Kourelis, Catherine Kovesi, Lena Lannutti, Allison Levy, Evan MacCarthy, Emanuela Mari, Areli Marina, Andrew McCormick, Gerry Milligan, Letizia Modena, Jacqueline Murray, Nerida Newbigin, Alexander Noelle, Jonathan Nelson, Jonquil O'Reilly, Sophie Pitman, Meredith Ray, Anna Reynolds, Diana Robin, Michael Rocke, Sarah Ross, Natalie Ruppel, Susannah Rutherglen, Lisa Saltzman, Monika Schmitter, Deanna Shemek, Nat Silver, Bruce Smith, Paola Ugolini, Abigail Upshaw, Alicia Walker, Evelyn Welch, Lynn Westwater, Kelli Wood and Amanda Wunder.

Marina Cotugno, Lia Markey and Amanda Luyster provided key assistance acquiring images. Pascal Cotte granted kind permission to publish his. For valuable help, inspiration and encouragement along the way, I am indebted to allies and accomplices including Diane Ahl, Angel Carreño, Anne Dunlop, Megan Holmes, Maria Loh, Emanuele Lugli, Peta Motture, Jacki Musacchio, Diana Bullen Presciutti, Andrea Rizzi, Mark Rosen, Allie Terry-Fritsch, Elly Truitt and Heidi Voskuhl. With affection and admiration, I thank Nathan Clark, Jonah Johnson, Sarah Kelley, Mark Metzger, Andrew Newton Schaftlein, Sarah Niehoff, Robert Rizzo, Scott Schaftlein and Ryan Whelan, and likewise my siblings and their partners, and my parents, Jinny and Tim.

I appreciate, profoundly, the support and labour of Alex Ciobanu, Amy Salter and Michael Leaman of Reaktion Books (and I apologize for any headaches that I caused them). This study would not have taken the form that it has, nor be nearly as incisive or exciting, without the intellectual generosity and guidance of Cristelle Baskins, Stephen Campbell, Sarah Cockram, John Gagné, Elizabeth Horodowich, Jill Pederson, Sean Roberts and Pat Simons. To Pat and Sean, who have challenged me to think critically about masculinity for more than two decades, I dedicate this book. I dedicate it as well to all those who – dispirited, burdened or broken by today's expectations and practices of masculinity – want to imagine and embody new, better futures. Looking to the past sometimes enables us to do so.

PHOTO ACKNOWLEDGEMENTS

The author and publishers wish to express their thanks to the below sources of illustrative material and/or permission to reproduce it. Some locations of artworks are also given below, in the interest of brevity:

Alamy Stock Photo: 7 (Riccardo Bianchini), 51 (Peregrine); Archivio Storico Civico e Biblioteca Trivulziana, Milan: 19 (MS Triv. 2167, fol. 54r), 26 (MS Triv. 2167, fol. IV), 71 (MS Triv. 1333, fol. Ir); Art Resource, NY: 28 (San Giacomo Maggiore, Bologna, photo Scala), 39 (Musée du Louvre, Paris, photo © RMN-Grand Palais); Beinecke Rare Book and Manuscript Library, Yale University, New Haven, CT (MS 446, fol. Ir): 44; Biblioteca Civica Berio, Genoa (MS M. R. Cf. Arm. 25, fol. 8r): 11; Biblioteca Estense Universitaria, Modena: 45 (MS Ital. 464, fol. 6v), 87 (MS Ital. 720, fol. 3r), 93 (MS Ital. 720, fol. 3v), 98 (MS Lat. 108, fol. Ir); Biblioteca Nazionale Centrale, Florence (MS Palatino 556, fol. 83v), reproduced by permission of Ministero della Cultura – Biblioteca Nazionale Centrale, Florence (all rights reserved): 10; Biblioteca Nazionale Centrale, Roma (MS Vitt.Em. 293): 88 (fol. 6r), 94 (fol. 7v), 95 (fol. 6r); Biblioteca Nazionale Marciana, Venice (MS Lat. XI, 53 (=4009), fol. 2r), reproduced by permission of Ministero della Cultura – Biblioteca Nazionale Marciana, Venice (all rights reserved): 74; Biblioteca Reale, Turin (MS Varia 75): 22 (fol. 8v), 23 (fol. 8r), 24 (fol. 5v), 25 (fol. 4v); Bridgeman Images: 29 (Mondadori Portfolio/Electa/Antonio Quattrone), 43 (© Musée Condé, Chantilly (MS 368 (1375), fol. IV)), 50 (© Raffaello Bencini); The Cleveland Museum of Art, OH: 46, 47; © Pascal Cotte/Lumière Technology, reproduced in Pascal Cotte, *Lumière on the Lady with an Ermine by Leonardo da Vinci: Unprecedented Discoveries* (Saint-Fargeau-Ponthierry, 2014): 77, 79; The Fitzwilliam Museum, University of Cambridge: 84; Gallerie degli Uffizi, Florence: 12; Herzog Anton Ulrich-Museum, Braunschweig (MS H 27 Bd. 67a, fol. 3r): 60; from George Hill, *A Corpus of Italian Medals of the Renaissance before Cellini* (London, 1930): 66 (formerly Museo di Capodimonte, Naples, now lost); Istituzione Biblioteca Classense, Ravenna (MS Cl 302, fol. 24v): 96; Isabella Stewart Gardner Museum, Boston: 82; The J. Paul Getty Museum, Los Angeles: 21 (MS Ludwig XV 13, fol. 8v), 36; Kunsthistorisches Museum, Vienna, photos © KHM-Museumsverband: 20, 40, 59; photos Timothy McCall: 42 (Gallerie degli Uffizi, Florence), 65, 67, 68, 69, 90, 99, 100, 101, 102, 103; The Metropolitan Museum of Art, New York: 80; The Morgan Library & Museum, New York (MS M.1148, fol. Ir), photo The Morgan Library & Museum, New York: 15; Münzkabinett, Staatliche Museen zu Berlin: 64; Musées

INDEX

Illustration numbers are in *italics*